YOU DON'T HAVE TO
BE YOUR MOTHER

Gayle Feldman

HAMISH HAMILTON . LONDON

HAMISH HAMILTON LTD

Published by the Penguin Group
Penguin Books Ltd, 27 Wrights Lane, London W8 5TZ, England
Penguin Books USA Inc., 375 Hudson Street, New York, New York 10014, USA
Penguin Books Australia Ltd, Ringwood, Victoria, Australia
Penguin Books Canada Ltd, 10 Alcorn Avenue, Toronto, Ontario, Canada M4V 3B2
Penguin Books (NZ) Ltd, 182–190 Wairau Road, Auckland 10, New Zealand

Penguin Books Ltd, Registered Offices: Harmondsworth, Middlesex, England

First published in the United States of America by W. W. Norton & Company, Inc. 1994
First published in Great Britain by Hamish Hamilton Ltd 1994
10 9 8 7 6 5 4 3 2
Copyright © Gayle Feldman, 1994

Printed in Great Britain by Clays Ltd, St Ives plc

A CIP catalogue record for this book is available from the British Library

ISBN 0-241-13439-0

YOU DON'T HAVE TO
BE YOUR MOTHER

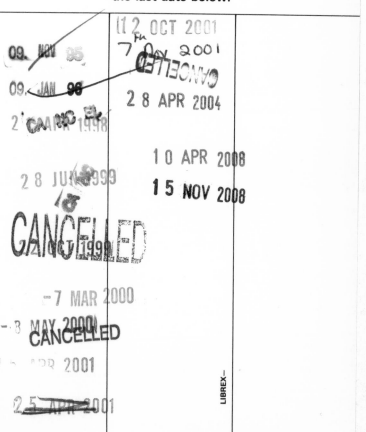

THIS IS FOR BEN

and in memory of
Bernice Borkofsky Feldman

If some messenger were to come to us with the offer that death should be overthrown, but with the one inseparable condition that birth should also cease . . . that never again would there be a child, or a youth, or first love, never again new persons with new hopes . . . ourselves for always and never any others—could the answer be in doubt?

From *The New Union Prayer Book* text,
Yizkor memorial service,
Yom Kippur

Acknowledgments

THIS BOOK IS DEDICATED TO TWO PEOPLE, MY SON AND my mother, the future and the past. Had it not seemed excessive to crowd the page with a third name, the man who has shared the present with me for twenty-one years would have been there, too. Without David Reid's extraordinary love, kindness, understanding and encouragement, I would not have been able to write this book, nor could I have come through the travail of the past few years so intact. There are no words to describe my gratitude to this man, my husband.

My Philadelphia family has been wonderfully supportive of a memoir that tells their story as well as mine. I'd like to thank Joseph Feldman, Sandra and Steve Benhaim, and Vickie Feldman for pulling together when it really counted and for reading the manuscript and wanting it to go forward. My father gave generously of his time, revisiting painful moments of the past in order to help me write this book. Anna B. Cohen and Sophie Frankel also allowed themselves to be interviewed for it.

On the English side, Diana Bramall is truly "an angel from across the sea," who flew here on wings provided by Richard Bramall and Colin and Betsy Reid. Thanks to Keith Reid for reading part of the manuscript and taking kindly to it.

I'm grateful to other family members and friends on both sides of the Atlantic—notably Jean Crichton, Brian and Diana Harrison, Nancy Jervis, Eric Marcus, Morris and Mary Rossabi, and Terry

6ACKNOWLEDGMENTS

10   Toll—for all they did to sustain us during a very difficult time. Our friend Jose Berlinka has kindly given permission to reprint the poem by his wife Jane that appears on p. 218.

Heart-felt thanks are due to the doctors, nurses and medical personnel who helped me give birth to a baby and survive breast cancer, and who graciously permitted their names to be used within the pages of this book. Special appreciation is reserved for Dr. Becky Brightman, Dr. Laurie Goldstein, Dr. Judy Schwartz, and Dr. Jeanne A. Petrek. In addition, I am very grateful to Jeanne Petrek and Laurie Goldstein for interrupting their hectic schedules to read the manuscript and for their valuable comments.

Many thanks are owed to the staff and publishers of *Publishers Weekly*, and particularly to John Baker, Michael Coffey, Daisy Maryles, and Maria Simson for their magnificent support. I am grateful to the Cahners Publishing Company for granting me a twelve-month leave of absence from *Publishers Weekly* in order to write this book. Equal thanks to the staff of Allen & Overy New York, who held it all together on David's end.

Despite being "in the business," I had never met my agent, Molly Friedrich, until after she had read the first chapter of this book and decided to take me on. She has believed in it from the very beginning. Thanks too to Sheri Holman.

I am grateful to Alexandra Pringle at Hamish Hamilton in London and Dorothée Grisebach at Droemer Knaur Verlag in Munich for their votes of confidence, and to Andy McKillop for his help.

Finally, this book was made better by the sensitive and thoughtful comments of my editor, Gerry Howard. I am glad that a man felt passionate about publishing this particular woman's book. He read every line, made me laugh when I needed to, and told me to "just keep writing." Most important, though, he allowed the book to remain my own.

Introduction

I AM THE DAUGHTER OF A WOMAN WHO DIED OF BREAST cancer in her forties, the age I am now.

I am the granddaughter of a woman whom I never knew as a living person, my mother's mother, one of the twin ghosts of childhood whose name gave me my own. She died of lung cancer in her fifties without ever having smoked a cigarette in her life. In those days, what started out in the breast often ended up, misdiagnosed, in the lung.

I am the wife of an Englishman whose younger brother married on the same day of the same month as my husband and myself. He and his wife had two little girls before my sister-in-law died of breast cancer in her mid-thirties.

And I am a woman who, at age forty, while in the eighth month of a first, much-desired, and difficult-to-achieve pregnancy, discovered that I had breast cancer and had to face not simply the imminent possibility of my own demise and the awful uncertainty engulfing the unborn child within me, but the knowledge that, should we both survive the passage to birth and beyond, everything would be different, changed irrevocably, the ghosts of cancers past intimate companions forevermore.

It seems to me that like some second, malevolently tangled DNA, cancer has twisted through my cells, providing a defining thread to my life as surely as the genetic skein that has given me large eyes, small bones, brown-black hair. As I grew from age eleven through fifteen and watched my mother die, my own chaotic teen years served as an outward mirror to the uncontrolled growth taking place within her body. Already I knew, even then, that my mother's death would be the formative experience of my life, and the paths I have taken and not taken to this day wind back to that crossroads so many years before.

Yet here I am, with a son nearly two years old, playing, squealing, chirping as I write, sitting in the study of my house in New York City, a house that I thought I might never live in or might already have died in.

Nineteen months ago, in part to try to make some sense of what had and was happening to me, I sat facing a blank screen and began to write. I had come late to the life of a journalist—having worked as one only for the previous half-dozen years—and it seemed the natural thing to do, to search for clarity through words. So much had been written about breast cancer but so much had not, and certainly not my experience of it, going from generation to generation, culminating in a *pas de deux* of birth and near-death.

Curiously, while this book has been taking shape, the passing months have echoed with public sound and fury surrounding breast cancer. Images and words have abounded, and in reading all these articles—for my eyes seem to have developed a special radar for the "C" word in print—so much has, time and again, been missing.

How can one who has not experienced cancer and a mastectomy write about it with verisimilitude? And how can one who has experienced it imperil her public image of herself as a woman by writing about it at all? In one sense, I am writing this book so that others may understand, may learn from my experience to help themselves. I hope this story of one woman, one family, may reach out to other lives and situations, may help the community of women and their families at large.

For me, it was only after the experience of cancer that I began to understand why I had made some decisions and not others, that

connecting links were forged to closed corridors of the past. Writing meant coming to terms with my personal history, with my
mother and the many legacies she left, but confronting the bond
between us and carrying on my own life meant affirming the fact
that I am not my mother. And so, in another sense, I am writing
this book in her honor, for memory's sake.

My mother died before I was ever able to know her as an adult,
and there is so much mystery that questions to my father, sisters,
and older relations can only partially unwind, never fully unravel. I
am writing this book for them, too, and with their help and encouragement. I am also writing it for my husband, as the record of
an extraordinary period in our time together, a passage we have
made in tandem with great difficulty and great love.

But most of all, I am writing this book for my son, Ben, so that
come what may, he will know something of me in a way that I have
not been able to fathom my own mother. Each day that I spend
getting to know him, seeing him change and grow and unfold
before my eyes, brings me more joy than I ever could have imagined. Since the doctors tell me that I may very well owe him my
life, a little explaining is the least I can do.

New York, August 1993

YOU DON'T HAVE TO BE YOUR MOTHER

Chapter One

I WAS NEWLY HOME, PROPPED UP ON THE SOFA, TRYING to make time pass before my husband would return. Because of the painkillers, I couldn't take in the words of the magazine, only the pictures. When I came upon the ad whose letters were big enough to be read across an eye doctor's examining room, it took a little while for them to form recognizably through the blur. "You do not have to be your mother," was what they said.

Eight days before, I had been forty years old and eight months pregnant. It had been an unexpectedly glorious time: friends said that I glowed, the way women carrying a new life sometimes do. In the photographs taken during those months, my image smiles back, undeniably brimming with great expectations and good health. My woman's body was growing a new person, cells multiplying astronomically, amazingly, into arms, legs, eyes, heart. What I didn't realize was that during those long and fruitful months, my body was also growing something else, cells multiplying astronomically, terrifyingly. The breast cancer that had convulsed my childhood, that had caused my mother to die at forty-seven after five terrible years, was about to overturn my life.

"You do not have to be your mother," was what the ad said. I stared at the picture of the bouncy, healthy young woman advertising athletic shoes, and repeated the words to myself wonderingly, remembering how as a teenager I had adopted a similar credo with the fierce determination of the very young. It was the only way that

18   I was able to make sense of what had happened to my mother. I set about distancing my life from hers, resolving to live as fully as possible, to experience everything I could beyond the confines of her life as wife and mother. I had spent many years in distant lands, living in China, France, and for a long time in Britain. I sounded more English than American as a result. I had established an identity in the world beyond home and family. But somehow, the distance between myself and my mother now seemed to have shrunk, just as she—all those years ago—had shrunk quite literally before my eyes.

I had taken the magazine from the hospital when I was discharged early that morning. It had been such a long day, like all the days of that week since the diagnosis. Days beyond fatigue, beyond fear, beyond feeling, having so much of all three that they were stretched to their thinnest and tautest for my husband, David, and me.

Although I had married at twenty-four, like many women of my generation I had delayed childbearing in favor of career, travel, and the pleasures of being a couple. In my case, the delay proved to have painful consequences: when we tried to start a family in our mid-thirties, we discovered that it would not be easy for me to conceive. So after the operations, the hormones, the regular visits to the infertility clinic, the kind but realistic assessments of the specialists, it had truly seemed a miracle when I finally became pregnant.

I found the lump in my thirty-third week. A small pimple had been resident on one breast for about a fortnight, and I suddenly realized that I hadn't examined myself since the early days of the pregnancy. I had always been punctilious in that regard, given what had happened to my mother, but the past months had found me so happily engrossed in producing a baby that the shadow of breast cancer had virtually—for the first time since my teens—disappeared from my mental geography.

I suppose it was the latent pull of habit that made me check.

About an inch from the pimple—which itself, when biopsied, turned out to be perfectly normal—I seemed to feel a small mound. David felt it, too. I made a note to tell my obstetrician, Laurie Goldstein, about it when I saw her the following week.

Laurie agreed with my suspicion. "It's probably a blocked milk duct, Gayle. One of those things that happen to pregnant breasts." But she called her colleague, Becky Brightman, to come over to take a look. Mammograms aren't given to pregnant women, for fear of exposing the fetus to radiation, but my doctors said that because of my family history, they could refer me for a sonogram.

Some women cope with the heritage of a mother's death from breast cancer by banishing it to a sealed compartment of the past, fleeing from the fear of their own genes. Others—and I fell into that group—try to keep fear at bay by being very matter-of-fact. I had never kidded myself, and I always knew that if there were any question of my body harboring a malignancy, I would want to have it dealt with as swiftly as possible. I told my obstetricians that yes, I would like to see their radiologist friend Mimi Levy-Ravetch. And undoubtedly it was that "yes" that saved my life.

I was very familiar with the sonogram procedure from the early months of the pregnancy, from my weekly 6:30 A.M. rendezvous with the technicians at the infertility clinic. Now, when Mimi's technician led me into the small, darkened cubicle, I didn't feel unduly nervous. She took the pictures and went away to show them to the doctor. I busied myself studying the machine, the equipment on the shelf, my face in the mirror. It was only after a longish time had elapsed and neither had returned that anxiety could no longer be reined in. And then suddenly, both women came into the room together.

Mimi said that the image was unclear. "I'll have to use a needle to aspirate some cells, which we'll send for analysis." She used the sonogram to guide the needle into place; it was painful, and the fluid was bloody. I wondered if that was good or bad; I wondered, but didn't ask. The results would be back on Friday at the earliest.

Mimi had been very straightforward, and her technician displayed the studied cheerfulness of the medical professional, but a small panic began to build inside me. Watching my mother die had put me into the habit of fearing the worst whenever I or anyone dear to me fell ill. Although I knew this was silly and irrational, the habit had proved stronger than my ability to break it. And this time, I could not shake off the feeling that something was really wrong.

I walked home slowly that Monday evening and was haunted by long-dormant scenes from childhood. I was eleven years old when my mother fell ill. After a few years, when the cancer really took hold, my father could not support the mental and emotional strain; my mother had always been his best friend and business confidante as well as wife. He had a breakdown and went away for a while. Relatives floated in and out.

When my father returned, his grief was still barely supportable, added to which his sign business was now in trouble. His workday stretched longer and longer into the night. My older sister was away at college, so I was left to care for my little sister, eight years younger than myself. Our mother was slowly disintegrating in our parents' bedroom, not speaking, seemingly unable to recognize us. Her bones were crumbling, and each day she seemed to shrink smaller and smaller into the vast whiteness of the bed beside which the nurse loomed. Even now, I am overcome by nausea when I go into an elevator or pass another woman on the street and catch a whiff of the perfume that nurse wore. Strong it was, and had to be, to ward off the smell of death.

In the evening, after I put my sister to bed and before my father returned, I sat in the kitchen and did my homework with the television on all the time. The nurse was there only during the day, and I was terrified of the night, of the dark room upstairs. I was fifteen when she died. My childhood had long since ended, although I was a child still.

After David came home that night, the goblins of the past receded. On Tuesday I returned to my job, and the routines of the office and of everyday life worked their reassuring magic. On Thursday morning, Mimi phoned and asked me something or other—I can't recall now what it was. I was a journalist writing against a deadline, and so I didn't pay much attention to the oddity of her calling before the results were due in. I went out for a very brief lunch with a friend, and was just settling back at the computer when the phone rang again.

We all know that someday we shall die. But as in the theater, where we suspend our disbelief for the pleasure of the play, we have also grown accustomed to suspending the knowledge of our certain mortality. We get on with living, and if any woman needs further persuasion, there is nothing like a baby developing inside her to convince her of the power of life. It was Laurie, my obstetrician, on the phone.

"I know you would want me to be straight with you, Gayle. The cells are malignant. That's why Mimi phoned you this morning."

How to describe the chasm that opened up, the moment that divided my life into before and after? Part of me was stunned, but in another part, images and thoughts and feelings flooded through in pandemonium. I could not speak. When sound finally did come, I was sobbing, and Laurie said that she would phone David, and that we should come to her office immediately.

My sobbing had summoned my lunchtime colleague to my desk. I had the reputation at the office of being cool, calm, composed. I could not answer Michael's fearful questions or respond to his shocked look with any assurances. I could only say through tears, forcing the words out, that something bad had happened and that he might not see me for a while. My maternity leave was due to start in just over two weeks. As I walked to the elevator, onto the street, and into a cab, I felt as though the clocks had stopped, as though I were living on a different plane, suspended out of time. I

22 wondered if I had given the cancer to the baby. I wondered if I would need a maternity leave at all.

As soon as David and I entered Laurie's office that Thursday, we were met by the familiar faces of Barbara, the office manager, and Irina, the technician. There was a silence in their greetings, a hollowness in their eyes, that communicated their knowledge of my condition. Laurie sat us down and told us that she had already talked with Becky and their other partner, Judy Schwartz, and had been on the phone to a well-known cancer surgeon, who would see me early that evening. Before then, I was to go to Mimi's office for a set of mammograms. They had all agreed that the way to proceed was to induce labor, since the hormones supporting the pregnancy were most probably making the cancer grow very fast. The baby had to be gotten out quickly so that I could be operated on. I could be admitted into the maternity ward either tomorrow or on Sunday. It shouldn't wait beyond then. Laurie looked at me, encouraging questions.

I had been shaky, but thus far had managed to listen and to respond. Although I would have to cede much of the control of my life to my doctors during the coming days and weeks, I knew that the final decisions had to rest with me, and that I had to be lucid in order to make them. But at that moment, all I could produce were little strangled sounds.

After twenty years of shared living, David knew what I wanted to say. He said it for me. "The baby isn't due for another five weeks, and hasn't shown any sign of wanting to come out into the world. What are the risks?" Grimly, he appended the coda: "Could the baby have cancer, too?"

Laurie spoke quickly, with her usual directness: "No way. It just doesn't work like that. The baby couldn't have cancer."

As to the risks of the early delivery, she said that the baby would be born at thirty-five weeks, and provided it was a good weight, everything would be fine. I had gained twenty pounds during the past eight months—enough, she reckoned. But she, Becky, and Judy had decided that I would be induced slowly, so as to avoid a cesarean delivery if at all possible. A vaginal birth, coupled with breast surgery a week or so later, would be physically exhausting enough. Two major operations in that time would be a whole lot worse.

It was already late afternoon when David accompanied me to Mimi's office. She was the sort of doctor who appeared to find words awkward—what, after all, could she say? But even then, shocked as I was, I recognized that she had done me a great service. A pregnant woman's breasts are lumpy and difficult to read at the best of times; not every radiologist would have bothered to do an aspiration.

I waited in the familiar small cubicle, and an unfamiliar technician walked in. I felt, as I would so often during the next few days, a freak. I was a pregnant woman, and I had breast cancer. I could not believe it, I could not get my mind around it, yet it had taken over my life and that of my baby.

The mammogram procedure was much more uncomfortable than usual; the tears that seemed to well up continually again washed over my face. The technician, an attractive black woman, looked at me with a calm, steady gaze. "It's alright, honey. You've got to hope for the best, hope that it's early and that they'll deal with it and you can put it behind you. My cousin had two little children under five when she and her husband were killed in a car crash. They didn't have a chance. You've got a chance. Remember that."

While the films were being developed, the technician stayed with me, and later, when Mimi was studying them, she sat with me again. It was clear that she didn't want to leave me on my own. Her simple kindness asked no questions.

I had learned during my pregnancy about the kindness of strangers. Not everyone would give up a seat on the subway or leave a

24 little extra room for me to pass, but many did. I like to think that they cherished instinctively—however hardened New York City had made their shells—the beginning of a new life full of hope and possibilities for us all. During the travail that followed, I was to be sustained over and over again by the warmth that flowed from many such encounters. The sight of me heavy with child, my husband at my side, tramping like refugees from doctor's office to doctor's office, statelessly suspended between birth and death, moved many whose grim business it was to deal with cancer routinely. Of course, not everyone was moved; not everyone behaved generously or even with civility. But it was those who did who made the difference.

We got to the breast surgeon's office at five o'clock. He had come back especially to see us. The office was in Mt. Sinai, the large teaching hospital where I had, with such anticipation, booked a maternity room for over a month hence. Instead, Laurie was arranging for me to be admitted at six o'clock on Sunday evening.

It was so late in the normal hospital appointment day that nobody was in the waiting room. Steve Brower came out and ushered us in himself. He began quietly and gently to tell us about himself, his background in research, and to provide a kind of oral primer in breast cancer.

He confirmed Mimi's analysis: the cancer might not be confined just to the area of the lump, where the cells had been aspirated. He picked up a film and pointed to some tiny white flecks in another section of the breast. Those, he said, were calcium deposits—calcifications—and could indicate more malignant cells. He didn't know whether the cancer was very early, confined to the milk ducts—noninvasive, or noninfiltrating, in medical parlance—or whether it had breached the duct walls and become invasive. If the latter, it could already have spread to my lymph nodes—the first place where it usually migrates—or been carried by the lymph or blood to another part of the body. It was rare for a cancer seen in several parts of the breast still to be noninvasive. Furthermore, since many breast cancers need estrogen to develop and my pregnant body was a veritable estrogen factory, it didn't look good.

Steve said he would wait for several days after the birth of my baby to let my body recover from the immediate effects of labor and delivery, and would then do a surgical biopsy on the breast. The biopsy results would determine whether I needed a lumpectomy, whereby only limited areas of tissue and some lymph nodes would be removed, or a mastectomy, which would take the whole breast and some nodes. Whatever happened, it would not be an easy operation because my breast would be swollen from milk and the extra blood that all pregnant women carry. There was the danger that I might bleed very heavily.

He went on to ask me about the pregnancy, about all the hormones I had taken in order to conceive. He wanted to know about any other medical problems I had had. Then he asked me about my mother. I had felt her shadow the whole time I had been sitting in his office. I kept seeing her face, the weary, set look it had assumed after she got ill. Relatives and friends always said that of her three daughters I resembled our mother the most, and I wondered if now my face, too, was assuming that stony cast.

I knew so little about the woman who had been my mother, and had known so little about her cancer until it was too late. Our parents kept the nature of the illness from us for as long as they could. Years afterward I was to learn that when she found the lump she was sent by our family doctor to see a specialist, who told her that he suspected breast cancer. She would have to have an immediate biopsy, followed most likely by a mastectomy. That day I remember because our parents returned and we children were shooed outside while our father and mother were inside together. Our mother was crying.

In another life, she had trained and worked just before and during the Second World War as a doctor's technician, so she was by

26 no means medically uninformed. But she could not accept the specialist's diagnosis, and went for a second opinion to a different surgeon at a famous hospital in our native Philadelphia.

That surgeon had helped many people—he had even treated the President—and he later was to have a building named after him. He told my mother that her lump was not malignant, that it was merely fluid that would need to be aspirated from time to time. During more than a year—a period that I remember vaguely—my mother visited this man's office for her regular aspirations. And then one day, in cancer terms so very, very much later, he was so very sorry.

She went away to the hospital and then to the nursing home in a distant suburb, where we were only able to visit her on Sunday. Finally she came home and had to rest every afternoon on the living room sofa. We were told nothing about the true nature of her illness, and we couldn't understand why our mother suddenly expected us to do a lot more around the house and got so upset when we didn't. I couldn't understand why the house seemed to grow so much quieter.

A few years later my mother started to have back pains, and she was sent to the hospital for what seemed to be the whole summer. My older sister was away at college by then. Somehow, in the intervening years, we had picked up some vague notion about our mother's breast cancer, and that summer we were told that she had to have another operation as well. They were going to remove her ovaries. The doctors weren't sure whether the cancer had metastasized to her other female organs, but in any case, late in the day, they had decided to put an end to the flow of estrogen that was supporting the malignant growth. By then the cancer was in her lungs, bones, and liver, too.

As little children, we had been used to going into our parents' room while our mother was getting dressed, but after her first operation she never let us into the room unless she was fully clothed. As I now sat in a breast surgeon's—my breast surgeon's—office, feeling the inexorable force that linked me to my mother, knowing that there were so many questions to which I could never have answers, I remembered one night from my teen years with aching sadness and regret.

My mother was having a bath. My little sister was asleep, my father wasn't home. I heard her calling to me, and I approached the bathroom door.

"Gayle, I can't get out of the tub, you're going to have to come in and lift me out." I remember standing there, frozen, dumb. I was afraid of what my mother would look like. I had never been able to face the scary scenes in movies; I had always averted my eyes. I knew that her body was disfigured, that she had kept it from us for the past three years. I could not turn the handle.

My mother could hear me on the other side of the door, and she called again. I don't know what I said or for how long I stood there. I began, in slow motion, to turn the handle, averting my eyes as though some curse would fall upon me if I gazed at her body directly. But by then, she had managed to hoist herself out. "You don't have to come in now," I heard her say through her tears.

I returned to the present. I sat facing a surgeon who would cut open my body. How much he would have to take away neither of us could predict. But whatever happened, this time, I knew there would be no looking away.

When David and I left Steve's office, it was after seven o'clock. We had spent more than five hours with doctors that day and were exhausted from having to concentrate, to hear what they were telling us. The landscape of our lives had changed forever, and we had to begin the painful adjustment to an unfamiliar terrain. For me though, during the weeks and months that followed, one rock would remain in place. Whatever happened, whatever I would look like after the doctors had finished with me, David would be beside me. I was a very fortunate woman.

As we walked home, we talked about how much there was to

do. In less than seventy-two hours I would be going into the hospital, and we had thus far prepared very little for the arrival of our baby. Our one piece of good luck was that we had the previous week engaged Amira, the woman who would be our nanny. But out of some unspoken superstition that invades so many parents-to-be, we had left off buying most of the paraphernalia that a new baby requires. In addition, I would have to put my affairs in order; there were bills to pay and my will to reconsider.

What we dreaded most, though, were the phone calls. We would have to let people know. How would I tell the news to my sisters, Sandy and Vickie, with our shared memories, knowing that my cancer, added to our mother's, meant that they were now even more at risk themselves? More terribly, how would I tell my father? I feared stirring the cauldron of memories that might spill over into one of his depressions, the legacy of those dreadful years. How would I let people know at work?

And how was David to tell his family, so far away in England? They, too, knew the trauma of breast cancer intimately. Keith, David's younger brother, had lost his first wife, Pat, to the disease when she was only thirty-four years old. Her illness was cut from the same pattern as my mother's, and David's brothers and sister and father had all borne witness to her slow dying. Keith had been left with two young children, and it was only recently, since his new marriage to Christina, that life had become more settled. How could we tell them that it was all starting again? How could we summon up enough hope to squeeze into our long-distance voices the reassurance that the trajectory of my life would not be the same as Pat's?

Chapter Two

AS WE SAT IN THE DINING ROOM, ALL OF THE ORDINARY objects, the familiar bits and pieces of our life together, seemed to take on the intensity of dreams. Everything was the same, and yet nothing was the same. I could not get around the sudden dislocation. The paintings, the Chinese teapots, the vase full of flowers, all of them stood out, noticeable, no longer the taken-for-granted background to a normal life. We felt like visitors to a museum of our past.

David, angled against the countertop, leaned toward the dining room phone. He had plonked the cordless unit from the living room onto the long glass table in front of me. I sipped the strong, sweet tea he had made. I normally didn't take sugar.

We had gotten back to the apartment an hour before, at 7:30, and had decided that tonight the only people we would phone would be my older sister, Sandy; David's law partner, Brian, and his wife, Diana; and my boss and good friend, Daisy, an Orthodox Jew whom I couldn't face phoning in the melee of office hours tomorrow, and who would be unreachable during the Sabbath that followed.

"Look, my darling, I'll phone Brian and Di to get us going. They already know what's up. You join in when you feel like it," David said.

So many hours ago, after David had first heard the word cancer over the telephone, he had stopped long enough to tell Brian before rushing off to meet me at Laurie's office. They were solicitors, partners in one of the major English law firms, now working in the New York branch office. Brian was a plucky, world-traveling New Zealander. My husband was an Englishman who in a very un-English move had taken up an undergraduate scholarship for college in America. He had loved it, but nevertheless returned home after three years and began to study law in London, while the American he had met at the University of Pennsylvania did an M.A. in French literature at Cambridge. I spent a year teaching English in France after that, and then we married. Nine years later, in 1985, David came back to the States to start up a U.S. outpost for the firm, while I transmogrified from London book editor to New York book journalist at *Publishers Weekly*.

Looking at them, hearing them speak, the two men seemed so different, and yet they were partners, professional secret sharers, and, more than that, friends. Brian—dark, peppery, aggressive—was quick to form opinions and to act on them; David, slim and pale, short reddish beard making up for the lack of thatch above his brow, was measured, patient, possessed of a kind of sweetness that seemed slightly at odds with his proper English demeanor and profession. My Chinese friends, meeting him for the first time in Beijing, pronounced that David had the air of a scholar rather than a lawyer. And they loved the fact that he played the clown about his baldness, joking rather than trying to hide or deny it.

David dialed the suburban number he knew by heart and smiled hard at me as it rang. "Brian? Yes, we only got back a little while ago. It's been a hell of a day, doctor after doctor. Gayle's going into Mt. Sinai on Sunday night. They're going to induce the baby and then do a biopsy a few days later.

"I'm coming in tomorrow to clear things up, since I don't know when I'll be around after that. We can talk in the morning. But we were wondering if you, or really Di, could help us out. We've got to get the things for the baby, and we don't know where to begin. Are the children up, or can you put Di on?"

I picked up the other phone and heard Brian telegraphing the news to his wife in the background. Diana, cool and blond like her name, had used the skills of a nurse to sojourn around the world before marrying and giving birth to their two young children.

"Hello, David . . ." came the flattened New Zealand syllables.

"Di, I'm on the line, too."

"Gayle, I'm really sorry. Just when everything seemed to be going so well. . . . Look, why don't we come shopping with you? We could all drive into the city on Saturday. Make a list and I'll fill in the gaps. And think about anything else you need, for you, rather than the baby. Oh, I can hear Max beginning to cry. He's wanting a feed. I'll talk to you tomorrow."

Di's words, "Everything seemed to be going so well," ebbed further and further away from the new shoreline of my life. She, more than many others, had understood how well things really had been these past eight months. Brian had joined David in the New York office three years before, just after he and Di had married. All of us knew that at our age it was time to get on with having children, and I marveled at how Di had conceived Jessica, and then Max, so easily. I, meanwhile, had my third operation to try to sort out my various gynecological woes.

As a result of that operation, Di and I got to know each other in an unexpectedly intimate way. The evening I returned from the hospital, my temperature soared and we discovered that an infection was festering in the wound. Nurse Di came to the rescue, crossing Manhattan every day for almost a week to clean out the incision so that it would heal properly. Quite a lot of talking got done during those visits.

I changed doctors, abandoning the specialist who was more interested in high-tech medicine and high doses of hormones than in taking care of the infection and talking me through my worries. I started seeing not a specialist but an ordinary gynecologist, Judy Schwartz, whose approach was both sympathetic and practical. Judy gave me the hormone clomiphene and Di followed my progress, cheering from the sidelines. Nothing happened.

It was after almost a year that Judy referred me to a specialist once again, Larry Grunfeld, at the Mt. Sinai infertility clinic. There was another operation, and more hormones, and then it worked. From the time the baby was conceived until this week, everything seemed to have fallen into place, indeed to have gone so well.

David got up to brew some fresh tea. The next call was one that I would have to make. As I dialed the Philadelphia area code and my sister Sandy's phone number, the knowledge of the words that I would have to speak, the knowledge of our family history, shuddered through me like the first chills of flu.

I was a very private person, and although I could be a good talker, chatting about this and that, offering opinions and advice, there was much about myself that I could share with only a few. I had always skirted around sharing certain things with my sisters; I was the middle one, and my younger sister, Vickie, never hesitated to remark on how maddening it was that I always seemed to be so cool.

When I thought about it, this girdle of silence had been with me from an early age. Our mother had drummed into our heads that "it's better to be a good listener than a talker. Don't tell people your problems. Don't go saying things all over the place. Keep it to yourself. . . ." Perhaps I was awed by this stricture, absorbed this taboo more deeply than my sisters, because of the way its terrible importance was brought home to me when I was very young. Because of something I did.

It was 1955, and I was four years old, when we moved to our new house in the newly developed area of the city that had been farmland only a few years before. "Fox Chase Road": I liked the sound of that name, the stories it promised, much better than the plain and simple "Stevens Street" we had left.

My father was a commercial artist. His business manufactured signs—neon, plastic, metal, even painted billboards. These signs—the giant cocktail glasses dipping and flashing above the bars, the jaunty cutouts of chefs twirling their mustaches on the pizza parlor plate glass, the mysterious characters and symbols adorning the Chinese restaurant walls—lit up and formed my childhood map of Philadelphia. Sometimes, when our father had to call on customers early in the evening, he would come by the house and scoop us up into his car or pickup, taking us with him "for the ride." It always seemed to me that out of the darkening night sky, all of the excitement, all of the unknown world of grown-ups and their adventures, was contained in those rides, in those beacons of light and color and movement that we drove by, that came out of my father's sign shop.

It happened the summer after we moved to the new house, when I was nearly five. The big red car disappeared and we began to ride in the pickup all the time. Vickie wasn't born yet, and Sandy and I didn't mind cramming together next to our parents on the front seat. In fact, we could see so much more riding high up in the truck. Somehow, though, the word *bankruptcy* entered my vocabulary. My father's business had gone "bankrupt" was what I kept hearing. To me, this sounded like such a big deal, full of importance, special. Something exciting, something to be shared.

So one day, when my mother sent me out of the house to play, I traveled from building to building, up and down the stoops of the semidetached houses on our side of the block, and wherever a child my age resided—and there were many, in this new development—I proudly told my playmates and their mothers that my father was bankrupt. It was after this got back to my mother that I learned the value of silence.

I cannot remember her words, or even how she came to know

34   what I had done—which of the neighbors had told her. But the intensity of her feelings, that I do recall, and their power to make me stand there, dumb with fear. She didn't hit me; she never did that. The fury was controlled, the burning in her eyes ice-cold.

"All your Grandmom Golde would have to do was to look at me, and I'd know, I'd do whatever she wanted. She never had to tell me," was what I remember her saying each time one of our childish infractions exasperated or disappointed her, each time we didn't do something she expected of us. Perhaps our mother never quite realized how much she had inherited that famous "look" or how devastating it could be. Certainly, I knew about keeping myself to myself after that.

Years later, I came to understand that it was my father who had dreamt up the designs, did many of the layouts, and sold the signs. He had left much of the running of other things to his partners. The business failed. Our car went the way of the business, but our father managed to hold on to the building and some tools. After the bankruptcy, he scraped together a little money and started a second time, on his own.

And now, here I was, calling Philadelphia, where my sisters and father had remained during the course of all my wanderings. My brother-in-law Steve answered the phone.

"Hi, Gayle, how're you doing? Feeling okay? Has the baby been kicking a lot and keeping you and Dave up at night?" he chuckled, this father of eleven-month-old Melissa and four-and-a-half-year-old Jessica. "I'll tell Sandy to pick up. She's in the hall."

"Hi, Gayle, how're things with the baby?"

I fought the constriction in my throat. "The baby is fine, Sandy, but the mother isn't so great. Look, I didn't tell you, I didn't want you to worry, but I found a lump ten days ago. The doctors said today that it's breast cancer. I'm going into the hospital on Sunday."

I had wondered if she would cry, but instead there was a momentary silence, like that silence so many years ago when I picked up the phone and was told that my mother had just died. I could imagine my sister, short and olive-complexioned like our father, staring, unseeing, into the big mirror in her old-fashioned, wood-paneled hallway. The image looking back would have cascading black hair, a long nose, lips thinner than mine, and panicky fear at the back of big, dark eyes.

I tried to keep my voice from cracking as we went through what had happened, what was about to happen, what was still so unknown.

"Gayle, what can I do? I can come up with the kids. Maybe I could leave Jessica here and only take Melissa. She won't be too much trouble. What can I bring? What about the baby, you need to get things for the baby. What if . . ."

"Sandy, listen to me. Please, don't come up yet. We'll need your help, but David and I have to work things out ourselves first. We're reeling, Sandy, reeling. We've asked Brian and Di to help us with the shopping . . . it's easier, they're here and you're in Philadelphia. The time will come for you to visit soon. I'll need all the visits I can get, but just not right now. The thing you can do now is to phone Vick and tell her. That would help a lot. Tell her that I'll speak to her tomorrow. I'll phone Daddy tomorrow, too."

When I put the phone down, I felt overcome by the weariness of having to say no. Often in our conversations with friends and relations during the coming days, David and I would have to stem the tide of offers, tamp down other people's need, so felt, so intense, just to do something, anything. The truth was that there was only so much they could do, and then only at certain junctures. There were times when, after coping with the attentions and questions of those near and dear, we'd simply fall back into the chair and weep, more exhausted, even, than before the phone rang. We felt as

36 though our lives were becoming public property. And we knew that they were being orchestrated elsewhere, that we were playing by the doctors' score now.

It was 9:30 P.M., and I phoned Daisy quickly, using many of the expressions I had just heard myself say to Sandy. Indeed, as the phone calls proceeded during the next few days, the questions and answers became a sort of catechism, almost automatic, rote. But we also had to talk about how things stood at work, about the article I had left half-written, about how the hungry pages for which I was responsible would be filled. In the end, Daisy cut through it all, saying simply, "Don't worry about anything here, Gayle."

We agreed that for now only a few people at the magazine need know what was really going on. Once the birth had taken place, she would say for public consumption that there were complications and so the baby was born early. I asked Daisy to phone Maria, my associate editor, to let her know what had happened; the two of them would have to step into the breach. I decided to tell Michael myself, given what he had witnessed earlier in the day, and would ask him to talk with John, the editor in chief. Daisy would inform the personnel office, and together they would wade through all the work-related bureaucracy that a serious illness entails.

After a quick call to Michael, we went to bed, but sleep was elusive. I could not summon up the concentration for a book, and my mind did not stop racing as I flipped page after magazine page. Finally, though, around 12:30, fatigue overcame my pregnant body and I dozed off. David's small light stayed on, late into the night.

We awoke early that Friday, the 27th of September, with no groggy transition from dreams to consciousness. As we opened our eyes and turned to each other, the adrenalin began coursing through us instantaneously. Over tea and fruit and toast, we worked out the plan for the day.

David would go to work and tell his small staff what was happening. It was an intimate group, eight people, and my husband, more than I at the time, comprehended that he would be depending on them not only to keep the office running smoothly without its head, but to help us personally in all sorts of ways, to copy and collect records and doctors' reports, to work out so many small, critical details.

I did not want to stay home alone, and so I would join David midmorning at the office, where we would tackle the phone calls to England, to my sister Vickie, to the doctors, to several close friends. Before then, I would start on a little necessary reading.

Working at *Publishers Weekly* as the book news editor is a bibliophile's dream; so many different volumes come my way, without my even asking. A lot of these books, when we've finished writing about them, are donated to the public library or passed on to colleagues. Some I bring home, so that a glance at our never-properly-organized bookshelves is like perusing the pages of a dictionary, with strangely disparate subjects knocking against each other cheek by jowl.

I knew that, scattered on shelves throughout the apartment, were a few volumes, collected over the years, that dealt with breast cancer. They were books I had never found time or inclination to study, but books that I at least had had the sense to save "just in case." I found three such, and the one I turned to first, the one that in the end proved to be most consistently of use, was cowritten by a woman surgeon, *Dr. Susan Love's Breast Book.*

I realized that what I knew about breast cancer was a mishmash of memories—anecdotal, uninformed, imprecise—and I had to find out so much, fast. Both David and I needed to embark on a crash reading course in cancer. Steve Brower had given us an introductory leaflet published by the National Cancer Institute. It mentioned a toll-free number through which people could obtain additional information and literature. I dialed the number and requested a half-dozen leaflets. Then I thought of Jean Crichton, a writer friend who had been operated on for breast cancer the previous

38 Christmas. She could bring to bear knowledge culled from hard personal experience and recommend some further reading as well. I phoned and left a message on her answering machine.

I wondered what my mother had done when she knew, finally, incontrovertibly, about her breast cancer. For me, there had always been the habit of reading, and I had access to so many books and to cancer networks with as-yet-unknown, untapped sources of information. But for her, in those days, in the early 1960s, three children and the demands of our father's business left little time for reading. And in any case, there was so little to go on, so much was hidden. Betty Rollin, Rose Kushner, Jill Ireland, Betty Ford . . . the women who would speak and write publicly about their breast cancer hadn't done so yet.

I turned to the jumble of books on the coffee table. Volumes about cancer and home medical encyclopedias lay on top of books about birth and babies. I had thought that the two weeks of my maternity leave that were to precede the October 30th due date would be filled with the words of Spock, Leach, Kitzinger, and Stoppard. Now there were just two days for so many books.

It was nearly noon when I reached the midtown office tower where my husband worked. Fortuitously, the week before, I had made an appointment to get my hair cut at four o'clock in the afternoon. I would need to keep that appointment, to make the effort, still, to look good. We would have about three hours, with a break for lunch, in which to make our calls.

As I walked into David's office, I did not want to look directly at Emma, the office manager, or Renee and Teri, the secretaries, for fear that I would cry. I tried to look straight ahead but could not escape their efforts not to stare, the shock still registering in the tense creases around their mouths.

My husband stood up and embraced me. "Let's phone Di first," was what he said.

Diana Bramall is David's older sister and, like our New Zealand

friend of the same first name, she's blond, blue-eyed, and trained as
a nurse. David and I have always been close with Diana and her
television director husband, Richard, from that time, twenty years
ago, when I first traveled to the big house in the English countryside to be introduced to my then-boyfriend's family. Diana, the
only daughter among five children, is the sympathetic ear of the
Reid family, emotional, unusually giving, deeply religious. She was
the one to whom Keith and Pat turned when Pat's cancer was
diagnosed. She'd seen a lot and then some.

Now my husband felt sorely in need of his older sister's emotional support, and David and I were going to ask a very particular
favor of her. Although we were immeasurably glad that we had
found a nanny before everything had blown up, we were both
concerned about the time, two weeks hence, when I would be
operated on and about the period immediately after I came home.
I might be gone for a week, and no doubt David would be spending a lot of that time with me at the hospital. How could we leave
this baby who was still inside me, my constant companion for the
past eight months, in the hands of a stranger, with neither of us
around? From a practical vantage point, Amira would only be a day
nanny, and we would also, now, need help at night. And because
times had changed since my mother's operation, and I would not
be going to a nursing home to recuperate, help would be needed
on that front as well.

Despite her willingness to lend a hand, Sandy had two small children to consider, who would make a stay in New York awkward at
best. Vick had a job that gave her very little vacation time. Since
Diana's three children were old enough, and we hoped that her
work as a family planning counselor was flexible enough, we were
going to ask her to come to New York. Still, it was a lot to ask, to
drop everything, leave her family, travel three thousand miles to
help us out.

They had been talking for a while, brother and sister, when my

40 husband passed me the receiver. "Oh, Gayle, you must be strong. I know you'll be strong. You will be. And David loves you so. You must hold on to that.

"David has asked me to tell Keith. Remember, you're not Pat. It's a different situation. They waited too long after she found the lump. That terrible GP who told her it was nothing to worry about. Your doctors are acting right away, and we've got to hope that it's still very early.

"I'll see what I can do about coming. I'll try. Richard and I will discuss it over the weekend, and I'll talk with the clinic next week. We'll all be praying for you."

I had started to cry when I heard her voice, and I could see that David's eyes were filling too. After I put the phone down, my husband took my hand. Like two frightened children, we sat there, wordlessly peering down at the bustle of the streets so many floors below, severed from the world that was ours just twenty-four hours before.

That night, I phoned my father. It was the call I had been dreading most.

"What? What are you saying?" was how he responded to the news. My father, in his old age, has become deaf in one ear. He talks a lot louder and is a lot more argumentative than he used to be. But the still-youthful voice spoke very quietly now.

"No, no, no. How could this happen? You looked so well when you were down two weeks ago. Who are these doctors? Are you sure about them? You know what happened with your mother. Maybe they could be wrong."

"Dad, it's because of what happened with Mother that I'm listening to these doctors. They're good doctors. There's no question. The only question is what they will have to do, how much they will have to take."

"Do you want me to phone your sisters?"

"I've already spoken to Sandy and Vick."

"Do you need anything? How's David?"

"You can't do anything, Dad, not just now. David's alright. We're bearing up. Why don't you talk to Sandy and Vickie? Maybe that would be a good thing."

"My God, what a life, what a life. Why? Your mother, now you. You know that I love you, don't you?"

"Of course I know that, and I love you too. I've got to go now, Dad. I've got to make some other calls. We'll be talking. You take care."

I put the phone down, and in my mind's eye saw an old man, short and slightly stooped, with still-powerful arms and hands, a good covering of white wavy hair, pencil-thin mustache, and eyes that were blinking, slowly, behind large glasses. Blinking in disbelief.

It was a surprise, still, to think of him as old, this man who goes to work every day, cruising around parts of Philadelphia that younger people avoid, selling and servicing his signs. Customers, just hearing his voice on the phone, assume he is a man in his mid-fifties; how many times he has told us, with undisguised glee, about their surprise when they discover he is twenty years older than that.

Joe Feldman's life crumbled when his wife died, and it took a long time, and another woman, Pearl, to put the pieces back together—although not quite as before. Never quite as before.

I walked upstairs, into our bedroom, and bent over to pluck from the bookshelf the slim bundle that I had taken from Philadelphia so many years before, carried to England, and then carried back across the Atlantic. Carefully, I crouched down and unfastened the large portrait photo that held the collection of smaller black-and-whites between its covers.

There they were, smiling up at me, the young couple with jet-black hair, laughing eyes. Like Clark Gable and Vivien Leigh, all the glamour and mystery of 1941. That beginning seemed a world away, but it produced us, my two sisters and me. So much change, so much happiness and unhappiness, but no answers, just questions. And yet, as I stared at my parents' youthful faces, at the possibilities for all that could have been, might have been, I felt, flowing up from the same deep pool, two streams quite separate but seamlessly parallel: an enormous sadness and an immensity of love. I clutched the photo to me, my eyes swimming. It was all a mystery and, whatever happened, would remain so. We just had to go on.

Chapter Three

DAVID TURNED THE KEY IN THE DOOR, AND WE WALKED
into the silence and dust of our new old house. After months of
looking, we had settled on this brownstone from another era on
New York's Upper East Side, barely modernized, as the place
where we would put down roots. We looked past the murky hall,
through the darkened dining room, and into the deep green of the
little walled garden. It was the garden that had charmed us.

We would be able to raise so many things here. We would be
able to grow a child here. Perhaps we had lived too long in houses
in London ever to feel really at home in a massive apartment block
in New York. We had thrown all our savings and more into this
townhouse, and the work had been proceeding feverishly so that
we could move toward the end of October, just before the baby
would be born.

It was the baby inside me who had spurred on the builders, the
painters, the plumber, the electrician. One of the tasks David had
undertaken Friday morning, before going to the office, was to visit
the house and tell all of them what had happened, that there was no
hurry now. The move, like so many things, had been put on hold.

I had wanted to see the house one more time, devoid of work-
men. And so in fading light, at nearly half-past five on a Sunday, we
were making this last stop en route to the hospital. The past two
days had been intensely active; we had hardly slept, hardly eaten.

Saturday had been unusually cold for late September. Brian and

44   Di came around as promised. We headed for the local children's store, and Di began whirling about, plucking blankets here, baby furniture there, undershirts, nightgowns, pacifiers, cloth diapers, all the things we knew we needed and many of the things we never would have had sense enough to buy. I could not keep up with her, and so my job was to stand by Jessica and Max, who had been parked in front of the fish tank, to guard them as they stared, fascinated, at the tropical fish. But as I, too, stared with them, I grew more and more preoccupied. Like those fish, I was walled off, isolated, horrifyingly exotic, worthy of stares, so different from all the ordinary big-bellied women moving about the shop around me.

Di must have noticed the look on my face. "Come on, Gayle, Brian and David can stand with the kids for a while. You come with me." We picked out some more items and then moved on to another shop. We managed to buy almost all that was needed to kit out a temporary nursery in our small guest bedroom.

For much of that afternoon, there was a tremendous relief in all the bustling about, in Max's coos, Jessica's questions, in my husband's initiation into the mysteries of diaper changing—he had missed the Lamaze session using life-size baby dolls, and Di had volunteered to let Max be the real-life baby for his first try. There was no false cheerfulness, but there was no heavy hand-wringing, either. Brian and Di just kept us moving along.

Late in the afternoon, Di and I went alone to the local lingerie shop. I had been sleeping in large T-shirts, but they would not do for the hospital.

"We're not going to look at price tags, we're going to look at pretty nightgowns, and we're going to get you some," was what she said.

We had to find gowns that would accommodate a postpartum figure, that would allow doctors ease of access to my chest and underarm, that later on would be high enough but not too high, not too buttoned-up and prim and sad. We succeeded in purchasing four that would be as nice as anything seen on the maternity floor.

In the evening, I phoned Eileen Conde, our Lamaze teacher whose main job was as nurse-training coordinator in Mt. Sinai's maternity ward. Vivacious, warm, with a small boy of her own, Eileen had been a wonderful teacher, and the couples in the class were all cheered by the idea that she might be around during our birthing travails. I had told Eileen about the lump after Monday's session, and she, like Laurie and Becky, had reckoned that it was only a blocked milk duct.

"Hi, Eileen, it's Gayle, from the Monday night class."

"Hi, Gayle, I recognized that English accent. What's up?"

"That lump I told you about . . . well, it turned out to be malignant."

"Oh, Gayle, what can I say? What are they going to do?"

"I'm going in to Sinai tomorrow night to be induced, and then Steve Brower—I guess you know him, being attached to the hospital—he'll do a biopsy and determine what kind of operation is needed. Anyway, Eileen, I wanted to let you know."

"I'll come and see you on Monday. And I'll let the nurses on the floor know about you, that you're one of my Lamaze students. I'll tell them what's happened. Don't worry on that score."

"Thank you so much. I didn't want to ask, but it would be such a help. It'll be a comfort to see you."

"I'll be there."

And now, here David and I were, at six o'clock on a Sunday evening, traveling in a cab up Madison Avenue on our way to Mt. Sinai Medical Center. My husband turned to me. "We're going to have to take it in stages," he said. "We'll break down if we try to face it all at once. You're going into the hospital to have the baby. That's what we have to think about, to concentrate on now. After the baby is born, we'll have to deal with the biopsy. After that, the surgery. And after that, the pathologist's report and whatever che-

46 motherapy or radiation you'll need. We've got to try to separate each step, that's the only way we'll get through the coming weeks."

I sat low down on the battered back seat of the cab, cold, almost inert with exhaustion. I held David's hand and listened and tried to accept his words as a child does, to believe in them, in their power to determine how things would be.

"Yes, yes, we'll take it in stages," I heard myself say.

We arrived at the hospital and took the elevator to the birthing floor. We walked up to the partitioned-off nurses' station. I identified myself and told the duty nurse my obstetricians' names.

"I'm sorry, we don't have you on our list of inductions."

"Eileen Conde is my Lamaze teacher. She was going to tell you about me." My voice sounded tired, unsteady.

"Well, I'm sorry, but you're not on our list."

Several people were milling around, and one of them, a young blonde woman, a doctor, yelled from the other side of the station, "Don't you understand? You've come on the wrong night."

I listened as David insisted quietly, "This isn't the wrong night. We're supposed to be here. There must be a note or something about my wife. Please look again."

The doctor glanced in our direction and said sharply, dismissively, "You'd better go home and phone in the morning. Why does she need to be induced, anyway?"

My husband rarely raises his voice, but he did now. All the anger at what was happening to us exploded from him. "We're here because my wife has cancer. She's being induced because she has cancer," is what he shouted.

Everyone lolling around the nurses' station froze like the statues in a children's game. Although this was a hospital, cancer was not a word that was heard on this floor. I covered my eyes and sobbed, feeling so completely cut off from all the normal mothers waiting to give birth and all the normal babies waiting to be born. When the tableau moved again, it was animated by the doctor turning and walking away without a word. The nurse who was in charge of registrations began to search frantically among the papers under the counter.

"Yes, here it is," she said to a colleague. She walked around the station, to the exit, and joined us out in the waiting area. I felt her arm encircle my shoulders. "I'm so sorry, Mrs. Reid. Please come with me. Please forgive us."

She led us to Birthing Room C, said that a nurse would join us shortly, and then left us alone. David squeezed my hand as, silently, we tried to calm down. We had never visited this area or the maternity floor itself; indeed, we were supposed to make the rounds with Eileen tomorrow evening for the last session of our Lamaze course. Now we were here for the real thing but without the usual overtures: no anxious middle-of-the-night phone call to the doctors, no rushed cab trip spent timing the contractions. There was just a baby inside me, not ready to come out.

The room was larger than I had expected and cheerful as hospitals go. It had unfaded wallpaper, fresh paint, and its window faced on Fifth Avenue, looking across to Central Park. Two young, attractive nurses appeared and introduced themselves as Phyllis and Chitra.

"We heard about what happened. Eileen had left a note about you, but not everybody was aware. We're really sorry."

"It's okay now," I responded. "It's not your fault."

"We've got forms for you to fill out, permissions for you to sign, we've got to take your blood pressure, examine you, all the usual. Around nine o'clock a resident will give you a prostaglandin suppository to try to soften the cervix. You'll be given another one in the middle of the night. One of your doctors will come in the morning, and you'll be hooked up to Pitocin intravenously, which should really get the contractions started."

"How long do you think it will take?"

Phyllis responded warily, "Your cervix is completely undilated, so it's difficult to say. We'll just have to wait and see."

David stayed with me for a while after they finished, and then it was time for him to go. We embraced. "I'll see you in the morning, my darling one. Don't worry. Just let them do their stuff. I'll be thinking about you." And then he was gone.

Chitra returned to sit with me, and we chatted about this and that, London and New York, our backgrounds and jobs.

"It seems kind of quiet here," I said.

"Just you wait until tomorrow. It won't be quiet then," she chuckled. "We've admitted quite a few women for inductions. A lot of people are having babies these days. I'd better go and see some of them."

A doctor came and administered the prostaglandin and then they both left. I turned on the television and heard Alastair Cooke introduce his umpteenth *Masterpiece Theatre*. It didn't matter that I had already seen the episode. I watched it anyway.

When I turned out the light, I could hear the drone of the buses passing along Fifth Avenue, the echo of footsteps walking away from the hospital entrance, the snatches of quiet conversation floating up from beneath the canopy below my window. Life outside the hospital continued on its way.

As I lay in the birthing room bed, I could feel my baby moving. Although like most first-time mothers I had been fearful about the labor, the pain of bringing a new person into the world, I felt curiously numb about it now. Like some detached spectator, I merely wondered when the pain would begin.

During the course of the pregnancy we had chosen not to know the sex of our baby, even though that piece of information was available to us from the amniocentesis and genetic tests. Not being able to refer to the baby as "he" or "she," we had gotten into the habit of calling it the "C.C.," for the "Constant Companion."

It was just the C.C. and me now—no David, no doctors, no

nurses. As I waited for the prostaglandin to kick in, I worried about all the fear and distress and the effect it must be having on the baby, wave after wave of it buffeting the small creature who was floating at my center. I thought of the sonogram images from a few months back, the marvelous being more akin to E.T. than to a fully formed flesh-and-blood baby. Was everything that was supposed to be there, there? Would my baby's eyes be ready to blink open into the hospital room lights five weeks early?

"Well, C.C., here we are together, you and me," I found myself saying. "You're going to come out into the world soon, a bit early. I know it'll be a shock, but it'll be okay. It's got to be okay. It's just got to."

At three in the morning I was awakened for the next supposi-tory, and then it was seven and light was streaming through the gap between the curtains. I sat up and opened them more fully, reveal-ing the miracle of New York's great park, the lung that enables the teeming city to breathe, to stretch, to renew itself. Despite the weekend's cold weather, the leaves still wore the green of summer.

I got up and showered, and at half past seven David phoned and said he would be in by lunchtime. At eight, my obstetrician, Becky Brightman, arrived. In her early thirties, a beautiful brunette with startlingly clear blue eyes, Becky breezed across the room and gave me a hug and kiss.

"So, how are you feeling? Everything okay? Let's have a look at you."

After she examined me, I finished breakfast while we chatted about my dramatic entrance the previous evening. Then Becky rose, saying, "Well, there's no sign of any softening. We'll hook you up to the Pitocin now. You'll start to feel a bit uncomfortable, but I hope it won't be too bad. We're not going to give you a lot to start off with, we're going to build up gradually. We don't want to end up rushing things and having to do a C-section."

They fixed up the IV and after Becky and the nurse left, I sat in

50 the chair next to the window and turned on the radio. During our early years together, David and I had lived in cheap furnished bed-sitting rooms in London, with shared bathroom and no central heating, no television either. It was in those days when we were too poor to afford a proper apartment or the modern conveniences that go with it that we discovered the companionship of the radio. Now, when I still could not find the energy for a book, I turned to the radio like an old friend.

I gazed out the window, at the park entrance directly opposite. A pretzel-and-soda vendor had already taken up his post, although business was scarce at that hour. I remembered it being a lot busier when David and I had passed through the entrance fifteen months before, as we were walking home after our first visit to Larry Grun-feld's office at the Sinai infertility clinic.

I remembered that visit so clearly. It was late on a lazy summer afternoon and, like so many couples sauntering under the shade of the trees, we were holding hands. But we were also trying to hold back the tears in our eyes, for Larry had just said that it might not be possible for us to have any children after all.

For a long time, we had put off starting a family. Most of the hesitation was on my part. If David had had his way, like his three brothers and sister, he would have opted for having children while we were still in our twenties. I was almost twenty-five when we married and had just spent seven years in universities. I was not ready to stay at home.

There were so many reasons, when I think back to those days. David's lawyering was extending later and later into the night, and he was traveling more. I knew that his hours would only get worse and that there would be even less time for home. I did not want the life of so many women around me, a child on my hands during the week and an exhausted husband on the weekends. I wanted to establish a career, a real life of my own out in the world.

There were other things, too. I loved many aspects of our London life: dear friends, the theater, the parks, the history, a certain kind of conversation, the sense of security that I felt as a woman walking alone down the rainy streets late at night. But despite my fondness for it, England was not my country. I was a foreigner there and always would be. Similarly, although we were very involved in the orbit of David's large family—his brothers and sister and father and his formidable Scottish mother—they could never take the place of my family, so very different, so far away.

Like other young Americans who've grown up with their heads lost in books, I had longed for the patina of European civilization, for a world far away from the middle-class Jewish ghetto of my childhood. And yet as the years passed, I began to pine for the ethnic rough-and-tumble of America's big cities. Although England was changing, its immigrant population was tiny compared to America, a place where everybody was an immigrant or only a few generations removed. I felt alien, beached on an island of such traditional homogeneity.

I wanted to raise a family amidst the hum and movement and color, the possibility, the sheer sense of space that America embodies. I wanted to raise a family in the place my grandparents had struggled to reach, the place whose ground had been so fertile for one such as me. Even if we could not move back permanently, I wanted, at least, to be able to spend a good stretch of time back on the other side of the Atlantic, to have a child of mine know something of America. Living abroad, I discovered how much I loved my own country, and feared that if I gave birth in England we would never make it back to the States.

And there was another reason why I resisted having children, something buried deep at the back of my mind, unacknowledged, unrelenting. It had to do with my mother.

As children and as adults, when we look for models in our own lives, whether we like it or not, we look first to our parents. What woman's role, of the many we undertake, looms larger than that of a mother? My memories of early childhood are quite dim, whereas the memories of late childhood and early adolescence scream out at me. And in those memories, motherhood and death appear as intimates, intricately intertwined, bound together by cancer.

In my twenties and thirties, the images of my mother inside my head were of a woman whose life was contained within the walls of her house, whose life withered in that world of husband and children. Being a mother and dying of cancer: the two went together, and I did not want that for myself. The simplest way to avoid it was not to become a mother at all.

And so, when I had my second laparoscopy in my late twenties in England—the first operation had taken place when I was twenty-one and still a student at Penn—and the doctor had said in passing, "Don't put off having children too long. You should really start trying by the time you're thirty-two," her words were filed somewhere toward the back of my brain. Pregnancy had been far from my thoughts when I had had those operations, anyway.

I had had them because my periods were so irregular, so heavy and painful. That's why I let the doctors poke about inside of me. My first period came when I was almost sixteen, that summer after my mother died, and it was a violent introduction to womanhood, erupting after the violence of my mother's illness had hardly begun to die down. They gave me synthetic morphine for a while, and then other drugs, but none worked well.

After the second laparoscopy, the doctors spoke of scar tissue and of a hormonal imbalance, of childhood infections and of too much prostaglandin. When they gave me something to limit the prostaglandin, for the first time the periods could be controlled. I did not worry about anything else.

But then we came back to America, I landed at *Publishers Weekly,* and I was no longer quite so young. My thirty-second birthday had come and gone three years before. If we were going to have a family, we both knew it was time to get started. We tried, but nothing happened.

The periods had become more irregular again, only this time there was excessive bleeding. My GP referred me to a gynecologist who also happened to specialize in infertility problems—just in case. The specialist determined that I had a uterine polyp that was preventing conception. It would have to be removed. He did a third laparoscopy and cut out the growth. In the process, he discovered that the tube on my left side had become blocked. He reckoned that as well as having had childhood infections that went undetected, I also had had appendicitis that had been misdiagnosed. The result of all this, the doctor said, was old scar tissue—adhesions—everywhere. He had tried to laser through them but had had to stop because of the bleeding.

It was after that operation that I got an infection, but the doctor didn't seem particularly bothered; he was more concerned about getting me pregnant and wanted to put me on a combination of very strong fertility drugs. I talked it over with nurse Di, and from her experience she agreed that it seemed a little extreme, given the infection and the fact that we hadn't yet gone through some of the basic infertility procedures. I turned to Judy Schwartz. When she sent us to Larry Grunfeld a year later, I was thirty-eight and time was running out.

I shall never forget that first visit to the Sinai infertility clinic. Larry, a young, intense man with a quiet voice and rapid-fire delivery, took my history, examined me, and did a uterine ultrasound. He invited David to join us in the consulting room and we talked for almost an hour, a very large parcel of time for a doctor to spend in conversation with one patient. His approach was very different from that of the previous specialist, who had been all action, no talk. We liked Larry and trusted him from the outset, but we didn't like what he said to us.

"Of course, Dr. Schwartz proceeded on the basis of the surgeon's report. But this ultrasound shows that you've still got a polyp. Either it wasn't fully removed in the last operation or it's grown back. Whatever the case, there was no way you could have gotten pregnant with it, and the clomiphene may have been counterproductive—it may have been making the polyp grow. From your laparoscopy report, I can see that one tube is blocked, and there's lots of scar tissue around the abdomen, which doesn't help.

"You've got a long menstrual cycle, every six weeks, and so basically, even if the polyp is removed, with one tube out of action, you'll only have a chance at conception every other cycle, every twelve weeks, four times a year. Because you've had a history of irregular bleeding, we don't even know that you ovulate each time, so it could be you've got far fewer chances at conception even than that. And you're thirty-eight, almost thirty-nine years old. I'm sorry to tell you that it may very well not be possible for you to have children."

We were stunned when the words finally came out. It was one thing to know that I had problems; it was another to be told, so matter-of-factly, what their logical outcome would be. We had tried not to face that possibility. I swallowed hard and the voice that emerged was quiet and tight.

"What can we do?"

Larry told us there would have to be another operation, but to guarantee that the growth would be excised completely, he would have to cut deep into the uterine lining. He would, in essence, remove most of it, and there was a risk of perforation. After the surgery, he would put me on Estrace, a hormone that would help to rebuild the lining. I would take it for several months and then he would give me clomiphene again. If that didn't work, the following month he would use a much more powerful drug, Pergonal, and if it too failed, we could try in vitro fertilization. But it was now or never, given my age; the clinic used in vitro techniques only on women under forty.

It was August, and I told Larry that I was due to travel to China for several weeks on business at the end of the month. I would have the operation at the beginning of October. And then I dredged up the question that had been lurking at the back of my mind after the initial shock of his pronouncement had begun to wear off. "Since this growth has recurred in my uterus, is there any chance that it could be malignant, with my family history of cancer?" I asked.

"There's always a possibility, but it's very unlikely."

And then I asked the other question, the one that had been preying on my mind for the past year or so.

"What about the hormones? Isn't there a risk vis-à-vis breast and ovarian cancer with them?"

I had never been easy about taking clomiphene; from the little reading I had done, I knew that there could be an association between hormones and cancer. Each month, I became irritable and nervous when it was time to take the pills. But each month I took them anyway.

"Yes, I have to say that there is certainly some risk. Connections have been established between reproductive hormones and cancer, and you've got other risk factors, too—your family history and your age. But what it comes down to is, do you want to have a baby? The decision is yours. If you want to have a baby, you'll have to do certain things. I'm sorry, I wish I could tell you something different, but I can't. And remember, even with the hormones and everything else, the odds aren't good."

Afterward, as we walked home through the park, I felt such a fool. How foolish I had been all those years is what I kept repeating to David, by way of apology. If only we had tried eight years ago, ten years ago. How could I have been so stupid to have put it off?

"We were both foolish," was his reply. "It takes two people to

56 make a baby. Maybe if we had come back to America sooner. Maybe if I'd been around more, hadn't worked so hard. There are so many maybes, my darling. All those years of using diaphragms and condoms, what a joke. Well, we'll just have to go on from here and do what they tell us. What else can we do?"

When, the following January, I took the first course of clomiphene after having had the fourth laparoscopy, I did not hold out much hope amidst the temperature taking and ovulation predictor testing that are regular parts of the infertility workup. I dreaded the prospect of Pergonal, which I would have to begin the following month.

But when I looked at the graph on my temperature chart, its shape was different from that of the previous months. And my breasts were feeling a little tender. I went to the clinic to be checked before work, at 6:30 A.M. as usual. I walked into the ultrasound booth, and the technician began the procedure. Then she turned to me, pointed to the monitor, and smiled.

"See that? That's where it's implanted. Congratulations, Mrs. Reid. You're pregnant."

I had been so lucky. No Pergonal. No invasive procedures. And now, here I was, eight months later, on a Pitocin drip, and everything had changed.

It was lunchtime already, and David walked into the birthing room bearing some sandwiches for himself and a few goodies for me to eat later, if I came off the drip. My munching had to be limited to ice chips while the drug was circulating through me. We had eaten so little the past few days, it was important for David at least to keep up his strength. I managed on adrenalin, pure and simple.

David also brought with lots of magazines and conversation about friends and relations. He had been manning the phone for a good part of the morning, fielding all the well-wishers' calls. Later in the afternoon, Eileen poked her head around the corner and joined us. Still later, Judy came by to say hello.

Chitra was right. The birthing floor was busy. We could hear the squidgy sounds of the doctors' and nurses' rubber-soled shoes rushing along the corridor. We could hear the trolleys being rolled back and forth, taking women to the operating room for cesarean sections. We could hear them rolling along to the maternity ward after the babies had been delivered. I got to know the rhythms of the birthing floor as few expectant mothers do; I had already been there far longer than most.

In the evening, a woman's screams began to be faintly discernible through the wall separating my room from the adjoining birthing suite. As I listened to them grow louder and her doctor's injunctions to hold on become more insistent, I felt anxious and unnerved. It was not so much that her pain would be a precursor of my own. What bothered me even more was that I felt so much a voyeur, separated from that mother's labor because nothing seemed to be happening to me.

Although the Pitocin had given me cramps, the pain was comparable to that of many periods I had endured. When Becky came to examine me early in the evening, she was amazed at how well I seemed to tolerate the drug. She summoned up a cheerful note when she said that there was still no real dilation.

"It happens sometimes. You'll see, tomorrow it'll all start." She took me off the drip for the evening, and ordered double doses of the prostaglandin suppositories for the night.

On Tuesday morning, Eileen stopped by and then Judy arrived and upped the Pitocin. In her mid-thirties, small-boned and attractive, Judy's large eyes looked tired beneath her straight, honey-colored fringe. She nevertheless stayed with me for quite a while, keeping me company, talking about her own life. Laurie dropped by later in the morning. My trio of lady obstetricians did not want

58   to let any fear show through their eyes. They were trying so hard to
keep us going, David and I both knew. They were our lifeline to
the baby and to the medical establishment, and we clung to them,
as simple as that.

For my mother and David's mother, the medical lifelines to
which they had clung for their first babies, during wartime, had
proved faulty. I don't know how old I was when I found out that
my parents had had a child before Sandy. That a son had been
conceived during the war and that he had died at birth.

My mother had worked as a technician for a general practitioner
back home in Philadelphia during the years that my father was in
the army. As children, part of the family mythology, recited again
and again but never enough to satisfy all our questions, had to do
with those early years of their life together. As usual, our mother
was quiet and it was our father who spun the tales.

Whenever he had a leave, even if only for twenty-four hours,
Joe Feldman would hop on a train from the camp in Aberdeen,
Maryland, and come north to visit his wife. His older brother, my
Uncle Mike, died fighting in the Battle of the Bulge, but by some
curious twist of fate my father was never shipped abroad. He has felt
guilty about his luck ever since.

There is a photograph taken of my parents during one of his
leaves. They're standing together in front of a statue in Fairmount
Park. He's in his uniform, eyes sparkling, having doffed his cap.
He's holding it in the middle of my mother's coat front. She's
laughing shyly, but also knowingly. They had just found out that
she was pregnant.

Other photographs of her, in her white medical jacket, smiling
above the microscope, doling out mysterious potions, seemed so
strange to us as children. They were of another woman, pictures
from another life, a woman who literally had another name. Dr.
Budin, the man she worked for, didn't much care for "Bernice"
and so he dubbed her "Betty." "Betty Feldman" is what is embla-

zoned in old English letters on the name plate Sandy has kept so carefully all these years. How she felt about being "Betty Feldman" we shall never know.

What we do know is that when her time came and the child was struggling to be born, Dr. Budin could not be found. Our father was back at camp in Maryland, and his wife's labor went on and on. There were too few doctors in the hospital, so many had been shipped off to war. How could they do a cesarean when her own physician wasn't around? When the baby was finally born, he was perfect in every way; perfect, that is, except for the fact that he was dead.

Joe got a telegram to come to Philadelphia and he traveled through the night. He was eager, expectant, but when he got to the hospital they wouldn't let him see his wife. Then they told him what had happened, that she had endured so much, that they had had to put her under sedation. When she finally woke up he was by her side, but they had pumped her so full of drugs that she could not see. She literally had gone blind. It was only temporary, though, and by the time she left the hospital she could see her flattening belly and the void in her arms where a baby should have been. Now, carrying my own child, I could imagine what she must have felt. Our father says quite simply that it tore her apart.

After Sandy and I came along, our parents still hoped for a boy. There were two miscarriages and then Vickie arrived. After that, it was too late.

David's parents had had one girl and four boys. But at some point he, too, discovered that there had been another child, the firstborn, a girl called Anne. Alan Reid was in the navy, stationed in Devon, when his wife, Margaret, was about to give birth. The baby needed an incubator, but there were no incubators in the small village where they lived. Before they could make it to the nearest large hospital in Plymouth, the baby had died.

During our first real vacation together, when David and I had scrimped up enough money to rent a cottage on Dartmoor for a week, we explored the villages that were dotted about the moors, tramping eight or ten miles each day. In one of those villages, we had a particular destination in mind. When we paid our visit to the old stone church, we found it in the burial register, the record of the sister my husband had never known.

I could not dwell on what had happened to them. I could not let myself think about those first children of our parents, lost to them forever. I could not let myself think about what would happen if my baby were lost to me.

Early in the afternoon, Judy reappeared. The cramps were much more insistent now, and I was beginning to feel very tired. The labor was dragging on very slowly. I had been on drugs for over forty hours, and had had to give up the chair by the window for the bed.

"I'm going to try something else, Gayle, if you're willing. I think it's time to try to stretch the cervix the old-fashioned way. It's going to hurt."

She called in a nurse, they positioned me further down the bed, and she spread my legs apart. David sat beside me. Judy put her hands inside me and began to prod. How far obstetrics has come, I thought. This is what it comes to when all else fails. I gripped David's hand and screwed up my face, hard. The pain was searing through me.

"I'm sorry, Gayle, bear with me a little longer, a little longer." And then it stopped, and Judy said, "I can't do any more. It just won't give." The worry in her face was undisguised now.

"Judy, does that mean the induction will go on for another day, that I'll have a third day of Pitocin? Is that safe for the baby?"

"We don't like it, but if we have to, we will. We're monitoring the baby. Everything's okay. Look, all that poking might get the dilation started. You've just got to hang in there."

David and I had been keeping each other's spirits up, but we were both feeling down now. "I guess I'll have to go out in a couple of hours and bring back something for tonight's dinner," he said, taking my hand. Neither of us felt much like eating.

That afternoon, a number of the nurses who had been looking after me during the past two days called in to see how I was doing. It was so rare for someone to spend this much time on the birthing floor; unwillingly, I was becoming something of a permanent fixture. After the initial shock of my admission, the nurses had been terrific. They were unfailingly kind and considerate, each in her own, different way.

I remember one woman particularly, a large-boned, middle-aged lady, Sarah Kathleen Hall. She made use of all three names when she introduced herself in a slow West Virginia drawl.

"Look, honey, I don't have much time because one of my ladies down the hall is near due. But I want you to know that I had cancer when I was younger, twenty years ago, and I got through. I'm the living proof that you can. You have that baby. You'll both be okay. And we'll be praying for you."

I would encounter, over and over again during the coming months, the generosity and warmth of the community of cancer survivors. The dread of the disease is such that many people, even close friends, choose not to reveal that they once had cancer—that is, until you become stricken and they find out. When they heard about me, men and women whom I knew well, and those whom I knew hardly at all, shared their stories, opened themselves to my questions, gave intimately and painfully of their past. I needed those stories, I needed to see, in the flesh, that you could do battle with cancer and survive. I needed it especially since I had seen cancer up close, and nobody—neither my mother nor sister-in-law nor a good friend, Jane, back in England—had made it through.

Around six o'clock, shortly before David was due to go out to buy the nightly care package, Judy returned.

"I'm going off soon, Gayle. Laurie'll take over. But I wanted to

62 have another look at you," she said. "My God, there's been some dilation, almost a centimeter. That poking must have done it. Gayle, I'm going to try to break the waters. David, go and hold her hands. She'll need it."

This time, Judy did not insert her fingers. Instead, she took up something that looked like the proverbial knitting needle. My nails dug into my husband's flesh as I gripped his hands tighter and tighter. I cried out and the sweat was trickling down my arms. Then it happened. I felt a warm rush between my legs, and Judy was shouting, "That's it! That's it! We're on the way."

David and I smiled at each other through the tears and sweat, and he said, "I guess we won't be eating that dinner after all." The relief was overwhelming, like a prelude to joy.

Judy said, "It'll go quickly now. That baby will be born sometime in the night. The Pitocin will really get to work, and you'll be feeling it, Gayle." Yes, indeed.

When I was first admitted, we had talked about how we would deal with the pain. I had opted to have an epidural anesthetic, which would be injected into the space around the base of my spinal cord and numb my lower trunk. I held off for a few hours, but then the contractions began to feel like the worst case periods I had known. The epidural was ordered.

Everything seemed to be happening at once. Laurie appeared in her green gown, having just delivered another baby. David was hovering over me, and the nurse, Mamerta, fluttered between the bed and the high-tech monitors. And there was another monitor doing its stuff. I don't know when it came on, or if it had always been on, but I became aware of the flashing images on the television. It was surreal. The program was devoted to President Johnson. LBJ was going through the travails of Vietnam, while I was going through my own trial, in Birthing Room C. Some of those disjointed images remain with me still.

The epidural was wearing off and Laurie told me to push. I felt so tired after two and a half days of drugs and contractions.

"Push. Come on, Gayle, push." Laurie was the no-nonsense one of the three.

"The head is crowning, I can see our baby's head crowning, my darling," David shouted.

"When I tell you to push, I'm going to count to ten and you hold it, Gayle. You've got to push that whole time."

Laurie counted to ten, once, twice, three times. And then I heard a wail and I saw tears streaming down my husband's face.

"You have a boy, it's a little boy," Laurie yelled.

And that is how, at ten minutes to midnight, on Tuesday, October 1st, fifty hours after the labor had started, Benjamin Reid was born.

Chapter Four

"A BOY, DAVID, A BOY. . . . MY FATHER WILL BE SO happy." Those were the words that tumbled out of me in the seconds after Ben was born. My father now had a grandson who would help close the wound of that first, wrenching loss, the boy-child whom he had had to bury almost half a century before. My body was so tired, but the tiredness didn't matter. David was holding my hand and I had never seen my husband look so joyous.

As Laurie placed the baby—our baby—in my arms, and I heard his little mew-like cries, I felt both a lightness and a rootedness to the earth. It was as though, for a little while, within the cocooned warmth of that hospital room, everything extraneous had been sloughed off. It had gone with the blood and sweat, the soiled sheets and damp blankets, leaving behind only the pure essence of new life. We had come through, we had the baby.

My whole being hummed with the music of those words: we had the baby. And he brought with him, that night, in his long and perilous passage through my body, the simplest, most powerful of gifts. He gave us hope and bound us back to life.

We had decided on the name long before. Although I'm Jewish and my husband is not, David had agreed that, according to the Jewish custom of remembering the dead in naming the next generation of the living, our baby would be named after my mother. Since she had used her Yiddish name, Bossie, with family and friends, we had decided that if the baby were a girl, we would jettison Bernice in favor of Becky. If the child were a boy, we had chosen Benjamin, and now here he was. The C.C. had turned into Benjamin Reid.

The afterbirth appeared and Laurie cut the cord. She weighed the baby, measured his length and head, cleaned him up a bit. Then she handed him to us again, swaddled, with a little knitted cap hugging his large, floppy head. "Happy birthday" its words proclaimed. The cap covered the soft, surprisingly thick nest of dark hair that had caused David to shout when he saw the head crown. Ben was a beautiful baby, with none of the puckered-apple, wrinkled-old-man look that we had been forewarned to expect. He was wonderful, he was our boy.

Laurie smiled. "He's a long one. And he weighs six pounds eight ounces, a good weight, even though he looks thin. He didn't have a chance to put on any fat—that would have come the last month. But he's fine. If he'd gone to term, he would have been a ninepounder, and you would have had to do a lot more pushing, Gayle."

She laughed with joy and relief. My trio of lady obstetricians had seen us through thus far. Laurie explained that Ben and I would be moved to area K-5, he to the nursery—the regular nursery, not the intensive care unit where so many premature babies spend their first few days—and I to the maternity ward on the same floor. She would go off now and leave me in the hands of the nurses, but at least one of the three would come to see me tomorrow. Despite the late hour, we phoned my father, Sandy, and Vickie, and shared with them our joy. Then David, too, departed.

Ben went down before me, while I waited to join him. There was a problem: I had requested a private room, but at the moment—it was past one in the morning—there was only one bed made up and available, in a shared room. I was wheeled down,

66 registered on the maternity floor, and conveyed to the bed.

"I'd like to see my baby before I go to sleep. Please, could you bring him to me?"

The maternity nurse to whom I spoke was young and clearly knew nothing about my case history. After the intensity of everyone on the birthing floor, she seemed curiously detached, tentative. As I came to know so well, nights were always unpopular, and many of the best nurses, those who could choose, opted to work days. The nurse told me, in a listless voice, that Ben was being cleaned and would be brought to me afterward.

I was wakeful, edgy with exhaustion. I needed the reassurance of holding him again, of feeling his breath pass gently over my flesh, of sensing the warmth of him curled up within my arms. Although my eyes were drooping, I did not sleep. The baby did not come.

A half hour passed and I rang the bell. Another half hour passed and I rang the bell again. The next thing I remember was being startled by the sound of a television blaring unwelcome noise in my direction. It was early morning already, about seven o'clock, and I had obviously sunk into sleep without having seen the baby. I had been awakened by my neighbor through the curtain, whose day, it seemed, began with the TV turned up full blast. I rang the bell, and a different nurse appeared, slim, black, well into middle age.

"I had asked to see my baby when I arrived here last night, and he was never brought to me. Is he alright? I'd like to see him now. Could I go to him, or could you bring him to me?" I tried to make my voice sound not too sharp, not too critical, although I felt worried and angry. I needed this woman to help me see Ben.

"I'm sorry, Mrs. Reid, the first place we like new mothers to go is the bathroom, and you'll find yourself light-headed just trying to get there. I'll help you, and later I'll come back and help you shower. We'll be bringing the babies along after the pediatricians have visited. I'm sorry you didn't see him in the night, but everything's fine. Don't worry." The nurse's name was Sybil Harper, and her words, delivered with a restrained kindliness, began to calm me down.

"Who's your pediatrician, by the way?" she asked.

Choosing a pediatrician was one of the things we had done during my prolonged stay in the birthing suite. We didn't have friends in the neighborhood with young children, so we had asked my obstetricians for a recommendation. They talked among themselves and were unanimous in suggesting Barry Stein, a South African who had relocated to Park Avenue. "You need somebody who's calm, who's really laid back, who won't add to your worries. That's Barry," is how Judy summed it up. And so, sight unseen, we had gone with their advice.

When I told Sybil his name, she said that Dr. Stein was already in the nursery, so I'd be seeing Ben very soon. I felt a whole lot better. Breakfast came and I ate with appetite.

The television was still blaring from behind the curtain. I pulled it aside, introduced myself to my neighbor, a North African woman, and asked if she could lower the volume. She obliged, and began to chat over the sound of the TV. Her English wasn't good, but it was good enough for her to inform me that "they will bring the baby to your breast soon. You are feeding him, no?"

The words of the perfectly normal question stung through me. How was my neighbor to know the woman opposite was not perfectly normal at all? It was the first of countless times that the question would be raised, always by women. Some would say with an interrogative lilt, "Of course, you're nursing Ben?" Others would ask, "How's the breast-feeding going?" Still others would enquire, "How long are you planning to nurse him?" There was forever the same assumption, from women with whom I had a passing acquaintance and from those whom I didn't know at all.

Each time it was painful. I would never know what it was like to suckle my baby, to nourish Ben from my own milk. That closeness we would never be able to share.

Judy had explained that I would be given a drug to dry up the milk, and the doctors hoped it would work by the time of the major surgery. On no account was I to be tempted, even for a moment, to put Ben to my breast. Doing that would stimulate milk production, which would be a disaster.

I told my neighbor that I would be bottle-feeding the baby, and when she looked querulous, about to continue the conversation, I smiled, turned away, and left her to the TV. During the coming months, whenever the question arose, I either told people the truth or, if I didn't know them well enough and didn't want to work through the inevitable chain reaction of shock, explanation, and embarrassed apology, I simply stated that I hadn't had enough milk, or that I had had problems, and so had to use formula. After a time, I became almost inured to the questioning. Almost, but not quite.

Our room was at the end of the hall, and a man appeared at the door. He was in his thirties, shortish, tanned, with long, burnished hair. "Hi Gayle, I'm Barry Stein. Ben's fine. How are you feeling?" The tones were relaxed, warm, unmistakably South African, layered with a thin veneer of New York. We talked for a few minutes and then he went off to see other mothers, other babies. Shortly afterward I could hear a trolley trundling along the corridor. At last my boy was coming. The nursery nurse gave him to me and left.

At first he was simply touch, feeling, the precious lodestone of all life nestled in my arms. Then I looked down at Ben, and looked again. Something was happening. The nurse was already well down the hall when I shouted. "My baby's turning blue, he's turning blue." The gods had truly made sport of me now.

She rushed in, took up the baby, and ran out again. A few moments later, I could hear Dr. Stein being paged over the intercom. I felt frozen to the bed, useless with terror.

How long it seemed I cannot describe, but Barry appeared again after fifteen minutes or so and said, "He's okay now. You know, he was fine when I saw him first thing. Sometimes when they're pre-mature, everything looks normal but then they have a little trouble breathing. Their autonomic nervous system takes a while to get going. I've had Ben brought down to the intensive care nursery, where he's getting some extra oxygen and will be monitored all the time. It'll be okay, don't worry, everything will be alright."

I felt tremendously nervous. I had entrusted my baby to this doctor whom I had only just met. Had he made a mistake when he first saw Ben and thought everything was fine? Was the baby really okay now? I had to tamp down the panic and try to be reasonable. I had to remind myself that it was Judy and Laurie and Becky who had told me to go with this man. I had to accept what he was saying. I had no other choice.

David would come soon, and he could go down and see the baby. I wouldn't be able to go myself until a little later. I rang the bell for Sybil to help me wash. At least I would be doing something then, not just thinking.

After I showered and Sybil changed the sheets, I settled back into the bed, but it was difficult to read. My mind's eye could not turn away from a small figure curled up in a glass box two floors below. Things were not made any easier by the cacophony of my neighbor's TV and constant chatter on the phone. Somehow she seemed to take up the whole room.

It was with enormous relief that I saw Eileen Conde poke her head around the door, accompanied by another nurse, whom she introduced as Collette Kramer. Collette was the chief duty nurse, and she came bearing gifts of reassurance and deliverance.

"Don't worry, the baby will be alright. This sort of thing happens all the time. When you go down there this afternoon, you'll see that Ben looks much bigger and healthier than a lot of the others. He'll be back up here in a day or two, I'm sure. Meanwhile, you're going to do some moving yourself. We're getting you out of

70 this room and into a single just after lunch. You need to rest as much as possible, and it'll be easier there."

The forms concerning maternity accommodation had said quite plainly that the number of private rooms was limited and it was not always possible to provide a single when requested. I knew that Eileen was doing all she could to help me and that she had enlisted Collette to do the same.

David arrived and immediately went down to check on Ben. While he was gone, Steve Brower turned up. Balding, with a thin dark mustache and the pallor of those who habitually overwork in closed rooms, Steve clasped my hand and said, "I heard you had a little boy. Congratulations, I'm so happy for you. How are you feeling?" His soft voice was warm and expressive, like his eyes.

I explained that I didn't feel too bad physically, just very tired. It was the worry about Ben, and about what would come, that was getting to me.

While Steve examined my breasts he said, "It'll be okay, you'll see. But I think we should do the biopsy on Friday. That way, we'll be able to operate next week and get it over with, and you can be back home with the baby the following week."

Of course, at our first meeting, he had said that the biopsy would need to be done a few days after the birth. Somehow, though, that sounded different from the reality of doing it the day after tomorrow.

"You mean, do the biopsy in forty-eight hours?"

"Yes, they'll discharge you from the floor here Friday morning. Then you can go down to radiology and have the mammograms and localization that will guide me during the surgery. Early in the afternoon, let's say one o'clock, you can come up to my floor and we'll do it under local. You'll be home later that afternoon."

By now, my husband had returned and joined us. I looked at him as I said, "If you think it should be Friday, it'll be Friday."

David shook his head in accord as Steve responded carefully, steadily, "Yes, it's best to move as fast as we can." He touched my hand, shook David's, and was gone.

"The baby looks okay, my darling. It's a little weird down there, but he's alright, he's breathing, and they're keeping a good eye on him."

Because it was moving day, lunch for me came and went especially early, and then the great trek to the other end of the maternity floor commenced. Suddenly there was space, light, and blissful quiet. Gratefully, I lay down and slept in the new bed while David dozed off in a chair. When I awoke, I felt better, stronger, and knew that I would be able to walk with my husband to see our son. Before we could do so, though, Becky Brightman appeared and hugged me.

"Let's take a peek at you. Everything looks good, remarkably good after such a long labor. I went downstairs to see the baby earlier, and he's beautiful. You met Barry? He's terrific, so don't worry. And let me tell you, you saw a rare sight. When I bumped into him downstairs, he was wearing a tie. I have never before seen Barry Stein wearing a tie!"

The atmosphere had lifted. David at my side, a new room, Becky joking around, flowers pouring in from family and friends, and the knowledge that I would soon be with my boy.

We three left the room together. I held firm to David's arm as he and I made our way slowly down the corridor, to the elevator, and to the intensive care nursery. There were notices telling us to wash our hands, to put on special gowns and hats. Like all the other parents, we would have done anything, anything they asked, to gain sight of our baby.

It was the noise that we noticed first, mechanical, not human. It came at us chaotically, like so many tennis balls shot from a practice machine gone mad. Each tiny, wriggling figure had exchanged one umbilical cord for another, one that attached it to a monitor beeping the technology of survival. The beeps were random, unsyn-

ּ◌ְ◌

72 chronized, like the twitches of the smallest, frailest looking babies that we saw, the ones who had been born addicted to crack. This was New York City, remember.

There were bright lights everywhere, overwhelming the feeble lights of the monitors. The nurses were moving between the banks of clear boxes, inserting their hands into the twin holes on the sides, touching the babies, checking and noting and moving on. It was warm and the babies were only wearing diapers. David led me to Ben. He was a good color, and I saw him move. I inserted my hands through the holes and touched him, offering what little comfort I could. What a strange new world for our boy to come into. Perhaps stranger still was yet to come.

Late in the afternoon, Collette walked in and kept me company for a while. I spoke with my sisters. Di Harrison phoned, and Judy stopped by. I was a mother, a new mother, and I was trying to take each hour as it came, trying not to think beyond that hour.

A little later, David joined me for dinner, which was ceremoniously rolled in complete with bud vase and cloth napkin, as though I were having a little rest cure in a good, small hotel. It seemed slightly funny, and of course I understood that such things were done to justify the unholy cost differential between private and semiprivate rooms, but I was grateful for the effort nonetheless.

I was immeasurably more grateful the following day, when Barry turned up and said that Ben had been stable through the night, breathing well, and that he would be returning to the floor later that morning. I got up, washed my hair, put on my best nightgown, as though preparing for the arrival of a lover long absent. My two-day-old lover was coming back to me.

Steve Brower again stopped by, and explained that a lady called Laura would be coming around that afternoon with some forms. Judy examined me, and Cathleen, my nurse, came by whenever she could. Eileen, my faithful Lamaze instructor, took time off from her job training other nurses to make her daily appearance. I knew that they were ensuring I didn't retreat into myself.

Just before lunch, they wheeled Ben in, and David and I took turns holding him. He was so delicate, so fragile. I felt awkward, afraid I would do something wrong, but slowly, sleepily, he took a little milk from the bottle, cradled in my arms. Cathleen gave us another demonstration in diaper changing. We had so many things to learn, but I didn't know when I would have the luxury of being able to learn them. For the next few weeks, so much of my time would be otherwise engaged.

That night, Thursday night, sleep did not come easily. I was going to have a biopsy for breast cancer the following day. It would be known tomorrow how much of my body would have to be taken away. The doctors would have a much better idea of how long Ben might have a mother. My thoughts turned to my own mother that night, to the woman who had carried me within her, the woman who had not lived to see me carry her grandchild into the world.

They did biopsies differently in those days. She had been having her aspirations for a year, but the pain and discomfort that she had felt in the right breast, that seemed to extend into her arm, drawing it to the earth, did not go away. My father recalls how she phoned the surgeon who had always reassured her that it was just "chronic cystic mastitis." He told her to come in again.

This time, when he felt it, the mass had grown larger and the doctor decided that an excisional biopsy should be done. My mother trusted this man. All was arranged.

She felt anxious that August day of 1963. Ann, our father's first cousin, who had been more sister than cousin from their earliest days, came along, as did our Aunt Betty, the wife of Daddy's older brother, Ben. After our mother had gone to see the first specialist and been told she needed a mastectomy, there had been talk among the family, and it was Betty, who worked in town and wore chic black dresses with lots of makeup, who had helped get the referral to the famous surgeon.

They arrived at the hospital after almost an hour, damp and enervated with the humidity of a Philadelphia August. My father, Cousin Ann, and Aunt Betty stayed behind. It wouldn't take too long, they were told. But time dragged on. Joe Feldman felt trapped inside the hospital waiting room. He went outside for a few minutes. The air did not move. He could smell the moist, earthy scent of the leaves. Perhaps it would rain.

Ann and Betty sat there in silence. This was a Jewish family, people who talked, who liked to talk a lot. Somehow there was nothing to say. While Joe was gone, their tight faces turned to each other and suddenly, without a word, dissolved in tears. Hours had passed. The nurses would tell them nothing. Their hearts feared . . . they knew not what exactly, but simply feared the worst.

The women took out their compacts, fixed their faces so that Joe wouldn't see. He returned and sat with them, but could not sit, and began to pace up and down the long hall. No news from the desk. Outside, the rain had finally come.

He resumed his walking. He noticed a porter and a nurse enter the corridor at the far end, wheeling a patient slowly along. They stopped for a minute, leaving their charge while they went to speak with the nurses at the desk. My father's route led him past the trolley. He barely took it in, but something made him look again. The face that was only partially visible beneath the sheet was his wife's, our mother's. She looked dead.

He ran to the desk, blindly, and the nurse and a doctor hurried to him. They had done the biopsy. There was a large, blood-filled cyst and behind it a hard mass. The tissue was rushed to pathology; it was cancer. The surgeon decided to take off the breast, then and there. They had signed the papers, after all, the consent forms. Remember?

A radical mastectomy. They did what they had to do. The chest muscles, the pectoralis major and minor, had also been cut out, as had twenty lymph nodes from under her arm. There was bleeding, a transfusion. She had opened her eyes briefly in the recovery room and gone back to sleep. She would be waking soon. Of course, she knew nothing.

They wheeled her into a room, with my father, Ann, and Betty following closely behind. They were in a state of shock and grief. And there was rage, rage at what the doctors had done, without telling them, without telling her. There was also guilt, the guilt of fellow conspirators, of wanting to hope, to believe too much. They had all urged her to have a second opinion, to go to a big name. They had all felt so much better when he had discounted the first surgeon's opinion. So long ago, so much time had passed.

She opened her eyes and saw them standing there, saw, through the anesthetic haze, their eyes. Somehow, she could not manage to move her right arm, so she lifted her left arm and felt—nothing. Nothing but bandages and dressings and drains. She started to scream.

The "one-step" procedure they called it, doing the biopsy under general anesthesia, rushing the tissue for analysis, removing the breast while the patient waited, insensible. The "Halsted radical mastectomy" took the breast, lymph nodes, both chest muscles. That part of the woman's body was no longer convex. It wasn't even flat. It was concave. So much easier, doing it that way, all at once, convenient, straightforward.

Until, that is, a few pushy, questioning women, in the free-for-all of the late 1960s, began to challenge the doctors, read the fine print, demand that the biopsy be done separately, as a thing in itself. They also began to question the terrible, disfiguring surgery. Did it have to be so radical, to leave them so caved in?

I was the beneficiary of their struggle. By the early 1970s, the medical philosophy had begun to change and the "two-step" procedure gradually became the norm. Not only that, but the Halsted radical gave way to the modified radical mastectomy, which left the major chest muscle intact and the woman flat, rather than just ribs and skin. Thinking had even gone beyond that now, with lumpectomy and radiation often an alternative to taking the whole breast. And yet, had things really progressed so much when, at the end of the day, breast cancer was still being treated not by vaccine or pills or preventive techniques, but by chopping off flesh and sinew, however little, however much?

I got up from the hospital bed, put on my robe, and quietly walked toward the nursery. The lights in the corridor had been dimmed. It was very late. The duty nurse shot me a curious glance, then smiled.

I looked through the glass window and saw him, sleeping peacefully, lovely in his slumber. That first night, when Ben was just born and we phoned Vickie, she had said, "I'm glad the baby's a boy." I thought of what my mother had gone through, and what would be starting for me tomorrow. Of course, I had understood what my sister meant instinctively, had thought of it myself. We didn't need any more girl-children with genes like ours. Vickie was right, I could only agree.

Chapter Five

I WOKE UP EARLY THAT FRIDAY MORNING, MY MIND RAC-
ing. I checked on Ben, who was fine, and ate what I could of
breakfast. I showered and dressed, having thought very carefully
about what to wear.

Yesterday I had asked David to bring the Liberty print blouse he
had bought for me during a trip to England last spring. It was a
beautiful blouse, a garden of small blossoms of every color brightly
planted on a black background. I had worn it all summer, growing
our baby inside me, the new life flowering beneath the flowers of
the shirt.

Today, though, I would wear it for very different reasons. It was
loose-fitting and buttoned down the front, easy to get in and out of,
especially if there were discomfort or pain. For all I knew there
might be some bloodstains; the pattern would hide them, and the
cotton would wash.

I put on the blouse, but when I glanced at my image in the
mirror, I felt overcome by sadness. I remembered a kind of inno-
cence now lost, a spring and summer of uncompromised fecundity
and hope. And yet today I would wear the blouse as my standard:
the flowers and colors defied the cancer, they were so redolent of
life.

I was due to report to Laura in radiology at 10:30. Steve Brower
had made sure that she was well briefed before she came to see me
yesterday. She had tried so hard to be cheerful, but it was obvious

that she was not in the habit of carrying her bundle of forms to the maternity floor.

I remembered the tears that had formed in Mimi Levy-Ravetch's eyes that day the cancer was diagnosed, when there was so little she could say. Like Laura, she came across new cancer patients each and every week, but my case had shaken her up. I knew, instinctively, that it had shaken Steve Brower as well. His card read, "practice limited to surgical oncology," but somehow, despite all he had seen, the duality of my situation seemed to act afresh on his soul.

David arrived around nine, almost simultaneously with Becky. She had agreed to be our rather unconventional *mohel,* to circumcise Ben before he left the hospital. After the deed was done, we hugged, and Becky bustled along to look in on some new mothers down the hall. I finished packing and, as an afterthought, stuffed a few of the magazines that had come with the private room into my bag. We arranged to donate to the pediatric ward many of the luxuriant bouquets that had poured in during the past two days. Others we would take home to cheer us up.

Judy came by, perched at the end of the bed while I sat in the chair, and we talked. She was the one whom I had known the longest, who had seen me through the infertility workup. She told me how to take care of myself as a new mother during the next few weeks. She tried to keep it light.

"Some people would tell you there are lots of things you should and shouldn't do. I think for the most part you just need to use common sense and listen to your body. But don't you dare have sex!"

"Sure, Judy, I really feel like it." We both laughed. Then we talked about the likely schedule of the next few days. We didn't have that much to say in the end; so much was unsaid, understood.

We had arranged for Ben to stay in the nursery until late afternoon. David would see me through the day, take me home, and then return to pick up our boy. It was time now for me to be discharged from one part of the hospital in order to enter another. We looked in on Ben, signed the discharge papers, and began the long walk through the meandering corridors to radiology.

My footsteps were weighed down by a tremendous clutching at the heart. Despite all the reminders—the visits from Steve Brower and Laura, the discussions with Judy, Becky, and Laurie—I had managed to feel, during my stay on the maternity floor, no more, no less than a mother. As I left the joy and light and new life behind, as I trudged down through the lower levels toward radiology, I became no more, no less than a cancer patient. And unlike Persephone, I had no idea when I might be recalled to full life again.

As soon as we arrived, David went back upstairs to collect my case and the boxes of flowers to cart home. He would meet me again in radiology as soon as he could. Laura took me in hand and introduced me to Andrea Abramson, an attractive woman of a certain age, the radiologist who would do the mammography and wire localization. I was very glad of the doctor's sex.

I undressed, and a technician began to take several mammograms. Despite the drug I had been prescribed, my breasts were engorged with milk, and it hurt when they had to be squeezed between the plates of the machine. Dr. Abramson explained what would happen.

"As you know, there are two areas that Dr. Brower is going to biopsy today. The mass can be felt, but the area of calcifications is tricky. What I'm going to do to help him is to put a very fine needle into your breast, pointing toward where the white flecks show up on the mammo. Then I'll thread a thin wire with a tiny hook on the end of it through the needle and position it right in the area of the calcifications. The hook will keep it there, and so Dr. Brower will know exactly where to operate."

She began to position me but was not happy about the angle. She asked me to move around, but that wasn't right either. We returned to a variation on the first position and then she inserted the needle. The sharpness of the pain was surprising and brought tears to my eyes.

"I'm so sorry. Normally it doesn't take this long and there isn't much discomfort, but with a breast like this, it's more difficult. I'm going to thread the wire through now. Oh, wait a minute, it's got to be just a tiny bit more angled. Hold on; I really want to get it right for you."

I felt nauseated and faint. I must have turned very white. I gripped the machine as she threaded the hook and wire through. My God, I hadn't expected the localization to hurt like this.

She exhaled slowly. "It's okay now, we're finished. It looks good."

When I went back into the cubicle, I dressed slowly as the tears crawled down my cheeks. I felt stupefied, exhausted. I looked at my watch: nearly noon.

I walked back to Laura's desk. "Your husband phoned, Mrs. Reid. He's on his way. A delivery of some baby stuff arrived just as he was about to leave. Can I get you something to drink?"

She brought me a glass of water. It was my hand that shook as I took it from her, and yet part of me still felt that it could not be my body, my life to which all this was happening, as though I were the intimate observer of somebody else's bad dream. Baby stuff and cancer. Baby stuff and cancer. I sat there for five minutes, then David walked in and put his arm around me.

"How are you feeling? I'm so sorry you've been waiting. Maybe I should have told them to come back later on, but it was the changing table and chest of drawers, and I thought we should have them in place. Let's get out of here. We can go to the cafeteria and have something to eat, or some tea, anyway." David kept talking as he guided me out of radiology. He could see the tautness in my face and knew that I was fighting for control, that if I opened my mouth the tears would flow again.

We sat in the cafeteria and drank very sweet tea. The time passed, and then it was ten to one. As we began to make our way to Steve's office, I could feel my whole body shake, tremors of adrenalin rushes shooting through me. The elevator took us to the twelfth floor. We got out, registered, and sat down to wait. The shaking would not stop, and yet I knew it was important that my body be still once Steve began to operate.

A nurse came into the waiting area and called my name. She explained that she would be assisting Dr. Brower and asked how I was feeling. My mouth and throat seemed to have filled with dust; I strained to make my voice work, and asked the nurse for something to drink. She returned with some juice and said, "Could you come with me now, Mrs. Reid? It's time to get you ready." David and I looked at each other, wide-eyed. My husband's face creased into a tense smile; he nodded his head and squeezed my hand. I followed the nurse through the doorway. Now I was on my own.

It was a fairly large room, with a dressing area curtained off at one end. The nurse stood outside while I undressed and put on a gown. When I emerged, she was wearing a green gown and a haircap, and gave me a cap to put on as well. Then she began to chat.

"What a terrible thing to happen, having a baby and discovering you've got cancer at the same time. It runs in your family, huh? How did you find it? Has your breast been hurting? Have you expressed any milk?" At first I tried to be polite and answered her, but the questions seemed to cluster thick and fast about my head like flies. I wanted them to stop, so I stopped responding and walked into the main part of the room where Steve was waiting.

"Hi, Gayle. We're all ready. Why don't you climb up on the table and we'll get going. I'll try to make you as comfortable as I can, but we'll be here for a little while. Two areas are involved and the breast is postpartum, so we'll have to take it steadily. I'll be telling you about everything that I'm doing, and you must tell me if you feel any pain at all. If you do, we'll top up the local anesthetic.

82 That's no problem." He sounded tired and looked, if anything, a shade paler than usual.

I got up on the table and put all my concentration, all my effort, into trying to control the shakes. A drape was erected below my neck. I could not see what Steve and the nurse were doing with their hands, but I could see his face, the tension visible even with the partial mask, and I could hear his voice, quiet and warm as always. I felt a cool liquid wash over my breast.

"I'm painting some Betadine on you and then I'm going to drape more towels around the breast." Steve turned aside for a moment. "Now I'm going to use a marker to draw where we have to go in. I'll be using a cautery to seal off the small blood vessels, to help prevent bleeding, so if you notice a slight burning smell, don't worry. I'm going to insert a needle now, filled with anesthetic. It might sting or burn a little, but it'll soon pass and then you shouldn't feel anything. I'll start to make the first incision after that."

The needle entered my breast, followed quickly by a burning sensation. Steve began to cut down through skin, through fat, through tissue, separating layer after layer of flesh, probing down toward the cancer itself. I had read in the books that I'd managed to consult before going into labor that the local anesthetic should head off any discomfort. Every few minutes, though, pain from the probing or the cauterizing—I didn't know which—would fan through me, and I would close my eyes, clench my teeth, and ask for a top-up. Although there wasn't usually supposed to be much bleeding, Steve seemed constantly to be calling for sponges and clamps, as well as the cautery itself.

When the biopsy was well underway, the nurse began her patter all over again, and there was no escaping it. "Look at that, now isn't that interesting. You can see the milk ducts. They're so full even though she's been taking those pills to dry her up. I've never seen anything like this."

I wanted to scream, to stop up her mouth, to shout at her. She was trying to make me less than a person, to reduce me to a breast, a freakish, cancerous, postpartum breast. Yes, I had milk ducts, but I could never use them, my baby would never be nourished by any of the milk that she was finding so "interesting." I wanted nothing so much as to make her feel all the pain that I was feeling with her every word.

Pinned there, I said nothing; nor did Steve. It was taking so long, so long. Finally, he glanced for a moment directly at my eyes and said, "I've finished excising the area where the calcifications are; I'm just going to deal with the lump now. We're sending the tissue over to pathology for frozen sectioning right away. We might hear something even before you leave."

Frozen sectioning, yes, I understood what he was talking about. I had studied French and Italian and Chinese and knew that you had to speak the language if you were going to live in a foreign place. I had entered this shadowy land so precipitously, only last week, but I was learning the language of cancer very fast.

Twenty-five years ago, the frozen sectioning process was gone through with every biopsy. In those days it would determine, as it did for my mother, whether the patient unconscious upon the table would be staying like that for a long time, long enough for the surgeon to perform a radical mastectomy as well.

The tissue would be rushed to pathology, where they would take a small part of the cancer and literally fast-freeze it, rendering it solid and hard. Then they would slice it ever so thinly, place it on a slide, stain it, and put it under the microscope. Although sometimes the final pathological analysis diverged from the quick findings of the frozen section, it would nevertheless provide an indication of the types and extent of the cancer, and what needed to be done.

Steve was talking to me again. "I've gotten hold of the lump now, Gayle, and you may feel some pulling as I take it out. That's it, now I'll sew you back together. It'll just take a little time." The

84 nurse had stopped talking a while back, and for some time there had been an eerie quiet, punctuated only by Steve's requests for instruments. A collective sigh of relief seemed to pass through the room. It was almost finished, almost finished.

Knowing that, I began to think of the next stage, as "what if" began to beat its insistent rhythm through my brain. What if the calcifications were not cancerous and I'd just have to have a lumpectomy? What would I look like, with a piece of my breast cut out? What would I look like now, when already a good chunk of tissue had been removed? What if the calcifications were cancerous, what then? There would be a mastectomy and, if it were invasive cancer, chemotherapy or radiation. But what if the prognosis were really bad, if whatever they could do were not enough?

"It's all over now, Gayle, you can get up and get dressed," I heard Steve say. The nurse helped me off the table and walked with me slowly to the changing cubicle. She tried to be kind, but remembering how her words had transformed me into a textbook curiosity, I felt anger flash through me once again. I could not look at her, I didn't want her help. I just wanted to get through that door as soon as possible, to collapse into David's arms.

I had brought a bra that I had purchased only two weeks before, in preparation for nursing. Steve had told me to come with the firmest one I could find, that the breast would need a lot of support after the surgery. The nursing bra was the best I had, but I felt sickened with the irony of it as I snapped it in place. I finished dressing quickly and looked down at my chest, maternally full, billowing beneath the black, flowery blouse.

I opened the door and walked out. David was waiting for me, but there were other people in the room, too. My eyes were liquid and I couldn't speak; I could see how full my husband's eyes had become. We sat there, holding hands, saying nothing. We waited, and heard the silence all around—in other people's muffled conversations, in the telephone ringing on the receptionists' desk, in the elevator stopping sporadically at our floor. Everything was silence, until a woman wandered through and called my name. We followed her to Steve's office.

He looked exhausted, his face a gray-white mask. The shreds of foolish hope that had remained in my heart disintegrated completely. We sat down, and Steve began to speak. "I've heard from pathology. It was in both samples, and they think it looks invasive. Gayle, David, I'm so sorry. We'll have to schedule the mastectomy. . . ."

I could hear my throat catch and felt the tears, dammed up for so long, begin to trickle down my cheeks. And then suddenly, in mid-sentence, Steve stopped talking and turned away. I looked at David, who was fighting to control his own face. We knew Steve was emotionally involved in my case, but this upset? We waited. One or two minutes passed. Slowly, slowly, he turned around to us. His face was ashen, drained. "Please forgive me, I . . . I think I told you I haven't been feeling well lately. I feel . . . sick. I'm sorry, I can't talk."

He buzzed through to his secretary, clutched the desk, and turned away. And with that, we could see that the man who had just operated on me was about to collapse.

Chapter Six

IN THE CAB GOING HOME, WE REPEATED TO OURSELVES, over and over again, the mantra that had been passed on by Steve's secretary. "It's only the flu, only the flu," she had said to us. Surely his indisposition could not have affected the operation that just took place. Of course we'd be talking to him on Monday and he'd be fine for the surgery next week.

We pulled up in front of the house, unlocked the street door, and climbed the stairs to our rented apartment, a duplex on the fourth and fifth stories of a brownstone much wider and grander than the house we were moving to. Trudging up through the building, my body worked so slowly, more slowly even than during those last few weeks of the pregnancy, slowed down by shock, by exhaustion, and by the painkillers I had been given before we left the hospital.

We entered our apartment and David hurried into the kitchen while I lingered amidst the soft, still light of the hall. I stood there, turning my head from side to side like a bird listening in its cage, noticing the sweep of the rooms from high ceilings to honey-colored floors, taking in the quiet all around. I felt like nothing so much as a ghost come back to haunt the place I had lived in many years before. So much had happened during the passage of one week.

I followed the trail of slanting light through to the sitting room, kicked off my shoes, and half-sat, half-lay on the flower-patterned sofa. There were vases of fresh flowers everywhere, my "welcome home" hastily arranged by David during his journey back from Mt. Sinai earlier in the day.

I could hear my husband setting out the tea things in the kitchen, listening to the messages on the answering machine while waiting for the water to boil. I vaguely discerned the tones and accents of Sandy, Vickie, Daisy, Di. My head felt as though it had been muffled in cotton wool, and my eyes were no longer focusing sharply, but there was very little pain in my breast. The pills were doing their stuff.

David walked in with a tray and sat down beside me. "Now you take it easy, my darling. I'll just have some tea and then go back and pick up the baby. Would you like some music, or a book or a magazine?"

"Could you turn on the radio, please, D. Reid? And there are some magazines in the side of my bag—could you get those?" My words slurred; the pills were taking the edge off so many things, physical things, but they were incapable of acting on the spiritual and emotional pain. The chasm inside me seemed to widen, to deepen. I felt as though I had no reserves left.

During the past few days, I had seen the other mothers dress, pack up, and leave the maternity floor, cradling their precious parcels in their arms, proud fathers at their sides. There was no such homecoming for us. I would only be here a few days before going away again, and God only knew what kind of shape I'd be in when I returned.

David kissed me lightly on the forehead and then set out. I listened to the music and picked up a newsmagazine, but it was useless, the words swam before my eyes. I began to flick through a woman's magazine instead, filled with glossy pictures of beautiful faces, beautiful clothes, beautiful bodies. It was hard to look at the

88 lingerie ads, the sexy clothes, the lovely half-naked forms, but it was hard not to dwell on them either. I flicked through again, and came upon an ad whose oversize letters proclaimed that I did not have to be my mother.

This time, it was more than the pills that made the letters swim before my eyes. The tears were coursing down my cheeks, and I allowed myself to cry hard, to sob, sitting on that sofa, waiting for my husband to bring our baby home to me.

Me and my mother, me as a mother. I remembered how set apart I had felt all those years, years when daughters normally have their mothers at their sides. How exquisitely, dramatically self-conscious the moment was each time the question was asked and I had to respond, "Oh, my mother, she's dead. She died young of cancer." Now I knew something, a little something, about what it was to be a mother, and the progress of my days, despite all my efforts to the contrary, seemed to be following the same path as that of the woman who had given me life forty years before.

My mother had once sat on a sofa like this, she had sat and been too tired to play with us, to do all the things we children had expected our mother to do. What would I be able to do, when would I be able to be just a mother for a while? For how long would our son have a mother at all? I felt outraged by the uncertainty hanging over our lives, over my baby's life. It was unbearable, insupportable. But somehow, for however long, I had to be there for him. I had to pull myself together.

David had been gone for almost two hours. The cab ride each way, even in clogged traffic, should have taken less than fifteen minutes. What was happening to him? Was something wrong with the baby? Why hadn't I heard anything?

At that moment, my husband was in a cab headed back home, trying hard not to cry. When he had gotten to the maternity ward, the shift had already changed and Collette and the other nurses we knew had gone. He went up to the desk and told the duty nurse that he was there to collect Benjamin Reid.

She looked at him quizzically. "We release babies to their mothers. Where is the baby's mother?"

"She was discharged this morning to have a medical procedure. We arranged with the duty nurse for our son to stay here until it was finished."

"Well, where's his mother? If the procedure is over, she can pick him up now."

David tried to keep his voice from rising. "No, you don't understand. She had a breast biopsy for cancer. My wife has cancer. I brought her home because she's too exhausted to do anything else today. Look, I'm the baby's father. We were told that there would be no problem in leaving him and coming back. Why can't you give him to me?"

The nurse softened and shook her head slowly. "I'm sorry, I don't mean to be difficult, but those are the rules. You may have read in the papers about those horrible cases where babies have been stolen. We have to be very careful. I don't have the authorization to release him to you. He'll have to stay here until I do."

"Well, who can give that authorization?"

"The chief nurse."

David's voice tensed. "Can't you call her? Please find her. This is my baby. I've left my wife at home all on her own. She's just had surgery and she shouldn't be alone. Can't you do something?"

It took more than an hour for the release to come. Weary and strung out, David traveled in a cab down Fifth Avenue clutching his son, trying to summon up some shred of composure to face what awaited him at home.

I could hear the key turning in the lock downstairs and a few moments later could see my husband carrying our baby in his arms. David came straight to me and placed our son in my lap. I sat there, holding him as we all quieted down. When he was fast asleep, David took Ben and laid him in the white wicker bassinet waiting upstairs.

That night, while we ate supper, I told David about the ad I had come across. Two sets of eyes filled again. We both felt shattered by tiredness, enormously sad, almost paralyzed with fear, but we managed to get through Ben's sleepy feeds, to change him, to comfort him. We were awkward and slow, brand-new at this, but we had to do it, to take care of our boy. Before I went to bed that night, I retrieved the magazine, ripped out the ad, and placed it in a folder in my desk drawer. I didn't have to be my mother.

I slept in the big bed on my own. When Barry had come to see Ben for a final look-over that morning, he had asked who would be taking care of the baby during the biopsy and whether we had organized any help for when we got home. We told him that our nanny, Amira, would start on Monday morning. During the past week, David had also arranged with the agency to have a baby nurse, Anne Marie, come in the evenings for the early weeks to see us through. For tonight, though, we would be on our own.

"In other words, you're winging it," Barry said with a laugh.

I had resisted the idea of a night nurse at first; irritated, I told my husband that we should at least be able to do the nights ourselves. But then David reminded me that I would not be around or capable of doing very much for a while, that I would need to rest. He couldn't do it all himself, look after both the baby and me and hold down a job. I yielded. That first night, he insisted on sleeping in with the baby.

"You must get some rest," he told me. When I looked at my face in the mirror, I knew he was right: I would collapse if I didn't. He got through the night fitfully, awakened every few hours by Ben's cries for food or by his nervous anticipation of those cries. I heard them, the first time the baby woke up. After that, I closed the door and slept through.

That Saturday morning, the phone rang while we were eating breakfast. It was my sister-in-law Di, phoning from London with good news: she would be able to come and help us for a week. She would book her ticket as soon as Steve had confirmed the date of surgery.

We phoned our friend Di Harrison to give her an update, and then phoned Sandy and Vickie and my father. My sisters were fretting, as they had done all week. We had talked every day during my stay on the maternity floor, and David had talked with them in the evenings as well, but there was so little we could say, so little they could do. We had agreed that my family would come up to New York to see us tomorrow. David was making the arrangements on the phone with my older sister when I suddenly heard his voice turn sharp.

"Look, Sandy, we know you want to do all you can, but it's not helping to have you worry at us on the phone. Diana's coming over to be here after the surgery. You know that'll be easier than your coming with Melissa. Di can concentrate on looking after Gayle and Ben without having to worry about anybody else. We'll need plenty of help from you later on, but you've just got to hold on till we ourselves know what we need.

"Of course Gayle wants to see all of you before she has the surgery, and she wants you to see the baby. But we don't want the visit to add to the stress. We're counting on you and Vick to make your father understand, to keep him from getting too upset. We want to have as nice a day as we can, we want the day to be in celebration of the baby. We just want it to be simple, to see you and be together."

I talked with my father after that. He wanted his lady friend Pearl to accompany them. I said no.

"Dad, please try to understand. I know that Pearl's been wonderful to you. She's a lovely person and I'm very fond of her, but she's not my mother. I want to be with you and Vickie and Sandy, and if you can, I'd like to talk with you about Mother. There are some things it might help me to know. It wouldn't feel right to have Pearl around when we talk about that. You'll just have to play it our way, Dad."

The resistance in his voice gave way. "Alright, alright, Gayle. I don't know what you're getting so upset about. Pearl cares about you, you know that, and I've been with her nearly as long as I was with your mother. She'll feel bad, but I'll do what you want. I'll see you tomorrow."

My father hung up and I sat back, exhausted by the effort of being so hard on him. I felt terrible. He was hurt, and Pearl would be hurt, but my hurt had to come first this time.

He would get over it. I know that my father is able to back down more easily with me than with my sisters. I think it is because I remind him a little of our mother, and because while Sandy was away at college and Vickie was far too young to understand what was going on, I had been there during those terrible months. I was the one who sat, day after day, and bore witness to the relentless unraveling of our family life.

I remember, when we were little, that our mother made it seem so special when he was on his way home. She would tell us, "Daddy's coming, Daddy's coming," and would look out for him, even though he'd more often than not be late. He was our emissary to the other world, to the far-flung corners of Philadelphia, and he would carry into the house some of the excitement and strangeness of that grown-up place. He would arrive bearing tribute, a brand-new gadget or a sack of pistachios or a box of cookies from a customer's shop. To us, they were always the latest gadgets or the tastiest nuts or the most delicious cookies, far nicer than anything we could buy around the corner ourselves. He would come home and scoop us up into the air and give us one of his bear hugs and be gay. She was not the only one who loved him.

But I remember what happened that summer after she died,

when it got really bad for him. He would sit in the big gray arm-
chair in the corner of the living room and hold his head in his
hands, unable to face the phone, to face other people, to face the
light of the world outside his suffering. On those days, I would
kneel on the floor at his side and remind him that he had to go out
and see his customers, go out and run the business. He would look
at me through eyes bloodshot with sleeplessness, and sometimes
mutter a few words in a small voice, not the voice of my father.
Then he would go upstairs and put on his business clothes and go
out. Sometimes he would drive around for hours and not see anyone. Other times, when Vickie was spending the day at a friend's
house, I would keep him company, staying in the car while he
made his rounds.

We never talked about these things afterward. As he struggled to
regain his spirits, his memories of that time were buried deeper and
deeper, and I went my own way. Now, contemplating my family's
visit tomorrow, I feared throwing my father back into his memories, feared it both for what it would do to him and for the effect
that would have on me. Although I loved my family dearly, I was
dreading their visit. I didn't know how I could cope if the wrong
things were said. Thankfully, though, there was so much to do that
I wasn't able to linger long over my fears.

Anne Marie, the relief baby nurse, arrived after lunch to allow
David to accompany me to the hospital for the preadmission testing. She was Jamaican, had trained as a nurse, and seemed nice
enough. But I noticed that there were dark circles under her eyes
and her words slurred with tiredness. I felt uneasy, leaving the baby
with this stranger, but we had to go out.

The waiting room was crowded with patients and their relatives
when we arrived. First there were the inevitable forms to fill out. I
tried to shrug off the uncertainty about Steve's health as I completed them. I'd be talking to him on Monday, that was sure.

After the forms came the chest X ray, the electrocardiogram, the blood and urine samples, the general physical. Between each segment we waited and waited. Once, when David had gone out to the pay phone in the hall to check on how our boy was doing, another woman, wanting to punctuate her boredom, tried to strike up a conversation.

"So you're coming in for a cesarean?"

The question took me aback for a moment, but of course, my belly was still distended. I smiled, shook my head no, and said that I had given birth to a son earlier in the week. Then I got up and went to look for David. I did not want her to pursue the topic further.

It was five o'clock by the time we finished. All was well when we arrived home. Anne Marie went out for a while, and David and I sat upstairs in the den, watching TV mindlessly while we ate our supper. When the baby woke up, I fed him while David looked on.

Ben took the milk very slowly. He was so delicate, so vulnerable, and I was fearful about whether I was doing everything right. Was I giving his head and neck enough support each time I picked him up? Was I burping him properly each feed? And yet Ben was such a calm, sleepy baby. Barry had said that a baby who starts out calm often stays that way. It would be a blessing to us if he did.

The feed progressed. While I listened to his little sucking sounds, I thought back to all the foolish worries I had had before and during the pregnancy. I came from a family of girls, and didn't want to know the baby's sex beforehand because I didn't want to spend half the pregnancy worrying about what I would do if it were a boy. Now, with Ben in my arms, I realized how silly I had been. The only thing that mattered was that he was my baby and needed me. I would do whatever had to be done and learn along the way.

David and I went to bed and Anne Marie took over. She would be sleeping in the guest room with the baby. We would be on the same floor, but at the other end of the apartment, separated by the bathroom, the laundry room, the den. I felt uneasy, unsettled, at a loss without the baby who had been inside me for eight months. But I was so very tired that that night I slept through, slept the heavy sleep of exhaustion.

Sunday morning Anne Marie hung around the house longer than we would have liked. Although she had worked in New York for a number of years, she was currently living in temporary accommodation and seemed none too keen to return to it. Finally, though, she left and David watched the baby while I went out and bought provisions for lunch. They arrived on time, my family who are always late.

They climbed the stairs, breathless by the time they reached the apartment, and walked in offering assurances that the journey had been good. They hugged me and David, each in turn, and smiled at the swaddled baby. My father was careful not to give one of his bear hugs, but held me a little longer than he was wont.

I was afraid of what they would say or do, afraid of three pairs of dark eyes swimming with emotion enough to swamp me, and so I recoiled stiffly and bustled about as best I could. But although the clouds of feeling gathered all around, they did not rain down and overwhelm me. Their eyes remained clear and their voices did not falter. Somehow my ever-emotional family understood my need for space. And gradually, like a wary cat, I sidled closer, settled down, and was able to heed their call.

We have many photographs of that day, and one in particular flashes up before my mind's eye when I think back to it. We are all together in the den, five figures clustered around a baby. My father is sitting by himself, on the sofa at the left of the picture. His heavy frame is turned toward me, almost as though he is half getting up, anxious to put his arm around me, to lend some physical support. He is smiling—we told him that he had to smile, it was an historic moment, a record that his grandson would keep—so he is smiling for the camera, but the shadows are also there, and sometimes when

I think about it, the expression on his face doesn't look like a smile at all.

I am seated in the rocking chair next to him, big glasses hiding the circles under my eyes. I am wearing my nautical pregnancy outfit, navy and white horizontal stripes on top, stripes vertically tilted on silk trousers below. My socks are white with little blue sailing boats cruising along them. There are earrings, big heavy blue and silver earrings that I normally wear only for important business occasions. Jaunty, I would look jaunty. I had to look positive for them, I kept telling myself.

Sandy is hovering above me, only her shoulders and head visible. She, too, is wearing stripes and smiling—perhaps our brain waves had met while dressing that day. Her stripes are red, but less bold than mine. The expression on her face is full of warmth, but the smile is crooked, just a little bit on edge.

Vickie is on the right, broad grin, big eyes, dark fluffy hair. She looks, as usual, a lot younger than her thirty-two years. The grin seems set, a permanent fixture. She is trying so hard to be funny. She even came prepared with her favorite radio station's joke of the day.

Vickie is leaning on David, who has put the camera on automatic. He hates being photographed, and this occasion is no different, but he nevertheless tries his best to look good. He is not even wearing his glasses, a great rarity. Maybe that is why the expression seems so startled, jumping out at me.

There is, of course, one other person in the picture. Ben— lovely, sweet Ben—is fast asleep on my lap, his neck supported between the thumb and forefinger of my hand. His mouth is open, his thin face silhouetted against the dark waves of my stripy top. His is the only face that isn't smiling.

And there is one person who is not in the picture, but who was with us nonetheless. She was in my son's genes, in mine and my sisters', and she flitted back and forth between our thoughts and conversation. Yes, my mother is there in that photograph, even though her image is absent.

That day, there was no arguing, no fretting, no raised voices, at least none that I can recall. My father came through for me, banishing all signs of the depression that I had feared. Instead, he and my sisters brought with them unquestioning love. We sat and had a meal together, sat as a family. We talked about little things, about what Melissa and Jessica were doing, about the baby in our midst. My father and sisters admired him and held him, each in turn. And then, after lunch, while Ben was asleep upstairs, our father sat and answered our questions about our mother.

"Of course, you girls meant the world to her. I guess we made mistakes in the way we lived, and God knows I would have done some things differently. We never went on a vacation, just the odd day here and there. But your mother, she was like that, she scrimped and saved and put everything into the house, into the business. She didn't seem to mind not going places, she was happy at home with you girls, until it all fell apart."

I could see Vickie soaking it all in, Vickie who was three when our mother got sick and seven when she died. How many times had she whispered to me over the years about how awful she felt at not remembering so much about our mother? How many times had she asked me questions that I, too, couldn't answer?

Our father was talking again. "I think your mother dreaded getting cancer, what with her mother and everything."

I snapped to attention. "Dad, what are you saying, what are you talking about?"

"Well, you know, don't you? I thought I told you. Your grandmother Golde, Golde whom you're named after, Gayle, who passed away the year before you were born—she died of cancer, too."

Sandy and I looked at each other, stunned. Vickie shouted an elongated "What?"

Questions began flooding through my head. "Dad, you never told us anything about her. You and Mother said when we were kids that she had died of some gallbladder problem. Of course, thinking about it now, I've not heard of many people dying from gallbladder problems, but cancer? Was it breast cancer?"

"No, it was lung cancer. But that was the odd thing. She was only in her mid-fifties and had never smoked a day in her life. Your grandfather Philip, he smoked, but he didn't die of cancer. Maybe, though, your grandmother somehow got it because of him."

"Well, Dad, here's another theory," I interjected. I remembered something I had come across during my crash reading course. "In those days, what was diagnosed in the lung sometimes started in the breast. For all we know, it could have been breast cancer."

"Well, it was cancer, whatever kind it was. And you know, Golde's mother, Sarah, she died of some type of cancer, too, and she wasn't that old, either. I didn't know Sarah, but your grandmother Golde, she was one hell of a woman, let me tell you. She had a real head for business, she was clever. Who ever heard of an immigrant woman from Russia in those days buying properties, investing in real estate? Your grandfather, he worked for the government; it was steady, but he didn't earn much. Golde took what he earned and saved thousands. She was the one who gave me the money to start the business again after the war.

"Your grandmother, she wasn't the hugging, kissing type: I don't ever remember her actually embracing your mother. But Bossie was the apple of her eye. There was a lot of love between them, and there was also respect.

"Golde had always been strong: even though she took in boarders on the top floor of the house, she never had anybody to help with the cleaning. But when the cancer got hold of her, the strength disappeared and the pain was terrible. It ate her up and she couldn't bear it. The doctor said he could do an operation, cut some nerves in her brain, that was the only thing that would give any relief.

"They went ahead with it, but something terrible happened. It wasn't a lobotomy exactly, I don't know what it was. I just remember that they shaved her head, and when she came out of it, she couldn't speak or recognize us. It almost broke your mother's heart.

"Golde ended up dying in a godforsaken nursing home, an awful place. It's still standing. And I remember one conversation we had after she died. Your mother said to me, 'If I ever get sick, promise me, Joe, that you'll never put me in a place like that. I never want you to put me in a nursing home like my mother.' I don't know if she had any ideas about cancer running in families, but I remember that conversation as though it were yesterday. That was the only time we ever talked about it."

Our father did not cry as he spoke about our mother and her mother. None of us cried, although our eyes were far from dry. I don't know how we held up, but we did. Perhaps it was the baby, we had to do it for his sake even more than for mine. He was, that tiny creature, beyond us, bigger than us. We fixed on him as a passenger fixes on the sea during a long ocean voyage, never tiring of him, the miracle, the mystery of him.

That Sunday, with the ghosts of what had been and what might be swirling all around us, Ben anchored us to life. In the evening, when it was time for my family to go back to Philadelphia, we did not dwell on the fact that I was going to have a major operation the coming week, that I would be receiving the pathologist's verdict of hope or despair, that whatever happened, things would never be quite the same again. In the end, we hugged and kissed, we didn't need to talk. We were a family, that was enough. And all of us felt better for it that fine October day.

Chapter Seven

MONDAY MORNING WAS NO DIFFERENT THAN THE MORN-
ings that had come before: we awoke with a start, fully conscious,
feeling as though we had not slept at all. Amira arrived at eight and
Anne Marie went off reluctantly. We were glad that Amira, whom
we had been able to interview at length, was now on watch. Our
nanny was Egyptian, born in Alexandria, but for the past twenty
years a resident of New York. There were those who raised their
eyebrows at her background, wondering if a Jewish mother, Chris-
tian father, and Muslim nanny wouldn't be too confusing for one
little boy. We understood their concerns, but Amira was the warm-
est person the agency had sent, and she assured us that she was
"modern."

We rather fancied building a multicultural household in this
patchwork of a city, and so we took her on, the thoroughly modern
Muslim. Although she would have to leap into the maelstrom and
survive pretty much on her own, we had to devote time to talking
with Amira about the way the apartment worked, about what we
wanted for the baby. Our days were consumed by talk—with our
nanny, with doctors, secretaries, friends, relations, colleagues—and
we had so little time left, far less than we ever could have imagined,
for the most important person of all, Ben.

I waited until ten o'clock that morning to phone Steve's office.
His secretary answered and in contrast to our previous conversations, she seemed distant, remote. It was the "don't call us, we'll

call you" policy, and it sent jitters through David and me, turning up the volume one more notch on the uncertainty drowning out our lives.

What was not uncertain was that we had to tackle the practical matters. First among them was to confirm that the surgery would be covered by my health insurance. I waded through the mire of medical bureaucracy at a time when no one should have to worry about red tape, but I was lucky. I had good coverage and knew that if I did what they asked, the bills would be paid.

In order for the insurance to kick in, I had to obtain a second opinion fast, and since Steve couldn't arrange it, Laurie did. The surgeon agreed, after some persuasion, that she didn't have to meet me; if she saw the mammograms, a letter from my obstetricians, the report from Mimi Levy-Ravetch, and the findings from pathology, that would be enough. It was David's office manager, Emma, who organized the ferrying to and fro. When the doctor finally had it all spread before her, we talked on the phone. She told me it was very simple: she agreed with everything the others had said. A mastectomy was in order, the sooner the better.

That evening, my writer friend Jean Crichton, who had been operated on for breast cancer the previous Christmas, responded to the message I had left ten days before.

"Hi, Gayle, I've been away and just got back. Look, this is not a club you want anybody else to join. What can I do to help?"

"Just talk to me, Jean, talk to me about what happened to you." We talked, and it was a great relief, hearing this woman who had made it to the other side of the river describe what the passage had been like.

I had met Jean early in my tenure at *Publishers Weekly*. She was warm and direct and good to work with. Although only a few years older than myself, she was a widow, and divided her time between travel and writing and her extended family. We got to know one another as editor and writer, but beyond that, we liked each other

YOU DON'T HAVE TO

as women. When her diagnosis came, I heard about it early on, and
Jean heard about my mother.

I had visited her in the hospital after her surgery; I had seen her
periodically in the nine months since, during chemotherapy, during reconstruction. Jean would appear in my office from time to
time, looking pale and drawn but always well dressed, carefully put
together. Her blonde hair thinned, but unlike so many people she
retained a pretty good covering throughout her ordeal, and she
always sounded plucky in spite of the nausea and tiredness. It was
only after the six months of chemotherapy were over and her body
began to return to something approximating normal that Jean recognized, by contrast, how awful she had felt.

She was through it now, while I was newly embarked on the
passage. But it was so good talking to her, so easy. No explanations,
no apologies. We understood each other very well.

Jean paused. "You seem happy with your surgeon. But you'll
want to be sure that he's absolutely straight with you. You'll want
that from your oncologists and from your plastic surgeon as well. I
shopped around, talked to a number of doctors, did a lot of reading
and thinking. What are you planning to do about reconstruction,
by the way?"

I had talked about it very briefly with my gynecological trio and
with Steve Brower. Steve had said, "You're a young woman still,
of course you'll have reconstruction so you can go back to a full
life. I can send you to some plastic surgeons, but it'll be easier if you
do that a little later on." Laurie had put it with her usual directness:
"You've got enough going on in your life right now. You don't
need anything else to worry about."

I told Jean that I was delaying any decision about reconstruction,
that I just wanted to get through the surgery. She responded,
"Well, the one good, if weird, thing about the mastectomy is that
you'll feel very little actual pain. Discomfort, yes, pulling under the
armpit where they remove the lymph nodes, yes, but pain—not

much. In fact, you'll feel numb there for a long time to come."

It was getting late, and we both knew it was time for the conversation to end. "You know, you've just got to hang in there. Look, I'm still here, after all. The baby's okay and that's wonderful, and you've got David, and he's being totally supportive, right? Let me know what happens about the hospital—I'll come and see you there. And if there's anything before then, just call."

Talking with Jean lifted my spirits. It was one of the few things that did that dark week, that week when we seemed forever to be on the chase. As well as trying to track down clues about when Steve would be fit to operate, we were also hunting for something else, something that was proving equally elusive. I needed blood.

When my mother had her mastectomy, she was given a transfusion—common enough then, with the Halsted procedure, but rare these days. A pregnant woman, however, has a greatly increased blood supply and there is a corresponding danger that she may bleed heavily during an operation. I lived in New York City, epicenter for AIDS, and my doctors counseled that it would be safest if family or friends could donate for me. I needed to find two healthy people who were compatible; I needed to find them during the next few days.

We already knew that my husband wouldn't be one of them. David had given blood regularly; he remembered that he was B positive. I was O positive, and he could not give to me. I phoned Sandy. She knew her type from having gone through two cesareans. She was A positive, like our father. Sandy said she'd phone Vick at the office.

Vickie would have to go to a lab or blood center in Philadelphia to ascertain if we were compatible, and if so she would have to travel immediately to New York. Even if she could do it, I would still need to find that second pint, and obviously I couldn't ask just anyone to drop everything to go and give blood. All of David's family and many of our oldest friends were in England, and several of our closest New York friends had moved abroad or to other cities during the past year. We were left with a small circle in the city whom we immediately started to call.

Brian and Di were incompatible; so were a couple of others. I phoned our good friends Morris and Mary Rossabi. Mary could never give blood again, having ruptured her spleen the previous year, but Morris, who had no idea of his type, was willing to give it a try. He arranged to go to Mt. Sinai later in the day. We were keeping our fingers crossed that Vickie and Morris would be my donors.

I spent the rest of that afternoon lying on the bed, rereading parts of Susan Love's book, perusing the pamphlets that had arrived from the National Cancer Institute, taking in as much as I could about what the next week would bring. The more I read, the more I could feel the waves of tiredness coming over me. Eventually I was swallowed down into the deep hole of a late afternoon nap. It was dark when David awakened me. "Time for dinner," he said.

Often when we sat at the table these days, my throat felt as though it had been blocked by stones. I could hardly eat and David was not much better. I remembered how, a few months after we moved to New York, our sister-in-law Pat began to deteriorate and my husband went back to England for long weekends to be with his brother. David would come home after each visit and shake his head disbelievingly, saying how Keith had gotten even thinner, how he never seemed to eat. Now on some days, it was only by force of will that we ate a proper meal at all.

Morris phoned during dinner. He had donated a pint of blood late in the afternoon, but it was the wrong type. Vick would go to a lab for testing first thing tomorrow, but we still had to continue the search to locate at least one, and possibly two, compatible people. I was becoming more and more fixated on finding those two precious pints of blood.

That Monday night we fell into bed completely strung out. My sleep was invaded again and again by dreams about childhood, nightmare wanderings, terrors about the baby. I would wake after each covered in cold sweat and listen to the infernal rumbling of the trucks lurching down Lexington Avenue. I listened, but could hear no sound coming from the room at the end of the hall. Finally, at about four in the morning, I had to see for myself, to make sure that he was alright. I got up and crept along the darkened corridor to the other end of the apartment.

The door to the bedroom was tightly closed, although we had asked Anne Marie to keep it always ajar so we could have access to the baby. When I opened it as quietly as I could, I saw that Ben was asleep but had managed to wriggle half out of his covers. Anne Marie, on the other hand, was well wrapped up, snoring slightly, impervious to him or to my presence in the room. I felt a sudden rush of anger. Were we paying this woman to sleep?

I covered the baby, went back to bed, and tried to rest. There was something about Anne Marie that disturbed me. Was it the circles under her eyes? The fact that she didn't have a place of her own to return to?

I felt a great sadness to be so dependent on strangers. When my mother died, we depended on a stranger then, too. Our father hired a housekeeper for a while, a woman whom Vickie and I never much liked. The house never felt quite clean, quite ordered after that. Our mother would have been unhappy with the way it looked, with what the woman bought, with what she didn't buy.

But of course, there really wasn't any alternative, no grandmothers to whom our father could turn. Golde was long gone and Rebecca, our father's mother, had died when I was five. I missed having grandmothers when I was growing up; I found it strange to hear other kids talk about something I had lost. Now my own sweet boy would never know either of the women who gave his parents life, would never know what it was to have a grandmother at all.

And my mother, after all those hard years, never had the pleasure of holding a grandchild in her arms. I would never be able to show Ben off to her, to make us both proud. I would never have the reassurance of knowing that the woman who nurtured me was helping to care for the new life I'd brought into the world.

Instead, there was Anne Marie. But it didn't have to be her. It could be someone else, someone better. And so the following morning, I collected my thoughts and explained to David that I was not happy about the nights. "Maybe it's irrational, but there's something that just isn't right. I think we should phone the agency."

My husband, who is not quick to change, who bends over backward to be fair, countered that it was just everything getting to me. "We need to have coverage during the nights, she's a trained nurse, it's quite reasonable that she should sleep when the baby does. She must have forgotten about the door. I'll talk to her about it."

Anger surged through me like floodwaters. I was about to snap but then thought better of it. Maybe David was right, maybe I was just reacting to everything with hypersensitivity. I tried to calm down, to let it subside. A little later I phoned Steve's office; still no word. I couldn't just sit there and do nothing, so I grabbed the phone and dialed my obstetrical trio. Theirs was a very busy, popular practice, but I had no trouble getting through. The word had gone out that whenever I called, they were to be interrupted no matter what they were doing. I never had to wait.

Laurie got on the phone. I could imagine her, dark and attractive, a mass of curly hair, arms akimbo, picking up in one of the examining rooms. The patient she was tending would be trying to figure out what was going on, but Laurie didn't miss a beat. "Look, Gayle, if we don't hear anything definitive about Steve's health by tomorrow, we're going to start phoning other surgeons," she told me.

Although the mass of the cancer is removed during the biopsy, malignant cells remain in the surrounding tissue. Those residual cells were used to justify the one-step procedure in the old days: doctors believed that the disturbance created by the biopsy could encourage them to spread and multiply even faster. These days, however, most surgeons say there is no harm in a brief delay, but still caution against waiting more than a week or two. In my case, given all the hormones pumping through my body, the timing was even more acute. We had to get things moving right away.

Almost as soon as I put the phone down, it rang again. "Hi, Gayle? It's Vickie. I'm at Sandy's. I came here straight from the lab. Look, I feel so bad, I'm A positive, the same as Sandy and Daddy. I can't donate for you." Again I was my mother's daughter. Vickie sounded shaken up, guilty for something far beyond her or anybody else's control.

My older sister got on the phone. I could hear my brother-in-law muttering something in the background. "Gayle, do you want Steve to go and be typed?"

"No, Sandy, that's okay. We'll sort something out here," I told her, my voice fading. Even if he were compatible, Steve had too much work on, so he would have to give the blood in Philadelphia. How would we get it to New York? It was too late, I couldn't face the hassle. "Anyway, tell Vick how grateful I am. She did all she could."

"Well, you know how much she hates the sight of needles and blood. She came here rather than heading straight for the office because she almost passed out when they drew the blood!"

I had to smile. Vickie was the family devotee of *Dracula* and "Dark Shadows." She got back on the phone, miffed. "I don't know why Sandy told you that."

"Because you did well, kiddo, even if you've been watching too many vampire movies." We both laughed, but when I put down the phone, I didn't know where to turn.

I told David that it seemed I'd have to depend on the regular blood bank. He could read the look on my face. "Gayle, we haven't exhausted all our possibilities yet. I'll phone Eric."

David and Eric Marcus had become friends while working as students in Germany. Both went on to study law, and when we returned to America the friendship flourished anew. Eric was now a partner in a big New York firm and, like most lawyers, he was always too busy, never had time to spare. David phoned, but as usual Eric was in conference. His secretary would leave a message asking him to call back.

It was evening already. Mary turned up, having traversed Manhattan bearing a chicken dinner, a little something she had whipped together for us the night before, after work. "You have enough to worry about, let other people worry about feeding you. Anyway, you need some chicken soup to keep up your strength." She smiled broadly.

We had finished dinner and the dishes by the time Eric got out of his meeting. Of course he and his wife knew nothing about the turn our lives had taken. During the initial moments of his conversation with David, I could tell he was asking the usual questions: "How's Gayle feeling? Any sign of contractions?" It was a shock to remember that most people thought the baby hadn't been born yet, wouldn't be born for another four weeks. David ran through the explanation on automatic and then asked Eric if he had ever given blood.

"You have, Eric? Do you remember your blood type?"

My husband's face creased into the first real smile I had seen in days. "That's fantastic. Can you get to Mt. Sinai tomorrow? Terrific, terrific, the earlier the better. Just give them Gayle's name and hospital number. We can't thank you enough." One donor down, one to go.

I let the machine answer a few calls—I just couldn't deal with them all. But one call I did pick up: it was Eileen Conde, wanting to know how we were getting on. We talked about the baby, about Steve Brower, and then I told her about my search for blood.

"Gayle, I'm O positive. I'll go to the blood bank in the hospital and donate for you tomorrow." She was absolutely straightforward, insisting that it was no big deal—but I couldn't believe my luck or Eileen's generosity. We hadn't known her very long and yet she was doing so much for us. Eileen, Eric, Morris, Mary, Jean, all the others—there were good people in the world and at last something was going right.

Anne Marie arrived for the nightly rendezvous. She went up and did the late evening feed. After an hour she came down again, just as we were about to go to bed. "That baby's blocked up, you know. We really ought to deal with it."

For the past few days the iron in the formula had been constipating Ben. The previous night Anne Marie had proposed a remedy: inserting a thermometer to stimulate the bowels. The thought of such a thing made us nervous, and when we consulted our baby books we were not reassured. The books said that such a maneuver, in an infant as young as our son, could result in perforation. Anne Marie insisted that she knew best from years of experience and training. She backed down eventually, but we knew we hadn't heard the last of it.

When we got into bed, David could tell that I was worrying about the baby nurse. He was too, but he tried to play it down. "Look Gayle, I agree, she's not ideal. But how do we know that the person who replaces her will be any better? You don't get the best people wanting to do nights. It's just for a few weeks, and Di will be joining us soon."

We fell asleep but my dreams turned fearful once more, and again I found myself walking to the other end of the apartment in the middle of the night. This time the door was open a crack, through which I could hear Anne Marie's deep, regular breathing. I looked in, but somehow couldn't make out the baby. I entered the room and still the bassinet seemed empty. Where was Ben?

I looked around frantically. He was lying next to Anne Marie, both of them asleep on the single bed. She could have crushed him in her heavy slumber. He could have fallen off the narrow bed.

I don't know how it was that Anne Marie didn't wake when I turned around and ran back through the hall. I shook David and said, "You'd better come with me, there's something you should see." He followed me to the makeshift nursery and I pointed to the bassinet, then I pointed to the bed.

David reached over and picked up the baby, returned him to the bassinet, and wheeled it down the corridor to our bedroom. Anne Marie slept through it all.

The following morning we did not shout. We did not want a scene. She said that the baby had awakened; she had picked him up to comfort him and had inadvertently fallen asleep. When she left the house, it was David who phoned the agent. He stuffed her pajamas, her slippers, her toilet things into a shopping bag and dropped them, with a check, at the agency. We would be on our own for a few nights. David would look after Ben.

Later that Wednesday morning, the phone rang. It was Laurie. David got on the other extension so he could hear the news as well. Steve had contacted his secretary and told her to tell my obstetricians that I needed to find another surgeon. The secretary didn't know what was wrong with him and didn't know when he would be able to operate again.

Laurie said that she had already conferred with Becky and Judy. They would try to get me into Memorial Sloan-Kettering Cancer Center. I knew, though, that no doctor would find it easy to rearrange a crowded schedule, to step into the messy middle of another person's case. I put the phone down and burst into tears. My husband was crying, too.

It was our lowest point since the diagnosis. We had clung to Steve Brower's warmth, to his caring, to his personal involvement. Suddenly we were cut adrift, sinking on a sea of uncertainty, unable to withstand this latest tide. We could not understand how once again everything had come crashing in on us.

Amira came up to check on the baby and found us crying. She mumbled an embarrassed apology and stood there for a moment, not knowing where to go. I turned my face to the wall and couldn't speak. David managed to say that we had had some bad news and needed to be alone. We would tell her about it later. How could she ever have imagined anything like this? Nannies had to cope with mothers' baby blues, but cancer? Was that what she had signed on for?

Taking care of babies was about nurturing new life, and yet here was I, an obscene reminder of our mortality. There were plenty of jobs in New York for experienced nannies, jobs with normal families whose joy was undimmed by the shadow of death. We were lucky that Amira hadn't turned tail and run.

The baby stirred and somehow we pulled ourselves together. Amira brought up a bottle and I started to feed Ben. After a while she reappeared with tea and sandwiches and took over the feed. We waited for Laurie, Judy, and Becky to crank up their medical machine once again.

The center of our life for the past five days had been the phone. All those calls about blood, conversations with doctors, calls from family and friends. The phone was our umbilical cord to the outside world, but as we sat there rigid, waiting for it to ring, the cord of life seemed to grow tighter and tighter around our necks.

I turned on the radio. After what seemed an age, the phone rang. It was Judy.

"Jeanne Petrek has agreed to see you at Sloan-Kettering at four. Call us when you're done."

Chapter Eight

THE SECRETARY'S NAME WAS BARBARA. "CALL HER," Judy had said. "She knows what she's doing."

The woman who answered the phone sounded clear and calm. She asked if I was familiar with the hospital; it was in my neighborhood, I had been there to visit my writer friend Jean. No trouble on that score.

They would need the mammograms, Mimi's report, a letter from my obstetricians, anything I could lay my hands on from Mt. Sinai—the pathologist's report, the biopsy slides, Steve Brower's notes. Some of it was with the surgeon who had provided the second opinion; some was in Steve's office; some was scattered about the hospital itself. David set off for the surgeon's office, my obstetricians' office, and Mt. Sinai. There was no time to spare.

Barbara told me to come to the ground floor of Sloan-Kettering's outpatient building on 67th Street, around the corner from the main entrance on York Avenue. I would have to register—that would take some time, she warned. Then I was to go to the waiting room on the third floor, where somebody would find me; she herself would have gone for the day. Dr. Petrek was squeezing me in and would probably be available closer to five.

I tried to phone Jean because the person I was about to meet had been one of her doctors, but the answering machine picked up the call. I wondered what she would be like, this woman breast surgeon. Sure, most of my doctors were women and I welcomed that kinship, but a breast surgeon—how did she do it, day in and day out?

I could feel my head pounding, my nerves and muscles were coiled tight; I stood up and began to pace the apartment. Ben was asleep, Amira out buying groceries. The bell rang. A new delivery of flowers.

The man placed the vase under the window in the dining room. I stared at them, green tendrils curling above blooms of deep purple, creamy white. They were especially lovely, these flowers, orchids from a publisher I admired, sent in celebration of the baby's birth. It meant a lot to me that he had sent them.

The orchids jerked me back to that other world, my working life. The publishing circuit—books, interviews, launch parties, article after article. How far away it seemed and yet it was still there, running on parallel time. It was painful to remember that, to feel so cut off from it all, to feel the sharp irony of what was and what seemed to be. And yet the flowers that had come pouring in were a reminder that there was that other world. It would be there, waiting for me to go back to. Sure, things would be different. I would be different. But there was another life, I told myself, and I tried to believe it.

Ben woke up and we began the feed, slow and sleepy. When we were halfway through I placed him on my shoulder for the burp. He was just a little creature, warm and clinging, a small animal of flesh and blood. I loved the smell of him, the sweet new baby smell, and I wondered if he recognized my smell, as the books said babies do. Did he know the difference between me and Amira? I worried about that. I would be going away and when I returned, who could say how much I'd be able to do, how long I'd be around? I wanted so much for him to know me, to know me as his mother. I couldn't remember my own mother's smell. Did she wear perfume? Were there traces of shampoo, of talc? For me, the only smell the thought of her conjured up was the scent of damp leaves, wet earth—the cemetery smell. I didn't want that for Ben.

David and Amira returned within minutes of each other, and I handed the baby to her. "Let's take a cab there and walk back," my husband suggested. "We're running a little late."

There was a lot of traffic as we threaded our way through the cross streets, but we were at the hospital in ten minutes. I remembered entering this place once before, the previous Christmas, to visit my friend after work. It was a wild night and the gusting wind, pushing frantically toward the East River, propelled me into the lobby before I had a chance to take anything in. I tried, that visit, to keep memories and fear in check, not to let the fact that this was the oldest cancer center in America and one of the biggest in the world unshackle the goblins within me. This time, there was no escaping, and the place loomed up before me, both familiar and strange.

We passed by the guardian of the gates and entered a large lobby lit by floor-to-ceiling windows. The heavy mock-leather chairs were grouped in clusters around oriental-patterned rugs. There weren't many people lingering at this hour of the hospital day. We walked up to the desk and spoke with the receptionist. She shared her space with a computer, and there were other terminals in the cubicles behind her. It was all very high-tech, geared up, a contrast to the down-at-the-heels preadmissions suite at Mt. Sinai.

As I sat filling out the obligatory form, I noticed a woman walking along the passageway toward the exit. She was young, nicely dressed, with an attractive face. She wore lots of eye makeup. She had no hair. I could feel the panic fan through me. I had to keep ahold of myself. I had to be able to talk to these people. I had to get through this visit. They were there to help me.

The woman at the desk took the form and began to input all the information. Why didn't she just ask me, I wondered? Or would that be too personal, not sufficiently businesslike? We sat again and then another woman appeared from a side room.

"Would you come with me, please, Mrs. Reid? I'm afraid we have to go through the insurance information and tie up a few more details before you can go up to see the doctor. I'm sorry about this, but I'll try to get it over with quickly."

She seemed a nice lady, and we were grateful for it. David put his arm around me as we followed her through the side door, into another room with computers. The clerk called up my file on screen—I already existed as a series of digits in the Sloan-Kettering memory bank—and she asked for my insurance cards. Then she asked about my employer, David's work situation, my history, my biopsy, all the while entering and storing the information in the electronic brain.

As we talked my fingers hooked together, rigid in my lap. I felt the strain of having to control my face, my voice, to keep from breaking down. I felt the shock waves from having entered such a place bounce through my still disbelieving brain. It was not easy, going through the whole thing, the potted history of my medical life and times, all over again.

I was alright until she asked about the baby. Then I crumpled, the fear and tiredness spilling over onto my face. The clerk immediately produced some tissues and sat back, saying in a very gentle voice, "It's okay, Mrs. Reid, it's okay. I'll leave you with your husband for a few minutes, while I go and get your blue card. We've just about finished anyway." I was not the first person she had seen break down in that chair. Nor would I be the last.

"I'm sorry, David, this is so stupid, all these tears. I just feel so tired, talking about it over and over again."

"It's alright, my darling, it's alright. You just sit quietly for a minute or two. We'll be seeing the doctor soon."

When the clerk came back, she produced a blue-and-white plastic card that identified me as a patient of Memorial Sloan-Kettering Cancer Center. She took the card and one of our credit cards and put them through for processing.

"Whenever you come here, just give the receptionist that card," she told me. "That's how we take care of all the billing." I had entered a very well-oiled financial machine indeed. Then the clerk fixed us with her eyes and smiled. "Good luck to you." She clasped my hand. I knew that she meant it.

We walked to the elevator and pressed three. When the doors parted we entered another large lobby area with armchairs, oriental rugs, piles of magazines. The lights were dimmed and it was preternaturally quiet in that long, high room: not surprising, since nobody else was there. It was as though all the patients and relatives who had come before us had vanished into thin air.

We sat and waited and already we understood perfectly the ritual of waiting. The life of the patient is more than anything else spent in that way, time parceled out into little packages of sitting around, staring unobtrusively, making small talk, glancing at magazines. Waiting for doctors, nurses, bureaucrats, for tests and results and meals, waiting for companionship to arrive. How many articles could have been written, how many feeds could have been done, in the time I had already spent waiting in hospitals?

I remembered how we used sometimes to wait for our mother, when she made those visits to the surgeon for her aspirations or for her checkups later on. It was a longish car journey, traversing Philadelphia from our home in the Northeast to the western part of the city. We would skirt around the center of town, passing by the Greek-columned art museum, boathouse row, the scullers on the river. We would shout out when we saw the statue of William Penn atop City Hall. Our father would have the radio on; he could always find the stations playing Frank Sinatra, musicals, or Mantovani. Finally we would get there. It was an excursion for Vickie and me.

We never came to that part of the city for any other reason. It was a strange place, foreign to us, part of the bigger world, what we read about in school. Sometimes when the weather was nice, we would wait in the car with the radio on and look out the window. There were all kinds of people, mixing together; they weren't just white, like near where we lived, or black, like where Daddy's shop was. There were faces even unlike those I had seen through the Chinese restaurant doors. There were tall, straight-backed men with beards and turbans, and ladies with long, wavy hair wearing gauzy lengths of cloth.

I don't ever remember stepping into the hospital itself. If it got too hot, we would climb out of the car and play on the patch of green nearby. We knew that our mother had come here to see the doctor, although we did not know why. We understood that this was a different place, connected to grown-ups, a world outside our family, only in this one way touching on it.

I resurfaced and looked at my watch. It was after five. A tall, slim, attractive red-haired woman around my own age was walking toward us from the back.

"Hi, are you Gayle Feldman Reid? I'm Dr. Petrek. You're all on your own, huh? Come with me, please."

She led us into a small, brightly lit room that was divided into two by a curtain. She pushed it aside and then pointed for me to sit on the examining table, and for David to occupy the chair. She stood above us, holding the thick sheaf of mammograms, reports, the box of slides.

"Well, so you had the biopsy—when was it—Friday? And the baby a couple of days before that. Uh-huh. Let me look at the mammograms." The words were spoken with a midwestern twang. She had sharp features, milk-white skin, and was wearing a flowery dress beneath her doctor's coat. Somehow portraits of Elizabeth I flashed through my mind. Like the English renaissance queen she had a no-nonsense air about her, although there was a slightly manic quality as well.

"I'll look at the reports later. Why don't you tell me about yourself, about your history."

I had to do it all over again. I pushed my voice and began to tell her about finding the lump, about the sequence of events since then. I concentrated every bit of remaining energy in an effort to keep in control, to speak lucidly, to remember anything she might need to know. The voice I heard telling the story sounded quiet, drained of all emotion, monotonous really. I felt withered, desiccated, as though there could not possibly be any tears left.

She asked me to talk about the infertility problems, the hormones.

"Very interesting," she said. Then she wanted to know about the pregnancy itself.

"Uh-huh. Well, I wrote the chapter on pregnancy in the breast cancer textbook. Although it doesn't happen very often, it happens a little more often than you would think."

I told her about the benign cyst I had had removed in England six years before, and then I told her about my mother.

"So let me get this straight now, she was premenopausal, about your age? Very interesting." She flicked through the file of papers and then looked up.

"You know, some women in your situation, premenopausal with a strong family history and cancer already identified in one breast, decide to have both of them off. We do a prophylactic of the noncancerous breast. Sometimes, of course, we end up finding cancer there, too."

Neither David nor I said anything.

"And the baby, everything's okay with him? Well, you're lucky that you found it when you did. Let's say you hadn't and had had the baby a month from now and started breastfeeding. You might not have noticed the lump. You could be dying within a year."

None of the doctors had spoken to me of death so baldly before. None of them had talked about having my other breast chopped off. I had walked into the room thinking that nothing could ever shock me again, and yet here I was, feeling shocked out of my skin.

"Well, I think I'd better examine you now." Dr. Petrek certainly wasn't prissy or fussy the way some doctors are. She didn't ask David to leave the room; she didn't even move him to the other side of the curtain. I was glad he was there.

"The biopsy incisions are healing well. Now wait a minute, you've still got this little lump here."

"Yes, that's the pimple I told you about, that set the whole thing in motion and caused me to be suspicious. Dr. Brower just reckoned it's a sebaceous cyst."

"I think he's probably right, but I'd like to biopsy it just in case. You seem to be quite calm about everything. We'll do it right now."

For a few seconds I didn't quite take in her words. I repeated to myself, "right now." Dr. Petrek began opening closets filled with gauze, sterile swabs, needles, all kinds of medical paraphernalia. While she was busy peering onto shelves, I relaxed a little. Not everything marched with quite such precision after all.

"I can't seem to find what I need. Usually there's a nurse who gets all the stuff. I'll go and find somebody."

After a few minutes, she strode back in, a nurse in tow. "Okay, so where do you keep it?"

"Here it is, it's all here. Do you want me to stay?" the nurse asked.

"No, I'll be alright on my own now," came the brisk reply.

Dr. Petrek poured antiseptic on the area and then a little local anesthetic. It didn't take long.

"Well, you tolerated it pretty well," she said when she had finished. "We'll send this for analysis. We may even get a reading before the surgery."

I got dressed as she continued to speak. "I operate on Fridays and Tuesdays. I can fit you in either the day after tomorrow or next

Tuesday. Of course you'll have to repeat the preadmissions testing, there's just no way around it. You can either decide now or tell my secretary, Barbara, in the morning. You'll have to talk to her then anyway."

"We'll phone Barbara in the morning." David looked at me quizzically as I said this.

"That's fine, but do it first thing. I'll be seeing you. Bye-bye."

When we walked out of the hospital, I took in great gulps of air. "I don't want to go home yet," I said to my husband in a tight voice. "Boy, how could she even talk about taking off the other breast? I think tomorrow morning I should phone Steve Brower's office to make sure there isn't any news. I don't think I can face changing surgeons. That's why I put off making the decision about when to be admitted."

"Hold on, my darling, hold on. Just calm down. Do you feel like eating or drinking anything? We could nip into a restaurant. I think it would be good for you to have some sugar. You look a little pale. We'll get something inside you, and then we can talk."

We walked into a coffee shop and were seated at a booth in the no-smoking section. We ordered some tea and danish pastries, and then began to talk.

"I agree she was blunt, but I'm sure she's a good surgeon, Gayle. Your obstetricians wouldn't have sent you to her if she weren't, and we're lucky that she's willing to squeeze you into her operating schedule. Look, she's telling it to us without the sugar coating. There's value in knowing exactly where we stand. You said that she operated on Jean, and obviously Jean's okay. And I think it wasn't a bad thing that she biopsied that pimple. What other choice do we have? I think it would be crazy to take our chances on Steve Brower's recovering soon enough. You've got to have that operation."

I sat and began to munch the danish and heard what my husband said. I was about to answer him but then suddenly began to cough.

I'm mildly asthmatic, and could tell that someone was smoking nearby. I glanced up and saw that a young woman, in the booth catty-cornered to ours, had lit up. She looked like a student from the college nearby, and was busy joking and flirting with the young man, presumably her boyfriend, seated opposite. They were strong cigarettes, meant to impress, and my coughing did not let up. I looked around—no free tables or booths—there was nothing to do but ask her to stop.

"Excuse me, I've got asthma and you're blowing smoke in my direction. Do you think you could stop until we've gone? We won't be long," I told her.

"Smoking is permitted in this row. She doesn't have to stop," the young man said aggressively.

"Look, my wife's just asking if you can put it off for a few minutes while we finish up here. Can't you hear her coughing?" David said.

"It's a free country. If you don't like the smoke, you can leave," the girl countered, tossing her head and laughing to match her boyfriend's bravado.

"Jesus, I'd like to throw that cup of coffee in her face," I snarled to David, half-hoping that the girl would hear my words. "What a little fool. She thinks she's immortal. Well, wait until those cigarettes turn into cancer in her lungs. She and her friend there don't know how lucky they are. They'll find out how smart and sophisticated they are someday." I was shaking with anger, and I could see that David was on the edge, about to take it further.

My husband leaned forward and said to the girl in a very tight voice, "My wife and I have just come from Sloan-Kettering. My wife has cancer. Now will you stop smoking that cigarette, please!"

The girl did not blink or react in any way other than to say, "So what? My brother had cancer." She continued to smoke.

I felt as though someone had slapped me in the face. Tears were welling up in my eyes, but I tried to keep them there. I did not want to cry in front of that girl. We got up, paid the check, and walked out. My brain was having trouble taking in her behavior, but part of me was appalled even more at the violence of our reaction than at those young kids' foolishness. I felt tremendously sad, and what had flared up so unexpectedly just as suddenly died down. It was as though there were no outer skin left to either of us anymore; we were just nerves, raw and exposed and ready to react to anything.

When we got home, we slumped down in the sitting room to finish the discussion about the surgery. I had gotten so used to Steve Brower, but I knew that David was right, and I remembered what Jean had said about wanting your doctors to be absolutely straight with you. Certainly, with Dr. Petrek, there was no question about that.

"Phone your obstetricians, if that will make you feel better, my darling." I decided to heed David's advice.

Becky was the one on call. "Look, Gayle, she's got a really good reputation, and it's a tough job for a woman. I wouldn't have any qualms. Just go with her."

And so I did. Dr. Petrek would be my surgeon, but we still had to decide whether I should enter Sloan-Kettering on Friday or wait until Tuesday. We remembered the donated blood, sitting in the Sinai blood bank for me, and thought about the hoops we would have to go through to get it transferred. We thought about another round of preadmissions testing. We considered the bad reactions I had had to general anesthesia in the past, and recognized how much better it would be if I could have an interview with an anesthesiologist before I was actually in the operating room. And we thought, finally, about the possibility of having one more weekend with Ben, before the surgery. Really, there wasn't any question. Tuesday it would be.

Chapter Nine

WE HAD FIVE DAYS IN WHICH TO PREPARE FOR THE SUR-
gery, and that Thursday morning we pushed ourselves into motion
early on. Our bodies were even more tired than usual, having lost
sleep to Ben's middle-of-the-night feed, but at least our dreams had
been easier, the undercurrent of fear about the baby nurse thankfully gone.

I phoned Dr. Petrek's secretary, Barbara, first thing. Often a
major operation on a Tuesday would dictate a Monday admission,
and all the testing and form filling would be done then. Instead I
would be admitted on the day of the surgery itself for a stay of up to
a week. I would have to phone Dr. Petrek's office on Monday
afternoon, after the schedule for the operating room had been set,
to find out when to turn up the following day. Meanwhile Barbara
would arrange for the testing to be carried out tomorrow and
would also see if someone from anesthesiology could talk to me
then. She would find out whom we should contact in order to have
the blood transferred. Judy was right. Barbara knew what she was
about.

As soon as I hung up, David picked up the phone and began to
dial the code for England. His sister answered.

"Hello, Di. Yes, we're okay, as okay as can be expected, and
Ben's fine, but it's been a real revolving door. We're having to
change surgeons, as I told you we might, and we're changing hospitals, too. Gayle's operation will be on Tuesday. Why don't you

try to get on a plane on Wednesday or Thursday? Let us know what you can organize."

After he and his sister had finished, my husband phoned the insurance companies and then phoned his office. Brian would tell everybody there and let his wife Di know as well. The next time the phone rang David passed it to me: my friend Jean was on the line.

"Hi, Gayle, I didn't want to phone you back too early. I know you've got somebody helping with the baby, so I thought maybe you would be asleep."

"No chance of that, Jean." I told her what happened. "So now we share not just a profession and a disease, but a hospital and surgeon as well. What a relationship!" I smiled in spite of myself. "What's Petrek really like?" I asked.

"I think she's great. As I said the last time we spoke, I like people to be straight with me. And she's got a lot of energy, which I think is important. She can be funny, too. Sometimes you need that."

I told Jean that I hadn't seen much evidence of humor bubbling up during our first encounter, but then, it wasn't exactly an encounter made for laughs. By the end of the conversation I had been very reassured by my friend's words. I felt again how good it was to have somebody to talk to who had been through it all before.

That day, our phone was never unoccupied for very long. Barbara rang back telling us that the person in charge of Sloan-Kettering's blood bank was called Helen DePalma. David phoned her straightaway.

"Well, Mr. Reid, it normally takes at least four working days for us to process a blood donation. Of course it will have to be re-tested," she said, after David had quickly sketched in the scene.

My husband was incredulous. "I don't understand—this is blood coming from another hospital—it's been tested and passed already."

"I hear what you're saying, Mr. Reid, but I'm very sorry, it's hospital policy. There's no way that any blood can be used in our operating rooms unless it's been tested by the New York Blood Service Center under our guidelines."

We had stumbled into the quicksand of medical bureaucracy once again. Since the blood would not arrive from Sinai until late in the afternoon or early tomorrow, everything would have to be done in half the usual time for it to be available. We had to face the possibility, after all we and our friends had gone through to get it, that the blood might not be released for the operation on Tuesday. It was totally absurd.

Still, Helen DePalma did not leave David without hope.

"Please believe me when I say that we'll try our best to expedite the processing. I understand your fears. I'll do all I can to make sure it's there." She was a stranger at the end of a telephone; we never even saw her face. Yet we were depending on her, and on so many strangers like her, to help us out. We knew that if the blood were waiting for me in the operating room on Tuesday, it would be because another human being had extended herself for us. It was as simple as that.

Later that Thursday I phoned my sisters and father to tell them of the new arrangements, and friends kept calling to find out what was going on. Di phoned back from London with details of a flight for the following Wednesday. Barbara came through with the name of an anesthesiologist who would see me early Friday afternoon.

That night, and for five nights thereafter until Di's arrival, my husband slept in with our son while I slept fitfully on my own. "You've got to get some rest, Gayle, I'll be alright," is what he kept telling me. But with each reassurance I had to ask myself, how would he manage to hold up? I knew it was a question he was also asking himself. He tried, of course, not to show his fear, but occasionally, when suspended for a brief instant between tasks, or when the phone rang bringing a voice or news he hadn't expected to hear, or when sometimes he looked over at me sitting quietly with

Ben, I could see him blinking back the terror that was passing across his eyes. How would he manage to hold up?

I depended on him absolutely, unquestioningly, as we both knew. David carried such heavy emotional cargo, shouldering his own shock and grief and fear as well as some of mine. The lack of proper rest added a physical burden on top of everything else. He wasn't even able to sleep during the day, there was just so much to do. My father, in the end, hadn't been able to cope with it all; David's brother Keith had done so, but at a very great price. My husband was frightened that he would break under the strain. He never talked about it to me; silence was another load he carried in his heart. All we could say to each other was that we had to take it one stage at a time. We repeated that over and over again. We would get through until Di came, and then there would be relief.

Friday morning I walked to the hospital on my own. "Are you sure you'll be alright, Gayle?" my husband had asked. Bills needed to be paid, and he had to sort out a few matters with the office over the phone. This was the first opening he had had for such things in the two weeks since the diagnosis.

"I'll be alright, I'll be alright, D. Reid," is what I told him. Ben was due for a checkup at our pediatrician's office at 2:00 P.M. If everything ran well at Sloan-Kettering, I would come home and grab a bite to eat and we would all set off together. Otherwise I would meet them at Barry's and gobble something afterward.

It was bright when I emerged from the dimness of the hall, and I stared at the traffic clogged with deliverymen. Although sometimes I would write an article at home, for the most part my footsteps were not heard near here at this hour of the working day. I had not stayed much around the house since those early months in the city, when I knew no one and spent my days combing the neighborhood to find things for the apartment. David was working all hours at that time, and I had nobody else to talk to, so I talked to the people in the shops. I roamed the streets, wanting to belong.

Once I had a job, once I seemingly belonged, the neighborhood became a place for weekends, for early morning rushing to the subway and evening rushing back. Now I found myself during the weekdays in the neighborhood once again. I knew I would be spending a lot of time here for at least the next few months. I remembered the loneliness I had felt amidst these crowded avenues once before.

I looked around. The street population was overwhelmingly female. I could see women out doing their morning shopping, mothers pushing their babies along. The ladies who lunched were making their preparations, already hitting the hairdressers and nail salons. Old people of both sexes were tottering to the bank or drugstore. Some were, like me, heading in search of a doctor. I walked due east, toward the river, toward the hospital, and realized how physically circumscribed my life in Manhattan had become. I had hardly ever ventured east of Second Avenue for the past five years. Now I knew that whenever I would venture this far east again, I would think of Sloan-Kettering. An association had been formed.

All of the testing went quite smoothly, the EKG, chest X ray, blood work, and general physical. When it was finished, I was directed to another part of the hospital for my rendezvous with the anesthesiologist. I waited and waited. When he eventually arrived, the youngish doctor apologized, explaining that he had been tied up in the operating room. I didn't mind the wait: I was so grateful for the chance to talk.

Although I had undergone general anesthesia for the four laparoscopies and the breast surgery I had had in London years before, I hadn't been able to talk with a doctor about it much before entering the operating room. By then it was always too late. The price I paid for blessed unconsciousness during the surgery was twelve or fourteen hours of convulsive sickness after waking up.

"Well, I think we may be able to do something about that," the doctor said to me. "I'm making some recommendations here, and whoever is on next Tuesday morning will have seen them. I think, using this kind of anesthesia, your experience will be better. At least we can try."

Although it was late and I found myself rushing to catch a cab to meet David and Benji at our pediatrician's office, I felt a strange kind of relief. We were crossing our fingers that the blood would be there, but apart from that, as far as the hospital was concerned, everything had slotted into place and the preparation was all done. I knew that Monday would be awful, that the fear would seep into every part of me, but until then I could concentrate on other things. The cancer patient could become just a mother again.

When I arrived at the Park Avenue office, the waiting room was crowded with women and children. It was not often that a father was the one to accompany a child there. Friday, I was to learn, was always the worst day to visit the pediatrician. Every runny nose or rash that had not seemed too terrible during the week suddenly loomed as a major crisis when confronted by the weekend. But Ben, being so very little, did not have to wait long—he was already being seen by the time I arrived.

"Hi, Gayle," Barry said when I rushed into the examining room. Ben, our tiny wriggling naked boy, was on the table, Barry and David bent over him. Barry turned toward me, planted a kiss on my cheek, and then turned back to the baby.

"Well, he's fine, but a bit thin. All babies lose some weight after they're born, but Ben should be putting it on again now. See if you can get him to take more formula. We'll weigh him again in ten days. Now, how are you? David told me about having to change hospitals. You've just come from Sloan-Kettering, right? Everything okay?"

"Yes, yes, it does seem to be okay," I told him.

"Well, I've finished here. Get Ben dressed and go back and enjoy him this weekend. And let me know what happens next week."

We walked the ten blocks home with our boy, surprised at how foreign it felt, this sensation of being able to do something normal, something entirely expected, to engage in one of the simple, taken-for-granted pleasures of being a parent. We felt so enormously proud. This was our baby asleep in the carriage between us, our brave boy who had been pushed into the world so rudely and had survived.

That weekend, we tried not to think, just to live for the moment, be existential, what you will. On Saturday there was the delight of going to the local art gallery and chatting about the pictures on the walls, after the owner and his staff had paid the requisite obeisance to our picture-perfect son. There was the joy of being able to return home to tea and cakes with a sleeping baby at our side, with no one else around and no phone calls from doctors to hope for or to dread. There was the happiness of sitting in the den, eating a take-away Chinese supper, and losing ourselves in a video. We lay there on the sofa and fell asleep in each other's arms. That was good, too.

On Sunday we walked up through Central Park to the Metropolitan Museum of Art. The leaves that had been so verdant when I stared out from my Mt. Sinai lair were brightening now, and we took turns posing for photographs beneath them. The object of the camera eye was almost lost to our pictures, snuggled as he was so sleepily within the knapsack one or the other of us wore. Once inside the museum we headed for an exhibition of Turkish tiles. We had developed an interest in Izmic pottery during the summer, when we had visited Istanbul for our final pre-baby fling.

I stared at the intricate patterns swirling out from the walls before us. Byzantine tiles, but how much less byzantine they were than the complex configurations of our lives. I thought about a photograph of us from that trip, taken as we stood high on a promontory above the Bosporus. I was five months pregnant, dressed in my black flowery blouse and Hollywood-movie-star floppy hat, while David was in his straw panama and summery checked shirt. We looked terrific. We went back to the hotel later that day and made love.

During the course of it, I remember thinking for a split second that I felt something on one of my breasts. I let it pass and did not notice anything again until that pimple appeared. I shall never know if what I felt in that hotel room in the heart of Istanbul was the lump I found three months later in my apartment in New York. But I realized with a start that if it had been and I had taken it up with the doctors on our return, there might not be a boy nestling against me now.

We walked back from the museum and made a few calls, had a simple meal, and around 7 P.M. our friends Morris and Mary arrived. They had left babies behind a long time ago, their own children having already grown up, but they would sit for us so that we could go to the movies. We needed to keep our minds off what was to come.

David's arm encircled me the whole time we sat there transported to Dublin, watching *The Commitments,* and for a while the electric shadows, as the Chinese call them, succeeded in blotting out the shadows that had been darkening our lives. We both slept better for the outing that night.

Monday morning dawned with lots of bits and pieces to put in place. We were still busy organizing them when the phone rang just after lunch.

"Hi, Mrs. Reid, it's Barbara from Dr. Petrek's office. We've got all the operations scheduled for tomorrow, and you're going to be the first. You have to be at the hospital at 6:30. Since you live nearby, we thought it wouldn't be a problem."

"Yes, that's okay, I'll be there."

I told David. "At least there'll be time to recover from the anesthesia before night," he reasoned. But as we filled the hours with our tasks, the call sounded again and again through my brain. It really was going to happen; this time tomorrow I would be inside Sloan-Kettering.

When there was nothing else to do, and the baby was sleeping sweetly upstairs, we repeated the ritual we had gone through two weeks before. We set out for the house.

As we turned into the street, Wilfredo, the friendly doorman at the apartment block on the corner, saluted us, having followed the progress of the renovations during the past few months. Now he doffed his cap, lips parting into a smile beneath the thin military mustache.

"When are you folks finally going to move in, then?" he enquired.

We smiled back, evasively. "Well, there've been some delays. Not too long now, not too long. We'll let you know," my husband replied.

This house is a very different sort of house from the place where I grew up. That house, my mother's house, is a memory palace whose walls and furnishings arrange and rearrange themselves like a house of mirrors through my most fearful dreams. Its magnetic force draws me back inexorably, so that when David and I return to Philadelphia, we find ourselves driving by a building whose smallness never fails to shock, given how large it looms in memory.

Our parents paid $16,900 in cash for the house. Our mother's father, our grandfather Philip, redeemed a $5000 insurance policy so they would be able to buy it without a mortgage. "No credit, no credit, pay in cash or don't buy at all," is what his wife, our grandmother Golde, had always said to them. She died five years before the house was bought, but a portrait photograph of her hung in the place of honor on the living room wall, across from the self-portrait sketched by our father's older brother, our Uncle Mike. It was Mike who had found the money to start up the sign business with our father in the late 1930s. Joe never got over the loss of his one true business partner when his brother died in the war.

Of course there were other dead relations in the family, grandparents and greatgrandparents whom we had heard about, whose pictures we saw, but it was Golde and Mike who seemed ever present during all those years we were growing up. They were real to us, twin ghosts hovering over our lives, over our house. But when our mother joined them there were too many ghosts for one small house. We, the living, could never feel easy there again.

But I wonder, did we ever feel completely easy there, even before that? Perhaps it's simply that the later memories blot out the happiness we once had known within its walls. Perhaps it's merely that the second house of childhood can never feel quite as cozy and secure as the first.

I remember when we moved there, to the new development, it felt so strange after the close quarters of the rowhouse on Stevens Street. There were great muddy swathes all around, vacant lots of tangled bushes and vegetation grown out of control. Within a few years it was all gone, had become a shopping center, a school, other houses on other streets.

But the land remembered what it once was, that first summer we lived there. The place seemed to fight back against the relentless new ground cover of concrete and tar. A plague of caterpillars seemed to drop from nowhere onto our hair and clothes. Their yellow furry bodies clung to the ragged patches of grass like a loose-woven carpet behind each house. The caterpillars disappeared after that summer just as mysteriously as they had come. The following year the ranks of houses had grown up around us, and the caterpillars never did return.

The developers had put all of the decoration into the fronts of the buildings, the best face forward to attract young families who might be driving by. There were stone and brick and shingle, and fast-growing evergreens beneath the big picture windows of each house. Around the back, though, it was all plain brick, utility poles, garbage cans, and concrete slabs where each family parked its car. The small squares of grass shared between each pair of houses seemed dwarfed by the grease-stained driveway running along them at the back.

We played in the driveway, not on the new front lawns fighting to take root beneath the burning summer sun. It seemed so ugly to me, that driveway, not like the pictures of the houses in the books I read. When I was big, I told myself, I would live in a house that was pretty both in front and in back. I would live in a house that was very different from the house in which I grew up.

And so I found myself standing in such a house, my husband at my side, that Monday night in mid-October. But I wondered how different this brownstone really was, this house that was pretty both in front and in back. Despite a lifetime's efforts to shake them off, the ghosts of my childhood had followed me here. The doors that I had locked against them back in Philadelphia had creaked open onto the streets of New York.

I was startled to hear my husband's voice. "We'll move before Christmas, you'll see. We'll spend Christmas in our new home and bring in a new year here. We'll put the cancer behind us." David said this, wearing his best smile, but his words echoed cheerlessly through the empty house.

We would never have bought such a place, planned such a move, if we had known what was coming. It was my husband's salary that would have to pay for the house, but he had no idea how long he would have to be away from work. The firm would be understanding, but what would happen if, in the end, he had to be both father and mother to our boy? He had saddled himself with such a mortgage! Would he be able to sell this place if he had to, with the real estate market so low? The bricks and stones and mortar of the house weighed very heavily on his soul.

David clasped my hand and we walked slowly through each room to take in the work that had been done, a lot more than we

YOU DON'T HAVE TO

had originally planned. While I had been consorting with doctors, my husband had been rejigging the arrangements at the house. He had even organized for the garden to be planted with spring bulbs. "It will be beautiful here, then," he told me, forcing conviction into every word.

That night I packed my bag. Two nightgowns with easy access to breast and arm; the usual toiletries; clock and Walkman; pictures of my husband and my baby; a few books, some magazines. I tried hard not to cry as I did the late-night feed, but some tears fell anyway. The tremors of fear were passing through me, making me feel cold as I sat there with Benji warm and unknowing in my arms. I closed my eyes and concentrated and tried to imprint his smell, his look, his feel on my brain. I wanted to carry them with me forever, wherever I would go.

Neither David nor I could get to sleep. It's always been like that before some crossroads in our lives—leaving for France or for China, starting a new job, buying a house. We crept along to see the baby over and over again. We had cups of tea until midnight, when it was "nothing by mouth" for me. We watched late-night television.

"At least we should lie in bed, my darling. Our bodies will get some rest that way, even if our minds can't shut off," David said.

And so we lay there reading and listening to the music on the radio for a while, until I turned to him. We had lived together for almost twenty years, and sometimes our dressing and undressing went by hardly noticed by either one. Sometimes, of course, our bodies were noticed more than anything else.

"Would you like to see what I look like, D. Reid, one last time, while there are still two breasts?" I felt a curious shyness come over me as I asked the question. My husband did not say anything. He merely nodded yes.

I went into the bathroom next door and took off my pajamas and looked at myself in the mirror. I had given birth almost two weeks before and my belly had become much less distended. I knew I had lost a lot of weight. No one would mistakenly think I was going into the hospital to have a cesarean section now. The linea nigra was still there, though, and my breasts were still full from the pregnancy. The wound from the biopsy had healed surprisingly well.

I walked into our bedroom, and my husband looked up at me. The deep wrinkles around his eyes creased into a smile full of pain. He held out his arms and I climbed into bed. He kissed me gently and we lay there for a while, exhausted, with no words left. There was no question of making love—that was not possible, the doctors had told us, for another four weeks. After a while, I sat up, put my pajamas back on, and lay back in his arms. We finally fell asleep, with the radio on for comfort, around two.

The alarm rang at 5:15. David made a cup of strong tea for himself and began to feed the baby. Amira would arrive at 5:45 and the car had been ordered to pick us up for the ride to the hospital at 6:15.

I felt completely awake, on automatic, going through all the motions of the morning. The clockwork mechanism of routine was sprung tighter still by adrenalin, sprung tight enough to keep hysteria at bay. By the time I was out of the shower, had dried my hair and brushed my teeth and dressed, David had dressed too and Amira was sitting with the baby in the den.

"Good luck, Gayle," she said with tears in her eyes. I bent to scoop up my son and did not cry. I had one last hold of him and then released him to her care. The adrenalin surged through my body, forcing me on. I went down the stairs, out the door, into the car, David at my side. We told the man where we were going and swiftly headed off.

Chapter Ten

WE GLIDED THROUGH THE STREETS OF EARLY MORNING Manhattan, a city strangely emptied of its bustle and its crowds. As the car moved forward we stared out the windows, not speaking, just holding hands. There were a few people, wrapped up against the hour and the autumn chill, who darted into coffee shops to fortify themselves for the coming day. Others were already hurrying to first shifts at twenty-four-hour groceries, restaurants, hotels. Mostly, though, the streets were clear, no sound of horns, no screech of brakes, no arguments, no laughter.

I remembered a car ride we had taken seven years before, when David drove me through London to Gatwick airport as I set out for a year in China. The feeling was much the same now, with time and space and great unknowns spread out before us, as though it would be our last ride together for a long, long while. We seemed to have ceded control of our lives to some larger mechanism that was directing everything, moving us along, whether we willed it or not.

The car pulled around to the hospital's main entrance on York Avenue. Several people were standing just outside, laminated badges clipped to pockets identifying them as members of staff. They were all smoking. I remembered from my previous visits the signs posted prominently as soon as you entered, prohibiting smoking once inside. I thought of the young girl in the coffee shop at whom we had shouted. I thought of an old Scottish saying, "There is nothing queerer than folk." We passed by, the smoke curling into the damp air, the still-dark sky. I wondered how many cases of lung cancer are seen at Sloan-Kettering in any given year.

The guard was at his post just inside, but the waiting room beyond him was empty and unlit. The whole place looked gray and forlorn. The guard followed us in and turned on the lights.

"You're a few minutes early. The admissions people will be here soon. Take a seat, please," he told us.

I felt terribly cold, although I was wearing a heavy sweater and hospitals are not underheated places. My gut was working over-time, and I had to ask the guard to point the way to the ladies' room. When I returned, another person had joined David in the waiting area, her small suitcase identifying her as a fellow patient. She was middle-aged, blonde, decidedly suburban. The woman sat there, fidgeting, and then automatically reached into her bag and took out a pack of cigarettes. When she lit up, David and I looked at each other, but couldn't bring ourselves to say anything.

"Well, they'd better get here soon. I've come all the way from Connecticut," the woman complained. After that, she and I kept a self-conscious distance, punctuated only by her coughs. There was really nothing to add.

The admissions clerk arrived and settled in for the day. He called my name and presented me with the consent form to sign. Unlike my mother, I knew what I was consenting to. I scrawled my signa-ture across it and then handed the clerk a copy of my "living will," which I had picked up on the day of preadmission testing. It was duly witnessed as instructed. No, I did not want to be kept in limbo on a respirator if something went amiss, I did not want to lie vege-tating on a bed as my grandmother Golde had done.

The nightmare of many a person waiting for a major operation is that something will go wrong, that the knife will slip or the heart will stop or, worst of all, that the wrong gas will be given and your mind, when you wake up, will no longer be your own. We voluntarily lose ourselves in sleep every night, but how many of us go gently, without fear, into that deep, vulnerable sleep of anesthesia?

The paperwork was finished swiftly, and David and I were led to a holding area, a room with eight beds in two facing ranks that could be separated by curtains. It looked more old-fashioned than any place else I had seen in Sloan-Kettering, like nothing so much as the wards I remembered from the National Health hospitals in England. Several nurses were sitting there, expectantly. One of them came forward, drew the curtain around my bed and told me to change into a green gown. David remained on the outside of the curtain. I felt bereft without him.

The nurse took my blood pressure and briefly examined me. She affixed a paper tag encased in plastic to each of my wrists—the white one identified me, the pink one identified the side on which the surgery would take place. I found the pink tag unnerving. Shouldn't they be able to remember which side the operation was on? The nurse opened the curtain part way and went out as quickly as David came in. She returned a few minutes later with a cap for my hair as well as some foam rubber shoes. I slipped one on each foot. They were surgical green, imprinted with happy faces. I stared at their have-a-nice-day smiles; such things, in such a place. I wanted to cry.

"Now, you'd better take your glasses off, Mrs. Reid, and give them to your husband. And oh, give him the wedding ring to keep for you, too," she said.

I stared at her. "My wedding ring? Can't you tape it on? That's what they've done in other operations."

"No, I'm telling you, those are the rules here. If you don't give it to your husband now, they won't let you into the O.R. They won't operate if you're wearing any jewelry."

I looked down at the thin gold band. It had always been a little too big for my finger and had become slightly deformed over the years. I tended to run it up and down, to play with it when I was nervous, but now it was going, another part of me being stripped away. Soon I would become just another unconscious slab upon a table, denuded of any personal identity, labeled only with hospital tags.

I handed the ring to my husband. "It's okay, my darling. I'll bring it back as soon as the operation is over." I could hear the dry tightness in David's voice. What could he do, other than stand beside the bed and hold my hand? By now, my companion of the waiting room was occupying one of the other beds in the holding area. I could hear a trolley approaching—were they coming for her or for me? The porters passed by my curtain and went along to hers. She was rolled away. I still had a few minutes left.

The nurse pushed open the curtain. I was glad to have more space, more air. I heard footsteps coming toward the room once again, but no sound of wheels accompanying them. A woman a little younger than myself appeared in semisurgical garb; not everything was in place quite yet.

"Hello, you're Gayle Feldman Reid?"

When I indicated yes, she took my hand and gave it a squeeze for a long moment. She spoke with a slight accent, Eastern European I supposed. "I'm Dr. Fischer. I'm the fellow here who will be assisting Dr. Petrek. I just want you to know that everything will be alright." She smiled the smile of someone who knows about fear and pain and the closeness of death, and I felt a tremendous wave of human warmth cross over from her to me. She touched my hand again lightly and nodded her head as if to assure me that really, I could trust her, I must believe what she said. "By the way, we have your blood. It was ready in time. I'll see you in the operating room." It would not be long now.

I looked at the big, plain clock on the wall. 7:30. I had been here for an hour. "They'll be coming for you soon," the nurse announced. "I'm afraid your husband has to go."

David put his arms around me and clasped me tightly to his

chest. "I love you," we whispered one to the other. "I'll go home now to our boy, and I'll see you later," my husband added. I smiled a watery smile in reply, and he was off.

Instead of the porters, though, the next person to appear was a woman dressed in street clothes, sixtyish, with short, wavy white hair. She seemed to have materialized from nowhere.

"Hello, I assume from your name that you're Jewish," was what she said to me. "I'm afraid that the rabbi won't be in till later. I'm the only one around at the moment. I'm Sister Elaine, and if you like, I'll just say a little prayer for you."

Shortly after my mother died, when I was still in high school, I came across a few of the works of the French philosopher Pascal. In one of them, he considers the question of believing or not believing, likening it to a wager. Although I've never been a religious person, like Pascal I have always wagered on the side of God. I answered Sister Elaine yes, she could pray for me.

She asked me a few questions, and I told her about Ben and my mother. She bowed her head and spoke for a few minutes, praying for me and my husband and our baby, praying for everything to go well, or, should it not, for me to find the strength to bear it, for my soul to find some peace. I began to cry when she was halfway through. When she finished, she turned to me and looked me straight in the eye. "Now you're going to go in there and get the shit over with and start living again."

Had I heard what I thought I heard? Strange words from a nun, and strangely comforting. In such a place as this all pretense was gone, anything could be said or done. Sister Elaine smiled at me and then vanished as quickly as she had come.

I could hear a trolley rolling down the hall and this time I knew it was for me. My body was trembling and my teeth began to chatter. I felt cold all over, as though wracked with fever, but there was no fever, I knew. The porters arrived and helped me up onto the trolley. The nurses covered me with green blankets and strapped me in, prone, my eyes fixed to the ceiling. The porters wheeled me down the corridor, turned the corner, and then stopped outside some big double doors. They pushed me through, into the bright lights of the operating room.

"Hi, we're all here now and everything's ready." Jeanne Petrek was speaking through a large, pointed, clear plastic mask that covered her whole face. I was sufficiently *compos mentis* to think how peculiar she looked wearing such a thing, like the proverbial creature from outer space. But of course, no surgeon could afford to be splashed by anybody's blood these days.

The anesthesiologist came forward and assured me that she had read the notes her colleague had left last week. "You should be okay afterward," she said to me. Then she and a nurse pored over the veins in my right hand and arm and finally inserted the IV. I was the star attraction under those white lights; people were bustling all around my body at center stage. I could hear Jeanne Petrek directing everything, and in between she and Dr. Fischer were talking to me, their voices reverberating through the din.

And then they were no longer there, and although I could feel that I was still hooked up to the IV, I sensed that I was in a much bigger room, with softer lights and muffled sound. I sensed other people, dull moans, the shuffle of feet, a rank of cots. "I have come through the operation, I have come through the operation," the words telegraphed repeatedly, wonderingly, through my brain.

My body felt heavy, but I moved my head slightly and a nurse noticed that my eyes were open. She smiled. "Can you hear me? You're in the recovery room. How do you feel?" Her words echoed down through the post-anesthesia tunnel.

I did not feel my stomach ratcheting back into reverse as usual; the nausea that I had felt after every other operation just didn't seem to be there. "I'm okay, I think. I'm glad to see you," my words traveled back to her, surprisingly clear.

She smiled again. "I'll get somebody to take you up to your

142 room." The nurse approached a porter and said something, then turned and pointed in my direction.

"I'm going on my break now. She'll just have to wait," is what the woman responded, loud enough for me to hear.

I felt as though someone had hit me in the face. I couldn't believe her voice, her words, the sullenness and disregard. The woman walked off.

The nurse realized that I had heard the exchange and trotted up to the bed. "Don't worry, I'll find someone else."

I lay there and stared at the big clock. Even without my glasses on I could make out the numbers. Nearly 11:30 A.M. Fifteen minutes passed while the nurse tended to other patients, glided between the beds, read the monitors, checked for signs of life. Another nurse was working the other end of the room, but no other porter showed up.

When the clock said 11:45, the nurse glanced in my direction and then appeared beside the bed. "I'm going to take you up myself," she muttered very quietly, through pursed lips. I knew she shouldn't be doing so; she could get in trouble for it. But I was so very grateful that she had chosen to care.

She rolled me along to an elevator and we began to journey up through the floors, each devoted to a different diagnostic procedure, a method of treatment, a kind of cancer. When we reached 18 the doors opened and she wheeled me out. We had arrived at the breast floor.

There was a big rectangular glassed-in doctors' and nurses' station at the core. We traveled around two corners and then stopped. She spoke quickly to another nurse through the partition and a moment later smiled down at me. "Good luck," she said, and went back the way we came.

The floor nurse logged me in and wheeled me down along the corridor to room 1828. It was a single. I had debated whether it would be better to opt for company or for rest, and had decided in favor of the latter.

"Would you like to be a bit more upright?" the nurse enquired.

I nodded my head yes and smiled. She adjusted the bed and moved the phone within reach.

"Will you be alright for a little while? I'll be back soon," she told me.

"Yes, yes, I'll be alright," I replied. I was aware of a great stiffness on my left side and so, carefully, in order not to disturb the IV, I reached for the phone with my right hand and cradled it between my shoulder and head.

It was one of those silly things that had preyed on my mind before the operation. Would I remember my own phone number coming out of the anesthetic? How would David know when to come to me? But my fingers remembered the sequence and then I heard my husband's voice on the line. Before I knew what I was saying, the words tumbled out. "I'm alive, I'm alive, D. Reid. Will you come now?" And he did.

Chapter Eleven

THAT FIRST AFTERNOON IN ROOM 1828, WITH MY HUSBAND at my side, I did not think about the limbo we had entered, the period of waiting for the pathologist's report. I did not question whether the cancer had migrated to the lymph nodes excised from under my arm, whether it had insinuated itself into the blood vessels of the breast that was no longer there, whether it had traveled onward to the lungs or liver or bones. I did not worry how I would get through the chemotherapy or wonder what I would look like with no hair. No, all that would come later. That afternoon David and I sat in the hospital room quietly marveling that I was still there, that the operation was over, that we were together again.

I looked down at my chest. I hadn't expected it—the left side wasn't flat at all. I put my fingers tentatively where there used to be a breast and felt a hard pressure bandage that had been placed atop the other dressings to keep the skin down. After a day or so the heavy bandage would come off. There would be no protection from flatness after that.

My husband slipped the wedding band back onto my finger, then held my hand and propped me up and turned on the radio. We listened to the classical music that he found. I slowly sipped some ice water and smiled up at him. Although later a wave of nausea did creep over me, it ebbed away as suddenly as it had come and I could not believe my luck in coming through, in the magic the anesthesiologists had wrought this time around.

I phoned my sister Sandy, who promised to phone Vickie and my father. "You sound so clear," was what she said to me. David phoned his partner, Brian, who would pass on the news to Di. Next my husband left a message for my obstetricians. The other calls would wait until evening, when David was at home. I felt very, very tired, but Sandy was right, my mind was clear. We sat there for a long time saying little to each other. Just being was enough.

A nurse came by to check on my temperature. It was slightly elevated, and they were giving me antibiotics through the IV. Then she checked on the drain suspended at my side. The nodes that had been removed to determine whether the cancer had spread through the lymphatic system—the most common route—had circulated fluid that my body now had to learn to redirect elsewhere. It takes time for the rerouting to occur, and if nothing is done in the interim, the fluid collects in great puffy pockets beneath the skin. As part of the operation, therefore, provision is made for drainage to take place.

Tubes are inserted through two small holes in the skin a few inches below the armpit, and these in turn are attached to a vacuum bottle. The liquid it collects is emptied and measured several times a day. It's bloody to start out with, but as the days progress it turns yellow and then almost clear. The amount gradually diminishes, until finally the drain can be removed.

There was a lot of fluid in the bottle that first time. The nurse took it away and then checked my temperature and pressure. She went out and returned, bearing a firm, blue-and-white striped pillow, less than half normal size. She placed it under my left side, saying, "You need to elevate that arm to help the fluid drain. Use the pillow to keep it raised generally, and three times a day, for twenty minutes at a time, we want you really to extend the arm. Use a couple of pillows and make sure that the hand is higher than the wrist and the elbow is higher than the shoulder. What we're

146 trying to prevent is a condition called lymphedema, where the arm swells up with fluid. But you look okay. You're doing fine."

Dr. Fischer came by to see me toward the end of the afternoon. "You know, we didn't have to use that donated blood. Everything went well." She took my hand in hers and I remembered how she had done so earlier that day. It felt as though an age had passed since 7:30 A.M. When she left, we knew that David should go home to check on our son.

I looked at my husband. "D. Reid, I'll be okay. You go and be my emissary to the kingdom of the Benj. I'll be better for knowing that you're with our boy."

"I'll come back in a little while, my darling. Amira said that she could stay till eight. I'll be back between six and half-past. I can grab something in the cafeteria downstairs and take it up here to eat. You get some rest, now."

I dropped into oblivion almost as soon as he was gone, and when I opened my eyes again the room was filled with the deep blue of early evening. I had been startled awake by the intercom behind my head. "Please indicate," it had crackled. I would come to hear that expression over and over again, throughout the day and into the night. "Nurse So-and-So, please indicate," "Please indicate where are the narcotics keys," "IV nurse to room X," "Nursing assistant to room Y." Perhaps, in the old days, when there were enough nurses to go around, hospitals were places of deep rest. Even in a private room, I discovered, they weren't that anymore.

Before going to sleep, I had pressed the button to lower the bed. Now as my mind was surfacing once more, I searched for the button to raise it up again. I couldn't manage to find it, nor could I hoist myself up under my own steam. I felt like a beached crab, legs wriggling in the air, body stuck on its back until the next wave came along. My whole upper left side felt stiff and sore. It wasn't that I was experiencing very sharp pain, no, that was not the case. I just couldn't get up.

I fished around the sheets again and at last grabbed onto a string. When I pulled it, I saw it was attached to the call button, and I "indicated" as soon as a woman's voice came through the static. About five minutes later a nurse appeared and put me upright again.

"I'd like to try to go to the bathroom," I told her.

"Don't you want to use a bedpan?"

I responded with an emphatic no. Thereupon we executed an awkward *pas de trois*—the nurse, my IV stand, and me—but I made it to the bathroom and was able to relieve myself. I was not going to be an invalid, no way.

"Until we check you tomorrow, anytime you want to go, don't try to do it yourself," she told me, as she settled me back in the bed. "You're pretty weak and could fall. Call on the intercom and one of the assistants will come and help you." The nurse turned on the brighter lights and then left. I waited for my husband to return.

The strange euphoria that I had felt early in the afternoon had died down, leaving me flat, allowing the questions to pour in. I wondered what Benji was doing at that moment, whether he was feeding or sleeping or somewhere in-between. I had to concentrate on myself, on my recovery, I kept telling myself, that was best for him as well. If I thought too much about the baby, if I lost myself in worry about whether he would forget me these days when I was not around, it would take longer for me to get out of here. That would do neither of us any good.

There was a knock on the door and the flower lady came in bearing two magnificent bouquets. One was from my sisters, the other from my obstetricians. They were there for me, my family and my terrific trio. This room needed their flowers, that was for sure. I looked around and saw tan walls pockmarked with white where previous generations of patients' tape or tacks had once been stuck. A lone picture conjured up a lakeside scene, all pine trees and cloudy sky. The decoration was completed by two bright orange

148 chairs with small holes in slightly sagging leatherette seats. No waiting room oriental rugs or plush armchairs here.

David returned, pulled up a seat, and began to munch a sandwich from the cafeteria. "Ben is fine," he told me. "Don't worry.
Everything'll be okay."

I ate a half-dozen packets of saltines that he had brought; saltines
had never tasted so good. We had consumed so little during the past
three weeks, it felt strange, this wanting to eat again. We watched
an hour of TV and then he helped me to the bathroom. When he
rearranged the pillows back around me in the bed, we knew it was
nearing time for him to go home. David had to make more calls
and try to get some sleep. It was night duty on his own once more,
but tomorrow, at last, his sister would arrive. The shadows on his
face showed how much he needed her help.

I switched back to the radio once he was gone. Around 9:30 a
nursing assistant came in to take my blood pressure, check my temperature, and empty the drain. I lay back with the music on when
she was gone and flicked through some magazines. As usual, the
night after an operation, I could not get to sleep.

The door had been left a few inches ajar and I could see the
private nurse attached to the room next to mine coming and going,
cleaning up, collecting supplies. The patient in that room was an
isolation case. I had overheard the nurses talking earlier and it was
clear that my neighbor had been confined there for some time. It
spooked me and I wondered if her body was riddled with disease, if
she was lost in that bed, in the last stages of breast cancer as my
mother once had been. I felt afraid of that room next door, just as I
had been afraid of my parents' bedroom so many years before.

A woman poked her head around the door. "Hi, I'm your nurse
for tonight. Sorry I've not been by sooner. It's getting late now.
Here, it's Halcion time." She held out a little plastic cup with a pill
inside. She stood there, unconsciously tapping her toe, wanting to
get on.

"Is that a sleeping pill? Is that what you want me to take?" I asked.

"Yes, you should get some sleep. You just take the pill now." The cast of her eyes belied the saccharin of her voice.

"I'm a little leery about the Halcion. I really don't think I want to take it. I've had enough stuff pumped through me for one day. Why don't you just leave it, and if I feel later in the night that I need it, I'll take it then."

"It doesn't work that way. You have to take it in front of me or else I throw it away. Look, most people take them."

"Well, I guess I'll just let nature take her course. You take it away. I can always ring later on."

She turned to leave, a too-bright smile frozen on her face. I was not cooperating. I decided I might as well brook further displeasure by holding her back a moment longer. At least I might be able to put part of my mind at rest.

"By the way, I don't mean to pry, but could you tell me what's wrong with the woman next door? Why is she in isolation?" I asked as casually as I could.

"Oh, she had a massive infection after her operation. They had to open her up again. She's doing a lot better now. Don't worry; it happens very rarely. But we don't want anybody else to get her germs."

I lay back with my eyes closed after she left, not exactly reassured. That lady wasn't a living ghost as my mother once had been, but her germs were right next door. I was glad that when last checked my temperature had stabilized to normal. I listened to the music turned low, and by eleven everything else grew quiet. My lids only occasionally snapped open when the intercom crackled to life. Sometimes I could make out the faint squidge, squidge, of a nurse's shoes hurrying past. But after a while, even the hum of the hospital died down to a lower key. Around one I finally dozed off, but I awakened again and the clock showed three. Nature called. I

150   had drunk a lot of ice water and apple juice that evening, and the IV was filling me full of liquid as well. I rang for somebody to help.

"What do you want?" came the response over the intercom. I stated my need. Ten minutes elapsed but no one appeared. I rang again, since the need had become quite pressing by then, and five minutes later I rang once more. My muscles were slack because I had just given birth, and I was afraid I would soil the sheets. Fully twenty minutes after the first call, a nursing assistant shuffled in.

"What are you ringing like that for?" she snapped. "You should be using a bedpan."

Was there so much for her to do at three o'clock in the morning? I felt both angry and afraid. She had kept me waiting until I was ready to burst, but I couldn't afford to snap back. I needed her help; I couldn't make it to the bathroom on my own.

I made myself smile. "Look, I've just had a baby and I've got tears that have been stitched up. It's more hygienic if I use the bathroom. I've been up twice already. Please, can you help?"

She looked me up and down and shook her head. "Come on then."

When I finished, got back into bed, and she had shut the door, I wondered why she didn't seem to care at all. I knew it was a low-paying job, bad hours, but still . . . I remembered the porter who had refused to take me up in the morning. I remembered the nurse who had come bearing the sleeping pill earlier on; she hadn't bothered to appear in my room either before or after that.

Many nurses and support staff were exemplary—I thought of Collette on the maternity floor at Sinai, of the nurse who took me up from the O.R. when the porter refused—but there were some who seemed to organize life not for the convenience of the patients but to suit their own. I remembered how, when I visited friends in the hospital in China, apart from the absolute basics, most of the nursing was done by patients' families. There was no pretense at other care. And yet caring was what patients the world over needed most.

I fell into sleep again, with the radio still on, but was awakened just before six by a different assistant, who came for the temperature, blood pressure, and drainage routine. I tried to go back to sleep for a little while but then realized I could sleep no more. I wondered how I could get myself up. Anything was worth a try. I held on to the bed and pulled, but that didn't work. Then I bent my knees, grabbed my thigh with my right hand for leverage, and pulled. Still the beached crab. I tried a second time and then made it, feeling stiff and in pain, but I was upright, that was the important thing.

I dropped my feet to the floor and woozily held tight to the IV stand. I got to the bathroom, washed my face, and brushed my teeth and hair. I felt human again.

It wasn't yet seven, and there was no sign of breakfast. On the table beside the bed were some apple juice and a few packets of saltines left over from the night before. My head spun. I needed some sugar, fast. I ate and drank all I could find.

I worked my way around to one of the orange chairs by the window and plopped down. I reached for the photos of Benji and David that were lying in an envelope nearby, and looked at them for a long while. My husband was having to be mother and father to our boy. Were they awake yet? Was David sitting with our son?

I tried not to feel too much the hollowness of separation from my baby. I tried not to let the yearning for his touch, his smell, take over my heart and soul. For these days, I had to concentrate on other things. I poked my nose into the flowers on the windowsill and took in their scent. There was freshness there, and life. The room was lightening. I put my feet up on the other chair and looked out.

In the space of a fortnight, I had exchanged one exclusive New

152   York City view for another. I had migrated eastward, but it was not exactly a migration of my choice. Gone were the earthiness of Central Park, the children and dogs gamboling across the street. Facing me now was a watery perspective, the East River, silvery and black. I could see cars beginning to crawl across the 59th Street bridge. A tugboat pulling a barge chugged along. Red letters spelled out "SILVER CUP" across the Long Island sky.

In the Mt. Sinai birthing room, I had been able to open the window and gulp in the freshness of the park, but my window on the eighteenth floor of Memorial Sloan-Kettering did not open for any outside air. This was a cancer center after all, and high windows might be too tempting for some.

Tiredness crept over me like river fog. I crawled back into bed and a few minutes later Dr. Fischer and another, younger female doctor came into the room. I hadn't expected to see anybody so early.

"Hi, we're sorry to disturb you at this hour. We just want to take a quick peek at you," Dr. Fischer said, sending another of her waves of warmth in my direction.

She bent down and lifted up the surgical bra and bandages for just a moment. I didn't look down. The two doctors nodded heads approvingly. "It's okay. Well, Dr. Petrek will come by to see you in a little while. Keep up the good work."

A half-hour later, Jeanne Petrek sailed in. "Hi, how are you doing this morning?" She smiled and sounded brighter, more energetic than I would have expected from somebody who had spent the previous day closeted in the operating room.

"I'm stiffer than I ever imagined, but not too bad," I told her.

"Well, your temperature's good, you're not draining too much. You should look at the incision as soon as you're ready. You'll look like a prepubescent girl again, on that side. It's not so bad. Well, I'd better move on. I'll see you tomorrow. Bye-bye."

I lay back in the bed and contemplated what it would be like to be "prepubescent" again, on one side only, to have lost nature's roundness and symmetry. In the brief time I had had for reading about breast cancer before the operation, I had seen drawings, but not photos of women after mastectomies.

My mother had had to study corpses as part of her medical technician's training, and she must have helped the doctor treat patients whose bodies had all kinds of deformities. But I wondered how long it had taken her to look at herself. For her, of course, it would have been far worse. She hadn't known what she was waking up to, for a start. The chest muscle had been removed and she, unlike myself, had been a large-breasted woman. I was small to begin with, and so with the right clothes, the before-and-after difference wouldn't be as noticeable.

"It's not so bad," Dr. Petrek had told me. But what would the scar be like? Even if I opted for reconstruction, the scar would always be there. I didn't have long to wonder, for my thoughts were interrupted by the arrival of a nurse, tall, young, with longish blond hair.

"Hi, I'm Tracy, I'll be your nurse for today and tomorrow. I just wanted to introduce myself. I'll be back later to do your bed and change your dressing, and if you like, I can help you get cleaned up and wash your hair. Is there anything you need right away?"

She smiled broadly. There was something relaxed and reassuring about her.

"Well, since you asked, I'd love a cup of tea."

"No problem. I'll just see to somebody down the hall and then make you some."

Ten minutes later she reappeared. "Here's the tea and some sugar. I brought you a little carton of milk as well. I've got a lot of family over in England, and I thought with that accent, you might want some milk."

"Thanks so much. You're absolutely right. I think I live on tea."

She beamed at me. "Breakfast should come up soon. I'll be back after that."

David phoned to see how I was. He would come by around noon. He had already been up for quite a while, had already finished feeding Ben and put him back to sleep. Breakfast arrived and Tracy returned an hour or so later. She walked me to the chair and began to pull the bed apart. She looked up at me. "I read your chart. How's your baby? It must be tough leaving him. Do you have any pictures?"

"Oh, he's just the best, the loveliest boy," I said, and offered up the envelope of photos. "That's him, that's Benj. And that's the proud father, my husband, David. You'll meet him later on."

"The baby's beautiful. Your husband's not going to bring him here though, is he?"

"No, I don't think this is the healthiest place for a newborn. Too many people with infections, too many wandering around with compromised immune systems from the chemo. But it's not easy being away from him."

I looked at her. She was a stranger and yet she was being kind to me. Here, as we sat in this room together, so many layers of my life had been stripped away and we found ourselves, she and I, in a position of utter intimacy. It all began to tumble out.

"The worst thing is that my mother died of breast cancer when she was only a bit older than I am now," I told her. "I don't want that to happen to him. I don't want to leave him without a mother, I can't bear the thought of that. He's so little." I felt my throat constrict and knew that I could not go on. Tracy knew it, too.

"Look, I understand what you're saying. My mother died of breast cancer and so did two of my aunts in England. I'm a candidate, just like you. My boyfriend thinks I'm crazy for working on this floor."

"I guess people like me are grateful that you do," I responded, with a shaky smile.

She took my hand. "Okay, the bed's all ready for you. Why don't you climb up and I'll give you a clean dressing. Have you looked at the incision yet? Do you want to see it?"

Not having been able to look at my mother's disfigured body, I knew I had to force myself, now, to look at my own. I could feel the dread course through me.

"Yes, I'd guess I'd better get it over with." I looked around and saw that the window curtain was wide open, that I could see quite far into the rooms in the building across the way. I laughed nervously. "Well, I guess the people opposite will get quite a show."

"I'll close it if you like, but don't worry about them. They're all doctors. They're oblivious to whatever they see from those windows anymore. They've seen it all."

Tracy began to remove the pressure bandage. Under that a plain surgical bra with thin, shapeless cups stretched across my chest. She began to unfasten the strip of Velcro holding it together. The sound of her fingers taking it apart made me shudder, it was like the sound of ripping flesh. The bra opened and dangled at my sides. Then there was only the gauze.

"Okay?" She looked at me for a second. I nodded, and gently she removed the final layer.

It was not nearly as bad as I had feared. I saw a long, thin line extending into my armpit, regularly crisscrossed by sutures. If this was anything to go by, Dr. Petrek had done a good job. It was all so neat, no lumps, no bumps, no breast. As I looked down, I felt my spirits lift, I felt curiously unfettered, happy almost. I was so glad to have looked Medusa in the face. I was so glad simply to be alive. The loss of the breast didn't seem to matter that much.

Tracy repeated the layering process in reverse. "Alright, now the fun part. You can have a hairwash!"

We walked into the bathroom and she drew the pastel-striped institutional curtain closed. I danced around the IV stand and washed myself as best I could. Tracy helped me wash my back. Then she said, "I'd be happy to do your hair for you, but if you like, you can do that yourself. The trick is not to wash it in the shower stall, but to bring the attachment over to the sink. It'll just about stretch. You can bend down and not worry about getting anything wet."

I decided to have a go on my own, and after she made sure that I was okay, Tracy went off to tend to another patient. I had brought with me a small bottle of French shampoo, taken from an expensive hotel. It felt wonderfully indulgent to use it and to feel clean again. I dumped the hospital gown and put on one of my own. I sprayed perfume on my neck and wrists. I put on a pair of earrings David had brought the night before. When I looked in the mirror, I saw a waxy pallor and dark circles under dark eyes, but I felt like a woman, not just a patient, again.

I climbed back into bed and picked up a book, but instead of reading, I thought about Tracy, living with the same genetic time bomb that was ticking inside of me. I was so lucky to have her as my nurse; we seemed to understand each other very well. Like her boyfriend, the only thing I couldn't understand was how she faced doing the job she did every day.

I drifted into sleep, but woke when I heard the intercom buzz into life. "The physical therapy session is ending. Those who would like to attend the discussion group should come now."

The nurses had already primed me about the therapy sessions. Each day there was an exercise regime, which I would begin to-morrow, once I was freed of the shackles of the IV. The exercises could be started the second day after surgery, and all of the women on the floor were encouraged to do them. The nurses said it would take six to eight weeks to get full mobility back in the arm. After the exercise sessions, which were led by a physiotherapist, the social worker took over. That was where I was heading now.

I put on my robe and slowly made my way out the door, around the nurses' station, toward the therapy room. Most of the women would already be there, having stayed on after the exercises. I went in and looked around. They were seated like wallflowers in chairs hugging the perimeter of the room, below the pulleys they had just used to exercise their arms. They were all ages, all sizes, all types, educated and not, some having husbands and children, some living on their own. A few already knew what stage their cancers had reached, but most sat there, still waiting for the knock that would bring the pathology report and knowledge of their fates.

There was a black woman ten years younger than I, with hair pinned up into a twist; a Belgian woman a year or two my senior who was also hooked up to an IV; a redhead in her early fifties, sporting good pearl earrings and impeccably coiffed; a brunette, about the same age, a housewife, Jewish like myself; a smoky-voiced Lauren Bacall type, handsome and sixtyish, in a beautiful silk robe; two others approaching the end of that decade, speaking with Central European accents, draped in big flannel tents.

Several others drifted in like afterthoughts, but more than a few of the name tags on the table remained unclaimed. Some women, it turned out, chose not to come. They were too depressed or fright-ened, too angry or too shy. They hardly left their rooms at all. The social worker began her spiel, asking us to pull the chairs closer together, saying that we were there because it might help to talk about what had happened, about our concerns and fears, about how we were planning to cope when we left the hospital.

To get us going, she told us, she had invited a guest. She went out of the room for a moment, and walked back in with a slim, spry, gray-haired lady in tow.

"This is Edith, a volunteer who comes here sometimes. I'll let her tell you about herself."

She was a woman who had aged gracefully and knew how to use

158 makeup well. She was wearing a muted silk scarf, some earrings, and a pendant dangled on her sweater, between her breasts. She looked around the room. "I'm here because I've had breast cancer, like all of you. I had a mastectomy thirty-six years ago and haven't had a recurrence since. You see, I'm proof that there is life after cancer."

She smiled, waiting for her words to sink in. The women's faces smiled back. Every one of us wanted to be an Edith.

"Now, is there anything you'd like to ask me? How are you all feeling? How are you coping?" she added.

I spoke first. "It's good just meeting you. That helps. I saw my sister-in-law die of breast cancer at thirty-four, my mother at forty-seven, and a close friend die of it in her early fifties. My cancer was diagnosed when I was pregnant, and two weeks ago I gave birth to a little boy. I want to be around a long time for him. It's good just seeing that somebody can make it." The others all inclined their heads.

Then the Belgian woman chimed in. "I don't feel physically as bad as I thought I would. But I'm worried about whether it's spread; I haven't heard from my doctor yet. And I know that this has changed my life forever. It won't be the same again, for me or for my husband." Several women nodded.

"In what ways has it changed?" the social worker asked.

"Well, there'll always be this uncertainty, this fear. It will always be at the back of my mind, whatever I do."

One of the Central Europeans piped up. "I am feeling so nervous these days, they have given me tranquilizers. I don't know if I will have to take them for a long time, I don't know what I will do without them. And I'm worried about the chemo, what will happen to me during the chemo? Tell us about that."

"I'm sorry, in my day, there wasn't much chemo," Edith responded. "There was just the mastectomy and radiation for some. But at least there is chemotherapy now, that's a step forward, that's the way I look at it. A lot of women I speak to say that it makes them feel that at least they're doing something to fight the cancer, that's how they get through the throwing up, the tiredness, and everything else."

The middle-aged Jewish lady shook her head. "I'll do whatever they tell me to do. Whatever happens, happens. I saw my aunt die of it, after a very long fight. At this point, I'm more worried for my daughters than for myself. I've already lived, seen things, done things. But my daughters, they're young women just starting out. I don't want to have passed this on to them. I've got to be strong for them, and I don't know how I'm going to cope." There were tears in her eyes.

"Well, I'm a lot younger than all of you," the thirtyish black woman interjected, "more like your daughters," she said, looking in the direction of the mother who had just spoken. "I'm not married and I'd like to be. How is this going to affect my chances with men? That's what I keep asking myself. I want to find out more about reconstruction. Did you have that, Edith?"

"I guess I'm not being much help around here. In my day, there was no reconstruction. There was just the radical mastectomy—not even the modified operation. I had to get somebody to make a prosthesis for me. There weren't many places that did it in those days. I could have had reconstruction later on, I suppose, but then I got used to the prosthesis. That's what you see me wearing right now. They're a lot better made, more natural, than they used to be. But if reconstruction had been available when it first happened to me, I think I would have done it. I was only in my thirties, after all."

The well-coiffed woman jumped in. "Well, I'm not in my thirties, but I'm having reconstruction. I'm not married, I don't have any children. I guess I'm married to my career. My feeling is, I just want to put all this behind me, I think that's the way we have to deal with it. My sister was here three years ago for the same thing.

We have no idea why this should have happened to us, there's nothing in our family. But anyway, I want to get out of here and back to my normal life. I'm not going to tell anybody at work; my boss knows, but nobody else. And I'm not going to tell most of my friends. It's just something that concerns me and my family and doctors; it's nobody else's business."

The Belgian woman looked at her, uncomprehendingly. "But you have to tell people about it. We have to be open. How else will there be more pressure put on the government, more money for research? How else will people understand what we're going through? More and more women are getting breast cancer, and not enough is being done. Think of what gay men have done to get money for AIDS. Breast cancer is nothing to be ashamed about, nothing to hide."

The redhead's cheek muscles tensed, her voice tightened. "Well, I'm sorry, but I disagree. This is my body, my business, it's not for public consumption. You do things your way, I'll do them mine."

I sat there, listening to the two camps. I could understand both. After all, I had only told a few colleagues at the office and a few close friends. I couldn't cope with phone calls and questions from too many people because explaining over and over again was such a strain. But the Belgian woman was right, breast cancer was nothing to be ashamed of, and yet for far too many women shame was close to what they felt. This was a defining element of our lives—not the only defining element, by any means, but something we'd carry around as part of us for the rest of our days. We had been forever changed by it and would have to face it every day. Hiding wouldn't help us or anybody else.

The tension in the room was almost palpable. The Bacall-type intervened, wanting to restore the peace. "I guess we all have to think positively, whatever way we can. We're all lucky in a way that we found it when we did. We've got to believe in our doctors, in the treatment they're giving us. That's the way I'm trying to look at it."

"Well, it's funny," Edith said, "I would have expected to hear a lot of you say some other things. I've heard you say you're worried about the cancer spreading, about the chemo, about your relationships. I've heard you say you're going to put it behind you, I've even heard you say you're lucky in a way. But I remember, when I was diagnosed and operated on, I just felt so sad, so sad all the time, and I didn't have anybody other than my husband to talk to. I didn't have any sisters, and anyway talking just wasn't done in those days.

"I was really depressed, I guess you could say, for a year or so. I was withdrawn and grieved for something I had lost, for a part of myself, both physical and spiritual. And after I stopped feeling sad, I felt angry, very, very angry. That was better in a way. Why had this happened to me, I went around asking myself. Why me? It took a good few years for me to begin to emerge. Now I wonder, don't any of you feel that way, angry or sad?"

We all looked at each other. "Yes, of course we do," I said quietly. "And you're right to draw it out of us."

We talked for a while longer, and then the social worker intervened. "Look, ladies, we've reached the end for today. Tomorrow, after the exercises, one of the nurses will present a session on lymphedema and on hand and arm care. Because of the type of surgery you've had, for the rest of your lives, you're going to have to look after yourselves in some special ways. On Friday, we'll have a session on prostheses and bras and we'll talk again. We'd like to thank all of you for coming, and if your roommate hasn't been with us today, we'd like you to encourage her to join in. See you tomorrow."

As I walked from the room, something Edith had told us echoed over and over again through my head. She would have had her surgery eight years before my mother had hers, I reckoned. "Talking just wasn't done in those days," she had said. That was not the culture of the time. The woman who had been my mother, who had taught me to keep myself to myself, didn't share her secrets, even with close relatives, even with my father. My husband and I were so much more open with each other than my parents had been back then. How did she live with such silence, I wondered? How did she manage to keep it from so many, even from us?

I shuffled back to the room, my IV pole like some battle-scarred standard leading the way. David had been waiting a few minutes already. He had brought along a sandwich for himself and some goodies for me. Lunch came up and then the young woman doctor, the junior member of the Petrek trio, returned to check me over. "Well, I think you'll be fine without the IV now. I'll get the nurse to come along and take it out."

After the deed was done, to celebrate my newfound freedom, David and I went for a walk to the pantry where the microwave resided. I would be able to boil my own water for tea now, and not have to wait for the nurses or nursing assistants to help. We walked back to the room with our booty, fresh hot cups of tea, and sat there together until our friend Di turned up to keep me company. David had to go home and then go off to the airport to meet his sister later in the afternoon. He would try to come back in the evening, but would call in any event.

Di and I talked for a while, and then she left. My boss, Daisy, arrived and I talked some more, but exhaustion began to carry me away. Daisy took her leave and after that I managed to get to sleep. When I woke up, a volunteer flower lady, different from the day before, arrived with more bouquets; another volunteer hauled in a cartload of library books; a nursing assistant arrived for the usual routine. The rhythms of the hospital were taking over, and there was comfort in knowing what to expect, in the set, enclosed world, in the small, safe surprises of what the flower lady or the phone would bring.

David came late that night, after supper, after his sister, Diana, had settled in. After he left, I slept through the night, and the following morning Jeanne Petrek walked in early. I told her that I had looked at the incision and congratulated her on the neatness of it all. "Well, I've got news. The pathologist's report will be coming down later today. They've been fast."

I felt a terrible fear pass through me. After she left, I phoned David to let him know. He would come by around lunchtime and bring Di. I didn't have any appetite for breakfast but ate it just the same. Tracy arrived, made the bed, and we chatted for a while, and then she went on to another patient. I couldn't sit there and wait. I had to move around. The nurses had said it would be good for all of us to walk, to build up our strength, to clear the post-anesthesia congestion from our lungs.

I grabbed my robe and began to circle around the corridor, slowly, again and again. Other women were also walking the route. When we encountered each other, we tried not to stare. Instead we smiled shyly and moved on. I stopped occasionally to take in the pictures, a whole gallery of colors and themes, places to escape to on every wall. Sailing boats, Caribbean scenes, summer landscapes, a Mexican boy holding an enormous yellow bouquet. There was also a rendering of some mountains that unfortunately resembled nothing so much as breasts, but at least we had something to look at other than ourselves. These were the landmarks of our stay here, and we came to know them well. I did my last turn around the corridor and made my way to the therapy room. It was time for the exercise session.

We were shown how to describe a pendulum with our affected arms, then told to hold our hands together and try to walk them slowly from the top of our heads down toward the back of our

164 necks. We tried to clasp our hands together and put them behind our backs; we lifted pulleys, attempting to straighten the affected arms above our heads. Finally we used little pegs to crawl the walls with our hands and mark how high we could get. Each day we would try to go a little higher, until our arms eventually straightened out.

We were told about lymphedema, how in my mother's day so many women's arms were swollen or weakened or chronic sources of pain. At that time they tended to remove scores of lymph nodes and again I wondered how my mother had coped. The doctors had taken twenty nodes from under her arm.

I'd only had nine nodes removed, Dr. Petrek had said, so it was unlikely that I would have much of a problem. However, the therapist told us that even women in my situation would have to elevate arms and do exercises for weeks to come. In order to avoid strain, we shouldn't lift anything heavy or put weight on the arm; no heavy shopping bags were to be held on that side. But the real danger would come from infection. We should all be extra careful about cuts or burns and shouldn't get cuticles trimmed on the fingers of that hand. There would be no more safety razors used to shave under that arm. Electric shavers, that would be it from now on. Even the smallest cut in that arm, if untreated, could have very serious consequences. Fewer nodes meant less lymphatic fluid to fight germs. An infection could set in with much greater ease. The therapist looked at us and said, "Any questions?"

A worry had been passing through my head, ever since she had told us not to lift. "I have a young baby. Surely I can pick him up?" I asked her.

"I'm sorry, you'll have to wait four weeks or so, until you're fully able to extend the arm, in order to do that. Even lifting a baby at this point could be too much strain. Somebody will have to lift your baby for you, and put him in your arms." I remembered what

Edith had said the day before, about feeling sad. What would it be like, being able to do so little, when I got home?

The session ended and I made my way back to the room. Lunch arrived and a little while later my husband's smiling face appeared around the door. "I've brought somebody with me, my darling!"

Behind him, I saw an angel from across the sea, his sister, Diana, a trained nurse and one of my favorite people in the world. She came up to the bed and put her arms around my back.

"Hello, mother of that wonderful boy," she said in her old familiar voice, smooth, low, and sweet. We hugged for a long time. "Everybody sends their love. Now let me look at you. Not too bad! How are you feeling? You've been through such a lot, such a lot. We've been praying for you."

We talked for a while about what had happened, about Benji, about all the family in England. I felt so grateful that she had come, that David's face was just that bit less tense.

"Now I've brought a few things for your Benjamin Bunny that I've left at home. You'll see them in a few days. But I've also brought something for you. Every woman needs a new pair of earrings from time to time, and this is one of them. Hope you like them."

She handed me a little box, which contained a lovely pair of silver and turquoise dangles. I put them on straightaway. It was like using that expensive French shampoo; they just made me feel better.

We chatted for a bit, then my husband turned to me. "My darling, have you had any further word on when the pathology will come down? We ought to be heading back, so Di can take care of Ben and let Amira do the shopping and run some errands. I need to do some paperwork at home, to go through some more bills, but I won't leave if you'd like me to wait here with you."

I did not want him to go, but he would be at the end of a telephone line as soon as I heard, and then he would come back to me. "You go on then, back to my rabbit, Benjamin Bunny as Di calls him. I'll phone you." They each kissed me, and were off.

I tried to read, but couldn't, and felt too tired to walk around. I lay back in the bed. The private nurse from the room next door was busy clearing up, going in and out. I thought about the patient there, and how I had been afraid she was like my mother. Now, as I waited for the verdict the pathologist would bring, I remembered what I could no longer put off. I remembered what the pathologist had told my mother, that second time around.

After the first operation, the pathologist had reported that although the cyst had been large and invasive cancer was dotted throughout, the lymph nodes had been clear. They hoped for the best. My father has told me that my mother tried hard to believe that she would live. But it all changed three years later, with the removal of her ovaries and the second pathology report, when she told Cousin Ann that she knew she was going to die. The doctors had found cancer in her lungs, liver, and bones. She would have known from her medical training that the lungs perhaps could be saved, but the liver, unless some miracle should occur, could not. There had been no miracles thus far.

It came back to me again, how she had asked my father, only that once, after her own mother had died, never to send her away if she got sick. Did she have a premonition of how she would end her days? She had made him promise to keep her at home, and so in that final year home is where she stayed. After a while, she rarely went out. She got thinner and thinner and began to stoop. She stopped changing from her bathrobe into day clothes, then stopped leaving the bedroom at all.

They hired the nurse when one day my father and Cousin Ann came back together and found her on the floor. She was half under the bed, dazed, hardly conscious, unable to speak. They had no idea how long she had been lying there. She must have tried to walk to the adjoining bathroom, a few paces from the side of the bed, but that day her bones had packed in. They could no longer support even her diminishing weight.

Vickie and I had been in school during the day, and when we got home, late in the afternoon, we hung around the kitchen as usual. Neither of us ventured much upstairs. Neither of us knew what had transpired. But we may well already have been home, one floor below at the other end of the house, at the time she had had her fall.

Spring came that year, but there was no renewal. And then, early in April, the nurse told our father it was just too much. She couldn't manage any longer on her own. Our mother lay there not communicating at all. They would have to send her away.

The hospital took her in. It was not something they often did, they avoided it if they could. But the surgeon had clout, and perhaps he had guilt; he had promised, when it came to the end, that he would help. In that way he did.

She was in the hospital for four weeks before she died. My father, Sandy, Aunt Betty, and Cousin Ann all visited her. Everyone thought it best if Vickie and I stayed home. By the end she had shrunk so much that they had to put her in a smaller sized bed, a kind of crib. I didn't know it then, of course. It was many years later that I was told.

I did not want to die of breast cancer, I did not want to take my leave in that horrible, lingering, painful way. Everything about my future hinged on what I would hear later today. It had been hard, the waiting, and yet part of me did not want it to end. At least to be suspended in limbo was not to know the worst.

I fell asleep and woke up around four. I went to make a cup of tea and then settled myself in the chair by the window and began to read. It was nearly five when I saw a flash of red hair in the corridor. Time slowed to a crawl.

Jeanne Petrek walked in the door. "It's good to see you up and about so fast, but I know that's not what you're waiting for me to say. Well, I've heard from pathology. It's all noninvasive, 'in situ' is what we call it. In cancer terms, you haven't even reached stage one. It's rare, especially given the size of the mass and calcifications and the suspicion of microinvasion from the biopsy. You are really lucky. You may even be able to go home on Saturday."

She stood across from me, smiling. I had been given back my life. It was better than either of us had dared hope.

Chapter Twelve

DAVID CAME TO THE HOSPITAL IMMEDIATELY AFTER I phoned. We sat in my room knowing we could plan a life together once again, hardly able to believe it, to take in such joy. We felt as though every atom of energy our bodies had managed to store was gone now, exhausted, used up. The thread of our lives had been so tensely wound. Now that the release had come we felt at a loose end, unraveled, all played out.

The pathology showed multiple areas, or "foci" as they are called, of "ductal carcinoma in situ"—DCIS. The ducts are the canals through which milk flows to the nipples. In addition, there was a single focus of another kind of abnormal cell, "lobular carcinoma in situ"—LCIS. I had read about LCIS and remembered that the lobules were where the milk was actually made. LCIS functioned as a kind of "marker" for cancer, Dr. Petrek had said. She had asked an oncologist to come and check me over tomorrow, and I would find out more about it then.

The Sloan-Kettering pathologist had reexamined all of the slides that had been submitted from Mt. Sinai, as well as the tissue from the mastectomy and axillary (underarm) excision itself. Although the Sinai doctor who had read the frozen section had noted in his report that the specimens were "highly suspicious for microscopic infiltration"—that is, for invasive breast cancer—close examination of all the slides subsequently revealed no definitive invasion. There was one other piece of good news as well. Despite the fact that the

169

cancer had not been limited to the mass and calcified area taken during the biopsy, the "deep margins," or borders, of the tissue the pathologist had studied were free of all malignancy. That was a very positive sign. Tomorrow the oncologist would talk about what further treatment I would need, but whatever that was, the prognosis was good.

I turned to my husband, using words to cover up the sudden shyness that I felt. "Well, my D., here we are. It looks as though you may be living with a single-breasted Amazon for some time to come. Do you want to see what I look like now, or would you like to wait until I get home?"

David's face smiled gently. "Yes, of course I'll look at the incision now. I didn't want to ask, in case you weren't ready to show it to me yet. Don't you worry, my darling. It doesn't matter. The important thing is that you're alive, that our boy has his mother. You are the love of my life, and losing the breast, well, it's nothing compared to having your life."

I wanted to do it quickly. I unbuttoned my gown, unfastened the Velcro, and removed the gauze. They had taken the pressure bandage off the night before.

"It's not so bad, really. Petrek was right." David bent over and kissed me on the forehead and held me to him. I could feel my eyes begin to tear. "It will be alright, my darling one, it will be alright," my husband said.

My mind wandered back over the three weeks since the diagnosis. Apart from the tension that had flared between us over the night baby-nurse, Anne Marie, there had been no disagreements, no sparks of contention between my husband and myself. Sure, we had been together a long, long time, and like any other couple, we had had our share of anger and frustration over the years. There had been times when we didn't speak to each other and times when we spoke too much. But these past weeks, there had been no question of not pulling together, no wasted words or deeds. I thought of the young black woman in the therapy sessions, the woman who had no steady man. I was so lucky to have mine.

We would not know whether I could go home Saturday until sometime Friday afternoon. It all depended on how much fluid was collecting in the vacuum drain. In my exercise class, there were women who had already been in the hospital for a week; two of them told me that they had been here for ten days, waiting for release from their drains.

The surgeons discharged some patients with their drains still in place, the nurses having taught them how to suction the liquid out. Those who had opted for immediate reconstruction generally had more fluid than women like me, and they also had more pain. For a modified radical mastectomy, the patient is generally on the operating table for a couple of hours. Those who have reconstruction with implants must add another two or three hours. The most complicated kind of reconstruction, using flesh taken from the woman's own body—from her abdomen, back, or buttocks—requires much more time.

During the normal reconstruction process—using artificial implants—the plastic surgeon either inserts a permanent form made of silicone gel or saline encased in a thin silicone bag, or, more usually these days, inserts an "expander" that is pumped up with saline fluid over the course of a number of months. If a permanent implant is used straightaway, it has to be small because there is not much room for it to fit behind the chest muscle. Using an expander allows for more flexibility. A "pocket" is created gradually, and when it reaches the desired size, the woman comes in for another small operation, during which the expander is removed and the permanent implant put in its place.

It all sounded like a lot more extra surgery to me, surgery that I didn't want or have to face. I was glad that none of my doctors had steered me toward that course. I could always do it later on, they said.

Thursday evening, after the phone had buzzed nonstop with family and friends, I got a decent night's sleep. The following morning I went to call on one of Dr. Petrek's other patients down the hall. After she had imparted her good news, Jeanne Petrek had stayed for a while to chat and then, just before leaving, asked if I would visit this woman, who was ten years younger than me and had a son of almost three. She was "not doing very well," my surgeon had said. What she meant was that the woman was depressed.

She had been operated on a few days before me, but had chosen to have immediate reconstruction and so had been slower to get up. She was due to go home early in the afternoon, after having been in the hospital a full week. Her husband was coming to pick her up.

I made my way to the room, which was all the way around the other side of the nurses' station. When I walked in I realized that I hadn't seen her before, certainly hadn't seen her at any of the therapy sessions. Other than chatting to her roommate, she was keeping herself to herself.

She was unusually pretty and looked younger than her years. The hospital hairdresser had recently come and gone, having washed and dried her hair.

"I want to look good, for going home," she confided. "I'll have to go to my hairdresser every week for a while, to have my hair done. I just can't raise the arm enough to do it on my own." I debated whether or not to tell her that I had been managing to do it myself. Would that make her even more depressed or would it encourage her? I felt pathetically indecisive. I held my tongue.

"Well, my pathology is pretty good," she told me. "It hasn't spread to the nodes. But I'm going to have to begin chemo in a few weeks. You're lucky, your son is so small. Mine is in the really physical stage, he's a handful. How am I going to explain to him that he can't just jump into my lap anymore, that Mommy's arm hurts and she can't play for a while? My mother-in-law is going to help for a week or two, but I don't know how I'm going to manage after that, what I'll do when the chemo starts."

She was a full-time mother, and her son, apart from a few hours in a playgroup each week, was under her sole charge. She didn't have a nanny and she didn't have a job outside the home to help take her mind off things. Her son and husband were everything.

I felt guilty for having more money and being able to afford good help, for knowing that I had available to me the distraction of an interesting job. I felt guilty for having a cancer prognosis that had better odds than hers. What could I say to this woman that would make anything any better?

We talked a while longer. I hoped just talking was a help. Then I went off to the exercise session and put everything I could into the routine. When we finished crawling the wall, a nurse came in and joined us. It was "show-and-tell." She opened a small case and began to take things out.

"These are some examples of the different kinds of prostheses available to you," the nurse began. "When your doctor signs your discharge order, one of us will come in and fit you with a temporary prosthesis, something like this, before you go home." She held up a cloth form that looked a bit like a miniature football. "We've got them in a few basic sizes, and the pocket in the back is open, so we can put more or less stuffing in according to your build."

She passed around the form for us to see. I recalled the padded bras we used to wear as teens.

The nurse continued. "Some women choose to have a permanent prosthesis that's not so different. It's made out of foam and it's light, like this. But it's often best to have one with more weight, to counterbalance the weight of your other breast, so some prostheses have foam on the outside and are stuffed with a kind of sand. The most modern ones are made of silicone and, as you'll notice when I pass them around, they feel a lot heavier than any of the others."

I was sitting nearest to her, and so she handed me what looked and felt like a pinkish brown slab of calves' liver encased in plastic film. It wobbled heavily. The substance in the form was also what was used in the majority of implants for reconstruction. I didn't like the look or the feel of it, or the idea of putting such a thing inside my body. Somehow the padded bra effect was more appealing, familiar, known.

The nurse finished off the session by talking about the kinds of wigs and turbans available for those who would lose their hair. I looked around at the other women's faces. It was good, it was essential, to be given all this information. What would we have done if the hospital hadn't provided it? But the session brought none of us any cheer. We were incomplete, we were different, we had suffered an irretrievable loss that by its very absence was there for all to see. Some of us would suffer even more public losses, if our hair went as well. How were we to face the world like this?

An answer walked in the door to see me that afternoon. My writer friend Jean came to call, came to the place where I had visited her only ten months before. She looked terrific. Her hair had returned to its natural fullness, she had just finished the reconstruction process, and her permanent saline implant was in place. She was wearing a lustrous silk blouse and turquoise jewelry from Tibet. She was trying to look her best for me, for herself, for the world at large.

She was a lot closer to me in age and experience than Edith, the volunteer from the other day. Jean looked at the photos of Ben and sat and chatted with me. She hadn't taken on any assignments for a while, and financially she didn't have to work full-time. I asked what she had been doing, what she was planning to do.

"Well, I want to travel more. I've always liked it and I've done a lot, but there are other places, more friends to see."

She wanted to use her time well, that was something we all wanted to do. Before the cancer, time was something loose around the edges, taken for granted, only guessed at, always there. Time had become a different concept to people like Jean and me.

When the nursing assistant came to check on my drain late that afternoon, she added up the fluid for the day and smiled at me. "You'll be going home."

David came that evening and to celebrate the good news we ventured down to the cafeteria together, practice for my reemergence into the outer world. We were like deep-sea divers, starting to decompress. We would have to judge how quickly or slowly we would be able to come up for normal air.

I remembered how, after I had spent nearly a year living and working in China and it was time to go home, I very much wanted to return to London, to be with my husband and friends; but I had also grown very attached to China and part of me would have liked to stay on there. So when I boarded the plane in Beijing, it was a good thing it took me not to London but to a week in Hong Kong. I didn't know where I would find such a land between two worlds to cushion the shock when I got out of here.

It was already nine o'clock when we returned to my room. The oncologist who Dr. Petrek had said would come to see me, Dr. Theresa Gilewski, had never turned up. We assumed that I'd be seeing her tomorrow morning instead. But a half-hour after we got back, a young, tall, tired-looking woman walked through the door. She had been on the go all day and could only come now to check me out.

Dr. Gilewski peered at the chart, then asked me a lot of questions, taking a long time over my family history. She began the examination, going from top to toe, feeling her way along the map of my body using the lymph glands as her route.

"I want to feel for any swelling, for anything abnormal," she told us.

I had never fully realized how wide and complicated a network the lymph system is. Her fingers crawled slowly over my body. A careful exam was especially important because Dr. Petrek had decided not to send me for the usual postsurgery scans.

Each day, during the therapy sessions, I had watched as several of my fellow patients were called down to radiology. Of course we had all had chest X rays before being admitted to the hospital, so the doctors knew something about the state of our lungs. But the other two places to which breast cancer usually metastasizes, the liver and the bone marrow, were uncharted lands. The scans would provide basic maps for now and would be used for comparison later on. I had felt nervous about not getting them, but had been assured that the pathologists' verdict obviated the need.

"We don't want to expose you to radiation if it's not absolutely necessary. Anyway, you've told us that you have arthritis in your neck, back, and knee. Those places will show up abnormalities and start you worrying over nothing," Dr. Petrek had said.

When Dr. Gilewski finally finished, I braced myself to ask her what would come next. What kind of radiation or chemical treatment would I need?

She looked at me quizzically. "Why, nothing."

I did not understand. It was late, after all, after 10:30. "What did you say?" I asked her.

She smiled. "I said that you don't need any further treatment at this point. With a diagnosis of DCIS and LCIS, a mastectomy is the treatment of choice. It takes away all the cancer. There would be no point in using radiation unless you had had a lumpectomy or unless we thought the cancer had spread. If all the cancer has been cut out of you, then you don't need to go pumping chemicals into your body to kill something systemically that just isn't there."

"But isn't there any risk that it might have spread?" David interjected.

"Yes, of course there is always a risk. The pathologist can't look at every bit of tissue. Maybe a cell or two or three has escaped and found its way somewhere else through the lymph or the blood-

stream. It could be lying low in some part of your body. Nothing is
cast-iron sure. But in medicine we have to work with probability.
The probability is that the cancer was contained. We would not
want to put you through chemo for that one percent chance it was
not."

She began to shuffle her papers together, to prepare to leave, and
then she turned to me again. "Of course, you'll need to be followed closely by Dr. Petrek and you should see an oncologist once
a year. You should watch your diet. We recommend cutting out as
much fat as possible—I mean you should keep it really low in fat.
And go easy on alcohol. On the other hand, there are some things
that we think might be especially good for you to eat—broccoli,
cauliflower, cabbage, and carrots too. There are substances in those
vegetables that may help fight cancer.

"Forget ever taking any hormones again. Some women in your
situation we would put on tamoxifen, which as you probably know
may afford some protection against recurrence. And since it's like a
hormone, it has the advantage of offering a measure of protection
against osteoporosis for women who can't have hormone replace-
ment therapy during the menopause.

"But there are studies which have raised the possibility that
tamoxifen may set off uterine cancer in some people. And although
it ends up bringing on the menopause, when you first go on it it
actually produces an estrogen surge. That wouldn't be a good idea
in your case, pumping more estrogen into a woman whose body
has just been producing huge amounts. Anyway, you're too young
to be made to go through the menopause unless it's absolutely necessary.

"But there is one thing, beyond adjusting your diet, that I think
you should do. Lobular carcinoma in situ acts as a marker. It shows
that a woman is at greater risk of having—or eventually developing—abnormal or invasive cells in other parts of the breast. But

178 that's not all it indicates. LCIS also signals a tendency to get cancer in the *other* breast. LCIS, added to a family history like yours, says to me that you should take the other breast off."

I was an automaton when she extended her hand. I shook it and then she was gone and I was left completely stunned. No chemotherapy, I kept repeating to myself. No chemotherapy. They had chopped the breast off, and that was it.

Except that wasn't it. Dr. Gilewski was repeating what Dr. Petrek had mentioned in passing that very first time we met. They should chop the other breast off. In the course of three weeks, I had been diagnosed with cancer, given birth to my baby five weeks early after two and a half days of labor, and had a mastectomy. Now they were telling me that really I should go out, come back, and have another all over again.

The sensation of not being able to catch hold of what was galloping through my brain took over. And on this night, when I had heard what so many women passing through this hospital long to hear—that I would not need radiation, not need chemo—when I should have felt wonderful, triumphant, I felt fearful and panicky instead. Other surgery aside—a very big aside—I was supposedly "cured," and yet I felt terrified, cut adrift. They weren't going to give me anything for those cells that might have escaped. I would have to live with the fear of them every day. My mother had once listened to a doctor who had told her nothing needed to be done. She had died five years after that.

David's face looked grim, mirroring my own. It was so late, it had all been so unexpected. "Look, Gayle, you'll have to talk to Dr. Petrek about it next week. And we'll get other opinions. You should see another oncologist at least." It was eleven o'clock and he had to go home. After he left, I tumbled exhausted into bed.

The following morning I woke up very early, while it was still dark, even before the drain lady came. I was going home. I would be with my baby in a few hours. The day I had longed for had come.

And yet I felt so unsettled. My thoughts drifted back to my mother's operations and to her homecomings. I could not remember any of them, and yet I should have been old enough to remember something each time. I could not remember who had taken care of us or what they had told us while she was gone. How had she felt when she saw us again, was it pleasure or was it pain? How would I feel seeing Ben again, knowing that the shadow, despite the good prognosis, would always be there? Again I could not fathom it, the mystery of how my body had produced a new life and propagated the seeds of death at the same time. How could I ever trust it again? How could I trust anything?

The drain lady came, then I got up and washed and dried my hair and felt better. I had packed most of my things by the time breakfast arrived. I began to pass through the preadmission ritual in reverse. Doctors and nurses filtered in and out, noting details on the chart, examining me, signing forms. Midmorning, the young male doctor who was covering for the Petrek team while they had Saturday off arrived to remove the drain. There was some discomfort when he pulled the two thin tubes out of me, but it was over quickly enough. Then he covered the area with gauze.

But although the drain itself was out, the draining process hadn't finished. Dr. Petrek's outpatient nurse, Anne Walsh, had come to introduce herself the day before. She had explained that I would need to see her twice a week for the next few weeks so she could aspirate the fluid that was sure to collect. A small, puffy pocket would develop under my armpit during the next few days. It was nothing to worry about, she told me, unless it became hot and red.

Between visits from doctors and nurses, I stared out the window at life beyond the confines of the hospital room. I could see the trees alongside the East River, their leaves already deep orange, gold, and red. The year had left the hot weather behind with my hardly having taken notice. I watched the cars carrying people across the 59th Street bridge, a bridge to another life that David and I once had known, a summer life, weekends by the sea waiting for a child to grow inside me, blissful in our ignorance about what else was growing there. I felt sealed off from that former life just as surely as the windows of this building sealed me off from the world outside. The outside world I rejoined would be different now, and I was both eager and afraid.

One of the nurses came in bearing the discharge papers as well as a little prosthesis form. She fiddled about with it inside my bra, removing a wad of stuffing and then adding some back. "Now they generally don't fall out, but be careful. When you go to get your permanent form, the shop will fit you with bras that have built-in pockets, or they'll use your own bras and sew you some."

I looked down at my chest after she had gone and felt a great, yawning sadness open up. I removed a bit more of the stuffing; she had made me bigger on that side than I naturally was. Probably they worried that most women walked out of the hospital feeling too small.

David arrived just after noon and we took a cab home. As we rode along the familiar streets, sprinkled with people going about their normal Saturday affairs, I felt as though I had journeyed from afar, as though I had just stepped off a plane, light-headed with jet lag and fatigue, and found myself speeding through the streets of Beijing or Istanbul. But this place that I had to make sense of was far stranger than that; it was where I would be living my life, it was merely my home.

We arrived outside the brownstone and trudged up the stairs. I did not hold on to the banister with my stiff left arm. The feelings were rushing over me and I could hardly contain myself. When we got inside the apartment, David sat me down on the small sofa and walked into the kitchen to turn on the kettle. I could hear my sister-in-law Di begin to creep down the stairs to join us in the sitting room. She did not want to wake the baby fast asleep upstairs.

As soon as I saw her, I could not help it—the tears began to flow. But Diana was a nurse and a mother and had known me half my life.

"It's alright, Gayle, you let it all out. It's often like this. It's just been too much, too much you've both been through. And now you're home and have to face it all and face the future, and you feel the fear and the let-down. Coming home doesn't take the problems away. But you'll be alright. You caught it early, not like Pat or your mother. And you've got the best reason to carry on—that baby sleeping upstairs. He really is the dearest little chap, and he needs you. You're his mother. You have a good cry, and I'll go and bring you a cup of tea."

Cups of tea go with stiff upper lips, they go with England. I had spent far more of my adult life in England than in America. And the English are great ones for showing how to muddle through.

Chapter Thirteen

THE DAY AFTER I LEFT THE HOSPITAL, THAT FIRST SUNDAY
I was home, the new routine did not seem so strange. It was a
Sunday after all, not a weekday, not a day when people were supposed to be working, out and about. I awakened on hospital hours,
just after 6 A.M., and felt as though I immediately needed to go back
to sleep again. But sleeping an hour and a half later, I soon found
out, really made no difference at all. The weariness and lassitude
still held me like quicksand in the big brass bed. My head felt as
though I were struggling to emerge from the haze of a narcotic
sleep, and yet I wasn't taking painkillers or any other drug. Gone
was the immediate, full consciousness I had awakened to for the
past three weeks. My nerves had slackened a little, and exhaustion
was all I seemed to feel.

I moved myself up in the bed, stiff and slow. I reached across
with my right hand to gather all the pillows and constructed a pyra-
mid on my left side, propping them up against the chest of drawers.
We had had to switch sides to accommodate this; David used to
sleep where I was lying now. I turned on the radio and raised the
arm, inclining it diagonally above my head. I would have to sit
there for twenty minutes, to allow any fluid to drain. This was the
ritual I would go through three times a day.

That Sunday morning, David brought in a mug of tea and some
toast for each of us while Diana fed the baby down the hall. Slowly,
slowly my mind began to surface from the pool of tiredness as I

sipped the tea. We got into a routine, with David bringing me tea and toast in bed every day. I felt so self-indulgent; I had never eaten breakfast in bed except when I was sick, and sickness like that, in all our time together, had never lasted for more than a few days.

After the twenty minutes had elapsed, the arm felt much less stiff. I began the exercises then. The pendulum, the back clasps, everything I had done in the hospital I now did here. I suspended the pulley from the hook on the inside of the clothes closet door. For weeks, three times a day, I sat with my back up against that door, raising my left arm as high as it would go and keeping it there for five minutes each time. It felt as though tight rubberbands were lining my armpit, stretched to their thinnest but never stretching quite enough. Sometimes I wondered, half-smiling to myself, what people in the apartment block opposite thought I was doing there, my arms bound by the pulley to the door.

For the final exercise, I stood up, pencil in hand, and crawled my fingers up the closet door, marking how high the left arm could reach compared to the right. I couldn't believe how much lower the left always seemed. Usually I was able to crawl a fraction higher each day, or at least match the mark made the day before. Occasionally though, I slipped back and couldn't reach that point. I tried not to worry but it sometimes got me down, and those times I couldn't help wondering if I would ever be able to straighten my arm again.

During the exercises, I often thought of my mother. I couldn't recall seeing her do anything of the sort, and yet how much tighter, with more than twice the number of nodes removed, her arm must have felt. What had she done, I asked myself? I should have some recollection—after all, I was almost twelve. It was Vickie who was too young to remember; she had only just turned four. How did my mother manage to pick up a four-year-old when I couldn't even pick up Ben?

I do remember her tiredness, something I now shared. Each day,

184   I would fall back into bed for two naps, one late in the morning, one late in the afternoon. I just couldn't manage without them.

That first Sunday, after I finally emerged, David sat me down, wanting to talk.

"Things have been piling up at the office, my darling. It's been three weeks since I've gone to work. Gayle, do you think you could manage if I went back this week?"

Of course, somewhere at the back of my mind, I knew it would come. I knew I would have to let him go. But my heart sank; I felt the panic close in on me and the only thing that kept it from taking hold was Di. She had to fly back to her own family on Tuesday night, but she would be there, while David was gone, for those first two days. I remembered again the time in Hong Kong between leaving China and going home to London. These few days with Di would be like that, the land in between the closed country of the hospital and the world outside my home.

She was anchor, she was company, she told me it would be okay. When I was so late to emerge in the morning on Monday and Tuesday, after all the time spent raising the arm, exercising, and the awkwardness at getting washed and dressed, I felt depressed at how slow I had become. And beyond that, I felt uneasy, cast adrift from the whole going-to-the-office routine and yet unable properly to establish a new routine with Ben. It was curious, confusing. Why didn't I feel joyous, to be at home, to be near the baby, to have the operation behind me? Di understood it all, and she told me what I needed to hear.

"It'll get faster. You just have to give yourself time, Gayle," she assured me, over and over again.

David had heard from the baby-nurse agency the week before. They thought they had found somebody suited to our nighttime needs, for with Di going home and David back at work, he wouldn't be able to do the late shift as well as function at the office. We had taken up the references, which all seemed fine. We had arranged for the woman to be interviewed by Di and me on Monday afternoon.

When the bell rang, the voice we heard over the intercom spoke in a musical, lilting contralto. "Hello, it's Hannah!" the woman trilled.

She climbed the four flights of stairs fairly quickly, a good sign of energy in someone whose sixtieth birthday had come and gone. Hannah was trim, neat, turned out in red patent leather shoes and matching bag. Like Anne Marie she was Jamaican, but apart from nationality nothing else was the same. She seemed warm but no-nonsense, highly religious, a person of decided views. Di and I exchanged glances. We took her on. She was just coming off another job, and would start on Thursday night.

On Tuesday afternoon, just after lunch, I was due to return to the hospital for the lymphatic fluid to be drained. Gradually, during the past few days, a small puffy pocket had been growing beneath my skin. Anne Walsh, Dr. Petrek's nurse, would aspirate it for me. I felt a little nervous about going back to the hospital, so while Amira watched Ben, Di and I set out together. It was a beautiful fall day and we should have needed no more than fifteen minutes to walk there, but it took almost twenty-five. I just didn't seem to have any energy, so unlike me, but I would have to get used to the limitations for a while. I would, as Di kept saying, have to give myself time.

Sunlight flooded the big, crowded room on the third floor, where all manner of people were awaiting their turns. It was like some modern day Babel, the buzzing of so many different tongues. Sitting down, I felt the rush of fear that I had known here before, but I also felt something else. There was a strange kind of comfort in being in this place. After all, they knew how to take care of people like me.

Anne Walsh, a friendly, good-looking blonde, assured me that everything was fine, there wasn't too much fluid, I wouldn't have

186 to return until Friday. I had put on some makeup before leaving the apartment and Anne commented on how well I looked—she was good at providing that kind of support, too.

But by the time Di and I walked from the outpatient pavilion I had begun to feel dizzy and knew that I had to get home. We climbed into a cab and as soon as I got into the apartment I went straight to bed. David came back from the office late in the afternoon, just after I woke up. He had to take Di to the airport. Amira would stay with me until he got back, since I couldn't be left to take care of the baby on my own.

We all tried hard not to be too emotional. We chatted and even managed to joke around. Di had splurged and bought Benj a one-piece outfit that turned out to be much too big. We put it on anyway, wanting her to see him wear it before she left. He swam in it but that didn't matter at all. With its outdoorsy pattern in green and brown, David dubbed it Ben's "huntin' shootin' fishin' suit" and we all laughed. But when it came time for them to leave the apartment, we held each other and the laughter had gone. "I'll phone you," she said.

While I waited for David to come back, I asked Amira to lift Ben out of the bassinet and place him in my arms. I sat there, in the big rocking chair in the den, and cradled him on the right side—it would always be that side. A great sadness opened up again. I could not put him to my breast. As I fed him the formula that he took so slowly—an hour to consume an ounce and a half—I wondered if it would have been different if he had had my milk, if he would have had more appetite, put on more weight. Certainly if he had gone to term things would have been different, I felt sure.

I loved him so much, more than I ever realized I could love, and I wanted everything to be right for him, I wanted the shadows to disappear from my life for him, even more than for me. He was such a good baby, a pleasure to be with. I wanted to be with him more than I could; there was no way I would be able to do even all his daytime feeds. The arm raising, the exercising, the naps, the twice-weekly visits to the hospital, and the fact that I simply could not lift him myself came between us. But it would get better, it had to get better, I told myself. I wouldn't feel like this forever. Meanwhile, we had to settle for what we could have.

The following day, Wednesday, I took two longer-than-usual naps because David and I were going out. It's funny how, when terrible things happen, we sometimes hang our hopes on the smallest details. David and I both loved opera, particularly Italian opera, and we gave ourselves the indulgence of a subscription to the Metropolitan each year. The first tickets of the new season were for October 23, and we had wondered, when we signed up the previous spring, whether we would make it that night, since the baby was due exactly one week later, on October 30. We had joked, insisting that first babies are always born late, particularly when you've got tickets to hear Placido Domingo sing Puccini.

Our baby came into the world not late, but five weeks early, a world in which everything had been turned upside down. For us, getting to that opera was more than just an evening to look forward to: it held out the promise of reemergence into the fullness of life.

And so we found ourselves headed in a cab to Lincoln Center eight days after I had lost a breast, twenty-three days after a baby had been born. As we crossed Central Park and looked up at the grandeur of the midtown skyline and the silhouettes of the trees, as we passed the twinkling lights festooning the garden of Tavern on the Green, it looked so much more beautiful than it had ever looked before. It was charmed, that evening, charmed with the gift of life.

When we walked into the opera house, I remembered how wide-eyed children feel, all dressed up in ribbons, flowered frocks, and patent leather shoes. I remembered how their eyes shine that

YOU DON'T HAVE TO

188 first time their parents take them to see *The Nutcracker* or a Broad-
way show. I looked nice, my husband told me, as we waded into
the throng.

We moved slowly through the crowd, our senses somehow
more acute, touched by the fragility and wonder of everything we
saw, by the wonder of our being there at all. But there was another
kind of fragility, one that caused David to hover anxiously at my
side, trying to protect me from sharp, interfering elbows or sudden,
awkward turns. There were so many people, and jostling would do
that wound on my chest no good at all.

"Maybe we should only stay for the first half," David said when
we sat down.

"D. Reid, I was a good girl, I took the long naps I promised I'd
take. I'm not going to walk out on Domingo," I responded. But in
truth, I wasn't sure I had the stamina to make it through. When the
music started, though, we were transfixed. It was *La Fanciulla del
West*, "The Girl of the Golden West," an opera we had never seen.
We were familiar with many of the arias from our records and
tapes, but the living voices soaring in the great hall moved us even
more. We did not leave halfway through.

It's a love story, of course, full of passion, desolation, foolishness,
hope. At the end, when the scaffold is up and the hero is about to
die and he's snatched back to life, given a second chance by the
woman he loves, when the cowboys and gamblers recognize what
it is they've lost and gained, tears were streaming down my husband's and my cheeks. We didn't feel any shame.

On that night we understood how lucky we were to be sitting at
the Metropolitan Opera in New York, to be carried away by the
music, to know as we had never quite known before what it is to
live, what it is to die. How lucky, to have a sleeping boy waiting for
us at home, to be together, to have seen each other through. That
evening, the emotion that had been so close to the surface for the
past month spilled out of us, feeling right and good.

On Thursday, though, I woke up to business as usual and had to put Puccini behind me. I was busy arranging visits to more doctors and receiving visits from friends. During the coming weeks, people often came to call in the afternoons, and I used that time to raise the arm. I sat propped up in the big bed, surrounded by cushions, feeling like some grand pasha holding court. Sometimes Ben would be lying there, my sleeping vizier, tiny and peaceful, almost lost in the covers at my side.

The dealings with the doctors were not always serene. I had spoken to Dr. Petrek about my fear of not having any further treatment, of being powerless against that one malignant cell that might remain. She thought Dr. Gilewski was right not to recommend chemotherapy, but she understood my fear and said there was no harm in hearing another oncologist's opinion. She suggested I try to see Anne Moore at New York Hospital. I already knew, from my friend Jean, how difficult it was to organize that—Dr. Moore was just too much in demand. Jean had tried and failed.

I phoned and was told that Dr. Moore would be out of town a good deal during the next few months, that no appointments for new patients were available until January, three months hence. If it were to be decided that I did, after all, need a short course of chemo, it would have to begin within a few weeks. I just couldn't wait for the new year. I made an appointment to see Jean's oncologist instead. I also arranged to visit Steve Brower the following week. He was just starting up office hours again on a limited basis, and I very much wanted to see him, to thank him, to hear what he had to say.

Perhaps, though, it was the habit of sheer doggedness, second nature to the journalist; perhaps it was the years spent navigating the bureaucracy of the National Health in England; perhaps it was seeing my mother die and being aggressive with doctors ever since; I phoned Dr. Moore's secretary once again. Before she could say no, I began to tell her about myself, about the baby and my mother

190 and my fear of not having chemotherapy. Her voice grew warm and friendly; she switched from the part of her job that was to guard the gates to that other part, the helpful, sympathetic ear.

"I'll talk to Dr. Moore about you," she promised. The next day she phoned back with an appointment in two weeks.

The following week I would be doctored with a capital D. I was scheduled to see Jeanne Petrek on Monday, Steve Brower on Wednesday, to see Laurie for a postpartum check-up on Thursday, to see Jean's oncologist, Dr. Tepler, on Friday. Was there life after doctors, I asked myself, or would it always be this way?

When I sat facing Jeanne Petrek that Monday morning, after she had looked at the incision and pronounced all was well, what Dr. Gilewski had said about the other breast—what Dr. Petrek herself had said that first time we met—was buzzing around my head.

"Look, this is what I think," she said to me. "We'll see how you do over the course of the next year and then we'll talk again. Don't think about it for a year, just put it out of your mind. I'll see you every few months, and of course you'll check the breast in between visits yourself." I knew, from my reading, the special significance of that first year after a cancer diagnosis. If any cells had escaped her knife and were of the really aggressive type, they would show themselves within that year. Two years is another benchmark, but it's five years without cancer that people yearn to attain. The statistics for long-term survival are really good if you last five years without a recurrence. My mother had gotten through the two-year mark, but never made it to five.

I entered Steve Brower's office two days later. It felt as though a long, long time had elapsed since I had sat there, since I had seen him on the verge of collapsing after getting through my biopsy. I felt unexpectedly bashful and when I was called in and he walked up to give me a hug, I could tell he was feeling the same. He still looked very pale. We chatted as he examined me.

"It was some kind of viral infection, they still aren't sure what it was exactly. And of course I'd been overworking," he said. He had also been very emotionally involved in my case. I wondered if that was what had tipped the balance and allowed the infection to take hold.

"Well, everything looks good and you're looking good," he said in his warm, quiet way. There was so much I wanted to say to him but didn't know how. I had grown to like Jeanne Petrek, to be very glad she was my surgeon, but I knew that at the time of the diagnosis, in those days before I gave birth to Ben and the days immediately thereafter, Steve Brower's exceptional warmth and caring had helped to carry me through. I was in his debt.

I was aware of an even bigger debt the following day, when I headed north again, to my obstetricians' office. As I walked in the door and Barbara, the office manager, looked up, I realized that the last time I had seen her was the day I received the diagnosis, when she had greeted David and me with frightened eyes, not knowing what to say. She and Irina, the technician, both knew what to say now. Nothing was fake or over the top. There was just a mutual, basic human joy in seeing each other again, in my having made it back from the other side, in a baby having been born.

Laurie, the woman who had helped bring my son into the world, was her usual earthy self. She examined me and said that the tears from giving birth had healed quite well, and that in another few weeks David and I would be able to make love again.

"Is everything okay with him, Gayle? I mean about the loss of the breast, the way you look now. I can't imagine, from what I've seen of you two together, that there would be any problem. But you know, there are people who can help if there is."

I assured her that everything seemed fine, but I took note of what she said. I couldn't really know for certain what would happen; we would find out in a couple of weeks. Then Judy and Becky came in for a minute, and we all stood around admiring photos of Benj.

It was impossible to imagine what I would have done without them. They were my doctors and they did their doctors' work, but they had given so much simply as people, each in her own very different way. They felt almost like sisters, and these rooms felt not like a doctor's office but like a family place. I could never find words with which to thank them enough.

That night, Hannah began looking after Ben. Of course we would have preferred to have done it all ourselves, but as she sat there in the rocking chair, singing quietly as he fell asleep, we felt reassured and we, too, were able to sleep. I needed that sleep, for the following day I would be very much on the go. I would be seeing Jean's oncologist, Dr. Tepler, but I'd have to stop off at Sloan-Kettering first, to collect photocopies of my records, something the ever-efficient Barbara had arranged.

When Dr. Tepler called me in, he sat reading the file for quite a while, then examined me and we talked. He was young and, like Dr. Moore, was attached to New York Hospital.

"I think the oncologist who saw you at Sloan-Kettering was right. From everything I've read here, you don't need chemo," he said. "Tamoxifen, well, an argument could be made perhaps, but do you really want to go through the menopause? You're too young for that.

"You've told me that you're going to see Dr. Moore in ten days, and she has asked for your slides to be read again, by one of our pathologists. Unless anything unexpected is found, you should consider yourself cured. But of course—I'm afraid there's the inevitable 'but'—you will always have to be very carefully watched."

Exactly one week later, as I walked to Sloan-Kettering, I marveled at how much my life hinged on a little box of slides. There were shelves and shelves of such boxes, all numbered and labeled and tagged, boxes of cancer fixed in glass, all stored within the pathology department walls. It felt so strange, going up in the hos-

pital elevator, walking to the accession desk, asking to collect my
slides.

This was not a public area; there were no oriental rugs, no comfortable chairs, no soothing prints to distract the mind. I showed
my blue card to the clerk, my "open sesame," and then he beetled
off. I looked around, peering at the table behind the clerk's desk.
Sitting there, wrapped in clear plastic, was something pink and red,
a hunk of stuff that wouldn't have looked unfamiliar in a butcher's
shop. I turned away, not wanting to gaze too closely after all, not
wanting to identify what part of a man or woman's body I had just
been looking at.

The clerk returned with the slides and I signed for them and took
them away. They would have to be brought back to Sloan-Kettering after the other hospital had finished. Wedged between those
layers of glass were the cells that had come out of me, cut out by
Steve Brower, cut out by Jeanne Petrek, cells that had been
analyzed and pronounced upon, that had changed my life forever.
As I made my way to Dr. Moore's office to drop them off, I felt
acutely aware of the fact that I was carrying my cancer cells on the
streets of New York in an ordinary canvas book bag slung casually
over my back. What if someone were to mug me? What if I were to
drop them? What if I were to leave them in a cab? What if, what if,
what if drummed through my head.

"What if these cells had never existed?" I asked myself with
some self-pity. "What if they hadn't been found in time?" came the
grateful reply.

Chapter Fourteen

AS SOON AS WE MET THE BESPECTACLED DOCTOR WITH the soft smile and honey-colored hair, we could understand why so many patients wanted to consult Anne Moore. She was plain-talking and unhurried, very generous with her time. We sat there for over an hour as she worked through our concerns. Although we were expecting no surprises, still we shared a surge of relief: her pathologist's report agreed completely with what Sloan-Kettering had said.

As to what else should be done, Dr. Moore echoed the other doctors' opinions: "I don't think chemotherapy is for you." But, looking at our faces, she added, "I understand your fears. Why don't we do this—if you like, I can raise your case for discussion at the hospital tumor board."

She explained that the tumor board was the monthly brain-storming session attended by the whole range of cancer specialists. The mix of factors in my case—pregnancy, family history, age, the lobular marker—would be sufficiently "interesting" to merit their time.

"Please put it forward," David and I said almost as one.

"Fine, then," she responded. "I'll make sure to ask for opinions about tamoxifen, and about the value of a prophylactic mastectomy of the other breast."

In spite of all we'd been told, we still secretly hoped that so much assembled brainpower, thinking collectively on our behalf, would be able to recommend a course of treatment that would somehow be absolute. Like every family in which cancer has struck, we longed to know that there was something else we could do, something more precise than changing our diet, something less drastic than taking off the other breast. And should a second operation be necessary, we wanted to be told that it would put an end to our fears, that breast cancer couldn't possibly recur if breast tissue wasn't there.

But there was no new, definitive answer when we spoke to Dr. Moore. Since I had had *in situ* cancer and was still relatively young, tamoxifen was ruled out once again. And as far as the prophylactic mastectomy was concerned, there were pros and cons. In the end, it was a very personal decision with no guarantees. It was a decision that had to be taken in the fullness of time.

Of course it was anticlimactic; our life together would have to be reconstructed with shadows still in place. Turning it over in my mind, though, I remembered something Jeanne Petrek had said early on. "You have to think of cancer in the long term, as something that might recur eight years, twelve years, twenty years from now. It's like living with a chronic illness that can be inactive for a very long time, and during that time you can lead your life normally. Sure, when there's a recurrence, you have to deal with it. But if you're really lucky, cancer will be something you'll watch for for the rest of your life, but you won't have to deal with again. Because you found it so early, your chances are pretty good."

And so as autumn began to wane and Thanksgiving fast approached, we had, on balance, much to be thankful for that year. When the holiday itself came around, I dressed carefully, wanting to look my nicest for David and Ben. David put on a tie and jacket, wanting to look good for the two of us. We bundled the baby into his portable cradle and made our way not exactly far afield—just around the corner to our local French restaurant. It was a little out of the ordinary, enjoying a Gallic version of the all-American feast, but then, it was altogether an unusual sort of Thanksgiving for us.

Traditionally we joined my family in Philadelphia for the holiday and long weekend, but this time, with Benj not sleeping through the night and me not yet up to speed, we decided to stay at home. We would go down to Philadelphia as soon as we could. My family would continue to visit us in New York until then.

But like the sights and sounds and scents we encountered on our constitutional after the meal—silhouettes of Pilgrim cutouts pasted across elementary school windowpanes, wind rattling through clusters of unswept city leaves, pungent smoke from an early wood fire curling up from a townhouse chimney—Thanksgiving, this first Thanksgiving with our boy, brought back so many memories. Our family was Jewish, so as kids Christmas never amounted to much: it was Thanksgiving, open to all comers, that was a great annual event.

Everybody would gather at our house, our aunt and cousins and our grandfather Philip Borkofsky, our only living grandparent, who would come dressed in his heavy three-piece suit. He would arrive out of breath, having insisted on making the journey by himself. He would have taken three different trolleys just to get to us. He would mop his brow, sit down slowly, and settle into the captain's chair. Then he and Bossie, his daughter, would chatter away in Yiddish while she put the finishing touches on the meal.

It's surprising how much we children accepted, didn't often question all that talk—the secret language of our childhood, only a little of which we understood. More surprising still, perhaps, to realize so many years afterward, that our American, English-speaking mother communicated to us in a language that wasn't her mother tongue.

When we'd interrupt them, Grandpop would give us a hug, and then we'd smell the cigarettes he smoked, the inhalers he used for his asthma, and the schnapps or beer he sipped whenever he came to our house. He'd talk to us in strongly accented English, interspersed with Yiddish here and there. His speech was distinctive; his writing was, too. My older sister Sandy was given checks made out to "Sendy Fledman," and my name always looked and sounded more like "Gaily" than "Gayle."

But despite its idiosyncrasies, after he came from Poland as a very young man, Grandpop learned enough English to land him that sought-after prize, a steady government job. He worked as a tailor at the Philadelphia Navy Yard, through the Depression, through the war years. He was a gentle man, quiet and retiring. It was his wife, Golde, who managed everything.

He depended on her for so much and saw her die of cancer before they were old. He turned to our mother after that—he and our parents were very close. Grandpop and Mother talked on the telephone practically every day. Perhaps that's why, when he knew his daughter was dying of cancer seventeen years after his wife had passed away, he fell ill himself and left us less than two months before she did. We children loved him very much and yet it's strange to say, I can't remember much about his passing; I was already too numb by then.

My memories of Thanksgiving, though, are clear, from before the unhappiness came. The whole house smelled good, it was noisy, it bustled from morning to night. We'd be wearing our best clothes and our mother would put aside her apron and look so nice.

She was not a woman who bought many clothes. Money didn't flow freely or easily for that kind of thing. Good food was another matter—no expense was spared—but dresses were handed down from one sister to the next, and she herself made do with blouses and skirts that had seen many years.

I don't recall my mother going shopping by herself very often. For one thing, although we lived in a suburban part of the city, she had never learned to drive. She depended on my father to take her places, or rode the buses or the trackless trolleys with us in tow. But when I was twelve or thirteen, her habits changed a little. She began to pay regular visits to the Rose Ackoff Dress Shop.

Although we would often go shopping as a family on a Friday

night or a Saturday afternoon, piling into the big station wagon for an expedition to buy food or things for the house, we never accompanied our mother to Rose's dress store, a trolley ride away. She either left my younger sister and me at home or took us on the trolley to our aunt's, deposited us there, and collected us when her shopping was done.

But I remember how she would talk approvingly of the shop and its general good taste, I remember her dressing up for the rare occasion in something she had bought from there. She would take her time over it and emerge transformed, a woman in black pumps or alligator shoes, glistening with jewelry our father had given her, wearing eye makeup and rouge. I remember her smile, only half ironic, the other half shyly pleased, when her middle daughter, on the threshold of adolescence, told her how beautiful she looked.

Rose—the forever unseen-by-the-likes-of-me Rose—and her shop were on my mind as David and I made our way to Miriam's New Beginning, the place where I would search for a prosthesis and a bra. Not every store suits a woman who has only one breast, and of course it was Rose's where my mother felt comfortable, where she felt able to shop. Although the prosthesis itself had come from another place, the clothes came from Rose. She could do any adjustments discreetly, efficiently, without making a woman feel a freak.

I had looked at all those prostheses during the therapy session at Sloan-Kettering, part of our crash course in preparation for life after breast cancer. Some had nipples, some didn't, there were big sizes, small sizes, light puffs, heavy silicone. They were aimed at making us presentable to the outside world. No Amazons we, although I had read about the women who did choose to show their asymmetry in public.

Although the statistics say that only ten percent of breast cancer patients opt for reconstruction, most of the younger women I was with had decided to take that route; if they hadn't started the process already, they intended to do it a few months down the line. My

doctors—Steve Brower, Jeanne Petrek, Laurie, Judy, and Becky—
all assumed that's what I'd do.

"You're a young woman still. Of course you'll want reconstruction when your body calms down a bit, six months, a year from
now." That is what they said to me, but I wasn't so sure.

The anesthesia would flow into my arm once again, and when I
was asleep the scar would be opened to put in the expander. Then
there would be trips back to the hospital every week for two months
to pump it up. After that, I'd wait another month and have another
stay, more anesthesia, for the "exchange" when the permanent implant—good for five or six years before needing to be renewed—
would be put in place. But still it wouldn't be finished, not if I
wanted the doctors to create a nipple. That would entail yet another
procedure later on. And as well as all that, a majority of the women
who have reconstruction at Sloan-Kettering end up choosing to
have work done on the other breast, for the sake of a better match.

Finally, there was the question of the implants themselves. It
wasn't just the news reports that made me leery of silicone, nervous
even about saline encased in a silicone bag. It was something
deeper, an instinctive fear I had known before. I remembered my
worries about taking all those hormones, how I had resisted the
infertility treatments in part because of that. The cancer may well
have borne out those fears; it was the baby who, in spite of everything, had made the hormones worthwhile. But I wasn't ready to
take something into my body again.

Of course I understood why many women choose to have reconstruction—how much easier dressing, going to the beach or
gym, facing the outside world would be. And for a woman who
was not as lucky as I, who was not in a loving long-term relationship, there were other, more pressing reasons to reconstruct a
breast. I didn't have to do so. Maybe someday I would change my
mind. My doctors and nurses told me that women have reconstruction two, three, five, ten years after their initial surgery. For now, I

had seen enough of the operating room. I could live without reconstruction. My husband said he could, too.

And so together we walked the fifteen blocks to Miriam Riera's, a '90s version of Rose's dress store. My nurse, Tracy, had told me about the shop while I was still in the hospital. Other patients had mentioned to her that they had gone there. The card directed us to what must once have been an old warehouse or factory, a large hulking building now converted to small offices and shops.

The elevator man took us up to six. "Are you going to the art gallery?" he asked, looking us over. I smiled and shook my head. "Oh, to Miriam's," he muttered, and said no more.

I felt headachy and sick as we walked down the corridor and rang the bell. David looked at me, smiled, and squeezed my hand. He was with me, I didn't have to face it on my own. When the door opened, we were greeted by a woman in her forties, short, with short reddish hair, hoop earrings, deep brown eyes. She ushered us in, a soft Hispanic voice speaking good English. She had to excuse herself: she'd be with us in a few minutes, she was on the phone. We sat down to wait in the windowless internal room.

I looked around and saw boxes of bras stacked high on shelves, racks of gaily colored swimsuits and lingerie lining two walls. In a small alcove off to one side an old lady sat bent over needle and thread. She was silhouetted against a dusty window facing on to a brick wall, and from time to time she glanced up and uttered something in Spanish to her employer.

Miriam finished her phone call, spoke to the seamstress, and walked over to us. She asked me when and where I had had the operation. She was warm and yet a little world-weary, a woman who had seen some ups and downs in her life.

"I was shown the different kinds of forms at Sloan-Kettering," I told her. "I don't want a silicone prosthesis. Since I'm small-breasted, I don't need anything like that." I tried to sound definite, unwavering, to ward off any hard-sell. In my mind, a foam puff

like the temporary one I had been wearing seemed less of a reminder of what was gone.

"Okay, I hear what you're saying," she responded with a smile,
as she lead me into the back and two curtained-off cubicles. Then
she turned. "Look, I had a mastectomy four years ago. I opened this
shop because I had trouble finding what I wanted. I'll show you
whatever you like. I have every kind of prosthesis you can imagine,
and then some. But listen to me, you're young and you should try
the silicone. Just see what it's like."

"But it's so heavy," I countered, in a less certain voice.

"Maybe they didn't tell you this in the hospital, but you'll find
you need the weight. You'll feel unbalanced, lopsided otherwise.
And let me tell you another thing. I have two boys myself. You've
got that baby. You'll want him, when he's a little older, to touch
something that feels like a breast when he comes to hug you. That
will be important to you both."

She showed me several foam-covered prostheses and then
brought out two different brands in silicone. One shape suited me
better, and I tried it on in two different sizes. In the end, Miriam
was right: David assured me the silicone form she recommended
looked better than anything else. But none of the special bras were
quite right, so we agreed I would go back to the department store
where I normally bought lingerie and purchase a half-dozen new
bras in the size I wore before having the baby. I would come back
later in the week to have the seamstress make the adjustments.

I felt emotionally drained by the time we got home, but
managed to perk up a little as soon as I saw our boy. I made some
supper, and as we ate we all sat together, Ben snuggled in his portable cradle, the center of attention up on the big table in front of us.
After we finished clearing up, Hannah arrived and I made my way
early to bed.

As soon as I walked into the bedroom, I glimpsed the box con-
taining my purchase sitting on the chair, and as I picked it up, all

that day's tiredness and nervousness came over me once again. The sadness poured out of me. I sat on the edge of the bed, holding the prosthesis, and wept.

David came up to say goodnight and found me sitting there like that.

"It's alright, my darling, it's alright," he said, his own voice catching a little.

"But this thing makes me feel the loss of the breast so much, it reminds me of what I really must look like, D. Reid," I said between sobs.

He held me while the crying subsided.

"You look like you, my darling. You look like an attractive woman, my woman. I don't want anybody else."

I held tightly to him, and when I looked up, I could see the image of that young man's face I had fallen in love with twenty years before. It was still there beneath the care-worn lines that had deepened so much these past few months. We had both been so exhausted, had been concentrating so hard on other things. Now we realized that two weeks had passed since the obstetricians had said I would be healed enough for sex.

We remembered their words that night, that night when for the first time since the diagnosis we made love. I was nervous when I took off the bra, but then, quickly, it was done. The skin on that side felt peculiar—half numb, half painfully sensitive. I didn't like the feeling of my "wound," as my husband began to call it.

But there was no trouble between us. And afterward we cried a little, not out of sadness, but out of relief. The unknowns were still there, but we had crossed another bridge, we had crossed it together, again.

Three days later I returned to Miriam's shop. She led me into a cubicle and I tried on one of the new bras. She began to put in some pins.

"We'll take it in a little here and here, and we'll create a pocket

for the prosthesis inside the cup. We'll sew some snaps onto the end
of the bra and pocket so you won't ever have to worry about the
thing falling out."

As she worked we chatted, and the conversation eventually
meandered onto the topic of my mother.

"Of course, there was no silicone in her day, but the prostheses
weren't too bad, I guess. Really early on, before your mother's
time, women had to make do with what they could put together
themselves or have made to order. And of course the operation was
so much more extensive then."

She had finished pinning all the bras. "Did you ever see what she
looked like, afterward?" Miriam asked in a quiet voice.

"No, my father was the only one who did," I answered, remembering that time my mother couldn't get out of the bath, feeling
dread surge through me once again. Quickly, I began to pull on my
blouse.

"Well, she would have looked a lot different from you and me.
If you want to see what women looked like with a full radical
mastectomy, I'll show you. I have a kind of library here about
women like us, and one of the books has photographs and is pretty
old."

I knew I had to face it now. "Yes, I'd like to see."

Miriam took me into the room where the seamstress sat. She
pulled out a volume and opened it, and I stared at a photograph of
a woman who was far more disfigured than myself. The chest muscles had been taken and so her ribs poked out. My throat felt dry
and tight, and I remembered my mother, those photographs with
high necklines, buttons all done up. In some of them, the fastening
seemed almost to extend into her face, into pursed lips, taut cheeks,
tense eyes.

"We are luckier than they were," Miriam said as she closed the
book. Silently, I inclined my head.

Chapter Fifteen

NOVEMBER GAVE WAY TO DECEMBER, AND SOON WE'D move. I'd been struggling to restore to active life all those things we'd put on hold, as gradually, gradually, my strength began to return. I stopped needing to raise my arm three times each day, although I still put it up when the stiffness threatened to return. And doing all those exercises had finally paid off: the fingers of both hands now met high above my head, and I could flap my arms as though newly blessed with wings. Besides all that, the day could stretch until four or even five; I fell into a nap then, but the tiredness wasn't nearly as bad.

I was able to spend a little more time with my son at last, and when I gazed down at Benj, it was a Reid face that returned my stare. True, his hair color was dark like a Feldman and by no means was everything about him English. But he was wont to have a certain intense expression, complete with furrowed brow and serious stare, that was pure Reid, visible in his father, his uncles, and his grandfather Alan.

"Mr. Po," David began to call him, and we'd both laugh at the thought of our two-month-old poe-faced boy. He also became "Mr. Chin," courtesy of the multiple chins that had begun to form now that he was putting on some weight. These were his "Chinese" identities, my husband would joke, and ascribe them to my sinological inclinations. But joking aside, what we loved most about our baby's changing expressions was that he had just begun to smile. Nothing could be better than that.

Benj and I, weather permitting, started to go out and about much more. I was still careful about lifting him from the bassinet and putting him into the stroller, and it was Amira who had to carry the stroller down the four flights of stairs. But we cruised around the streets together and each day traveled the three blocks to inspect progress on the house.

We'd interviewed movers and decided on a firm. I'd begun to sort through the accumulation six years in America had brought, to discover high shelves or dusty corners in which sealed, forgotten boxes lurked, full of bits and pieces of a London life that now seemed long gone. Some days I foraged around the neighborhood seeking all the things the house would soon require, while on others I sifted through shelves of books, searching for a few dozen we might give away. Mostly I tried to keep very busy, not to think too much. I didn't want to have time to dwell on the strangeness of being at home.

I had worked for sixteen years and was a student for six before that, so I'd been used to being out in the world a good long while. Although people from that other life regularly phoned and sometimes came to call, although our spacious apartment was a far pleasanter place than a tiny cubicle at work, still, sticking to those rooms made me a little edgy, even with Benj smiling, gurgling, binding me to life. The new house beckoned and I'd be happy enough to heed its call, to put this apartment behind me, to give this chapter of my life the closure moving on would provide.

It was curious, this insistent, buzzing uneasiness, hovering about my head, but at the same time it seemed familiar, not entirely unknown. Indeed, I had felt it once before, the summer after my mother died.

I was fifteen then, and my sister Sandy was living away from home, working during her final vacation from art college. Vickie, eight years old in July, was spending a good part of each day at camp. Every morning I took two buses to attend a typing class at a high school in another neighborhood, but the heavy summer afternoons seemed to stretch endlessly on after that.

Because I had chosen to leave the neighborhood in order to attend the Philadelphia High School for Girls, one of the two "academic" public schools that drew students from across the entire city, my friends were scattered all over the place and were often not easy to reach. That summer, many were away at overnight camp, on trips with their families, or at jobs. I couldn't depend on them to fill up the time, nor could I get a job: my class ended at 11:30 and I had to be back by 4 P.M., when Vickie returned. I hated spending time alone at home.

In an odd way it hadn't been so bad during the school year, although my mother was dying at home. The school, my friends and their parents, and my teachers drew me out of the house. One of my best friends, Amy, used to keep me company several afternoons a week. Once the final bell rang, we'd pick up our books and head down Broad Street to Linton's restaurant. There we'd settle in a booth and order two Cokes or two cups of tea and two apple brown Bettys. We'd talk for an hour while we pecked at the food, and it was the talk that drew me there.

It had got so, in those days, I hardly seemed to eat anything at all. I'd have some orange juice and an aspirin for breakfast—somehow I came to believe that an aspirin a day would ward off everything bad—and I'd munch a piece of bread en route. For lunch, I'd buy a couple of rolls and butter from the school cafeteria, usually nothing more substantial than that.

For supper, I would sometimes make the few dishes that Aunt Betty and Cousin Ann had taught me to cook. But Vickie and I were also eating a lot of canned food those days, macaroni and cheese, Campbell's soup, tins of tuna doctored into "tuna surprise." Our father, except for the days when he would sit in the gray chair, silent and depressed, was out seeking work, trying to bring in whatever money he could. Where he grabbed his food many an evening was a mystery to us.

But with summer, I no longer had the school routine to provide a refuge away from home. And yet it became impossible for me to stay alone in our house. The reminders of my mother, of illness and death, loomed everywhere. I was frightened of what I had seen and only vaguely understood; I was frightened of what the future held. Cousin Ann had already taken me aside and said that there would be no money after Girls' High. I would have to win a good scholarship if I wanted to get away. Occasionally, if I let it, a panic would radiate through my body. I would go upstairs to the bathroom, close the door, and begin to cry. The tears would ripple into shudders until I would finally sit back exhausted, dry.

During the last few months of her illness, my mother had become incontinent, and sometimes when the nurse was too busy and there had been an accident, the job of washing her urine-soaked sheets would fall to me. Cousin Ann had told me to use lots of disinfectant every time I did such a wash, but I was terrified that I'd get cancer from handling the sheets, that it would remain behind in the washing machine, that it would find its way into our clothes and somehow invade the rest of us. I was terrified I'd get cancer from touching the things in her room, from the dishes we used, from the air we breathed. I couldn't let myself think about it or speak with anyone about it. I just had to get out of that house.

Between the time my class ended and my return to meet Vickie late in the afternoon, the library, the department store, the donut shop, became my havens, anywhere lots of people were around. Previous summers, when it was hot, I used to like to spend whole afternoons curled up, reading in my room, but now I felt comforted sitting at a crowded table in the library hour after hour.

I didn't have any money to spend on clothes, but I would ride the trolley or bus to the shopping center nonetheless and wander down the racks of blouses, dresses, miniskirts, the aisles of makeup and perfume. The salesladies patrolling the aisles in some of the stores must have come to know my face pretty well, but every time anybody approached, "Just looking" is what I would tell them and move on.

On some afternoons, I ended up in the department store, at the soda fountain counter. I would sit there, slowly eking out my root-beer float. On the hottest days, when just the thought of walking from the library to the big store made me sweat, I would hop around to the donut shop down the street instead. I'd sit on a stool nibbling at a cruller or sipping something cold to drink, and listen to the waitresses and the cops bantering back and forth, trading joke after joke.

I would concentrate intently on other people's conversations, trying to drown out the ones playing over and over again in my head, for before my mother had stopped speaking, before her brain gave way, she had begun to talk a lot. My quiet-voiced mother had begun to shout. We didn't understand, for a long time, why everything we did always seemed to be wrong, why she sometimes got so upset with our father, why she didn't even seem to want us around. The anger spewed out of her as it never had before.

But now, as I looked at the people sitting at the counter next to me, I seemed to understand a lot more. I told myself fiercely that I would get through two more years of high school and then make my escape. I would put all the unhappiness behind me, become a different person, lead a different life. I would be somebody out in the world, not a woman tied to her home with children, a woman waiting to die.

And with the help of my teachers, I did just that—I won a full scholarship to Penn. I moved to a part of the city that could have been another part of the globe. I didn't go back to Northeast Philadelphia very much after that.

Vickie went to live with Sandy, who by then had gotten married. I missed her, having taken care of my kid sister for the best part of three years. I worried about her, about everything she had seen, what a child should never have to see. That was the one thing that didn't feel quite right about my being away. Vickie had had so many changes in so few years, so many different people setting different courses for her life. I had hoped, secretly, I would be able to take care of her once again, after I graduated and began to work. But I fell in love with an Englishman and went too far away. Vickie stayed put.

My father after a few years met Pearl, and began, painfully, to glue the fragments of his life together again. I went on to France, to China, and finally ended up in New York. I had left a certain time in Philadelphia far behind, or so I had thought. But the feeling of never being quite comfortable spending weekdays at home remained, a reminder that lingered on. And now I found myself once again at home, preparing for our move.

The moving manager came to inspect both the apartment and the house. It would be tough for the men, although we would only be traveling three blocks. They would have to take everything on their backs down from the fourth and fifth floors of our walk-up, then carry it all up again, throughout the four floors plus basement of another brownstone house. A big, young crew would have to do it, and the next date such a crew would be available was Friday, December 6th.

When the manager told me this, I smiled and heard myself respond that that date was fine by us. After all, a Friday move was always considered best. Inside, though, I was more than a little shaken up. As I'd learned since that summer so very long ago, whatever you do to make yourself into a different person can never fully work. Your past is always your past, it's always with you; you can escape only up to a point.

December 6th, the day we would move to our new home, our new life, was the day my parents had gotten married so many years before. My father had received official permission and a weekend furlough from the army camp in Maryland. The rabbi had given him and my mother a special dispensation and had married them on a Sabbath. My parents spent their wedding night celebrating with their friends at the Cadillac Tavern in Philadelphia, but they woke the next morning to news about a place called Pearl Harbor.

The war changed everything. My father's beloved brother, Mike, who had guided their fledgling sign business from the start, died fighting in Europe, and the child who would have been my brother died a few months after that. My father was to spend many years looking for that brother, for that son. But like a rainbow, five years to the day after my parents had been wed, my older sister, Sandy, was born. Life did go on.

We would be moving on what would have been my parents' fiftieth wedding anniversary. We could only hope that the date would bring another rainbow for us.

◊ ◊ ◊

That Friday came, and the birds flew again above Benji's head long before most other things were done. Once the boxes appeared and the men arrived and our apartment was turned upside down, our baby looked to us with unsettled eyes under finely drawn question-mark brows. How could two months of life make sense of so much noise, so many people, such uprooting all around?

But that night, in his new room, he didn't have to take any of it in: his father had seen to that. For amidst the chaos of that long, long day, David had remembered Benji's birds. There they were, tacked high on the wall, ready to greet him when it was time for bed.

In the old place, we could never decide if it was the Chinese birds or our faces that our boy had smiled at first. They had always been there, printed on the long strip of cloth hanging above the chair where he was fed. Now as I sat and rocked, dusty and tired, the baby in my arms, white wings silhouetted against green and purple and pink spread out above our heads. Our boy was nestling into sleep. His birds were there and we were home.

That first weekend Vickie and our brother-in-law Steve came to help, with Sandy on watch in Philadelphia with the kids. Like an Amish barn raising, everybody lent a hand, everybody did their bit. I organized what I could, but mainly looked after Benj; the others unpacked and humped and cleaned. When we sat down to our take-away meal in the evening, we all felt ready to drop.

But Ben's room had everything in place by the time they were gone, and I had a kitchen ready for use. They had helped us a lot that weekend, but that time together helped my family a good deal as well. At last some of the nervousness and feelings of impotence of the past two and a half months had found a release. Our house was baptized into the family as it echoed with their laughter and their work.

That work continued during the next few months, but always there was something else to do. David, Amira, and I pushed ourselves, the sorting, cleaning, arranging, the buying that never seemed to stop. Our night nurse, Hannah, returned to Jamaica in mid-December and we decided to go it alone after that. And then the holiday season was upon us and we celebrated in our new home, just as, only half believing, we'd promised each other we would.

By the middle of January, when most things had found their place, more suddenly arrived to be absorbed. They came in crates from England, and had belonged to David's mother. She had died suddenly in March 1990, and after a time, even though my husband's father had stayed on in their house, its contents were divided up. The four other children had had their lots, while ours sat waiting in England until we moved.

From the layers of tissue and bubblewrap and cardboard opened all those memories of the Queen Anne house on the hill. It was a place the likes of which a girl from Northeast Philadelphia could

212   only have conjured up from books. I remember the first time I set foot in that house, that Christmas I was twenty-one. As I walked along the annex, through the kitchen, down the hall, toward the sitting room where I would be introduced, what I felt was not simply the nervousness of meeting my young man's parents: it was the self-consciousness of having entered a totally different world.

The piano, David's grandmother's piano, which his mother had promised him while still alive, was what I now welcomed most. I had had lessons as a girl, my husband had played as a boy, and one day we hoped to hear our own boy scale its keys. The piano felt normal, felt right. The other things, as I unpacked them in a brownstone in New York City, felt part of another life.

My mind placed each object not in some well-suited corner of our house but in memories of the English country house where they'd belonged. The delicate-legged French desk in the large entrance hall, the oxblood Chinese vase near the sitting room hearth, the portraits of David's great-great-grandfather and his quiet, dark wife facing each other on the dining room wall. There had been so many beautiful things in the many rooms of that house that some of them, like the carved parrot or the Japanese scholar's prints, had languished in corners, hardly noticed at all. Now they were strewn about our living room floor.

And as they emerged from the mountain of wrapping paper, so too stepped my mother-in-law, Margaret Reid. She was a big woman, large-framed, handsome and tall, made bigger still by having brought six children into the world. She was strong-willed, intelligent, never easy, although charming in a lady-of-the-manor sort of way. When she relaxed, a hint of Scottish cheekiness allowed itself to be heard beneath the soft Scottish burr she never lost. Mostly though, what she had constructed for others to meet was the grand facade of both her person and her house.

Like many who've lost a mother when young, I had hoped another might take on some of that role. But I had uprooted myself, was a stranger in a foreign land, and perhaps inevitably, things with Margaret didn't work quite like that. Our relations were sometimes cordial, sometimes strained, always conducted according to the rules of a culture not my own. Certain things were simply never discussed; others mistakenly assumed. But we knew each other a good long time, and peppered through those years were intimacies we shared. More than that, I'll remember her because of the things I learned. Indeed, I learned from her a great deal.

She was so much her stubborn father's daughter that of course she spurned his plans for her life. She refused to go to university in the late 1930s, even though, unusually for a woman, she'd won a place. Instead, she put her considerable intelligence into marrying young, raising children, creating gardens, furnishing homes. The finest house, the culmination of her life, was the Suffolk hall, bought when her husband, Alan, was about to retire.

I learned about houses from her, about gardens, about maintaining a certain kind of standard, stamping things with a very personal style. When I think of the English countryside, I think of her. The avenues of lime trees intoxicating in their sweetness, the freshening breezes and ever-changing skies, the gentle quiet of the rolling hills each dotted with its church tower are with me still because of Margaret and her house. The glories of old roses, carpeted lawns, herbaceous borders, hedges of singing birds, all these I knew from her—as well as the relentless, back-breaking labor that made them so.

It was her house where my eyes were opened to another sense of history, quite unlike that which I had gleaned elsewhere. But I also learned what happens when a good mind is too often left fallow, about the loneliness of a life where a house, however beautiful, is all that remains once the children have gone.

She had been very good with young babies, but our child will never know her living face. These things that I was unpacking, along with what he will hear of her from us and those across the sea, are all, apart from the genes that he carries, that our boy will have of his Scottish grandmother.

Eleanor and Celia, my young nieces in England, may be able to remember a little about their grandmother when she was alive. But I know, even now, that the person they desperately struggle to recall, as my sister Vickie tried when she was a child, is not their grandmother but their mother, the woman whom they lost to cancer when so very young.

Yes, the memories of Pat tumbled out from all those English things, alongside the memories of Margaret Reid. After all, we both went to the big house for the first time that same Christmas, although our lives diverged a great deal after that. Pat and Keith married quickly—the following summer—and seven years later Eleanor came along, then Celia a few years after that. It was when Pat had only just finished putting Celia to the breast that her fingers stumbled across the lump.

Like Margaret she was strong-willed, big-framed, handsome, and was not really interested in pursuing a career. She stayed at home with the children, was not one for being out in the world. She lived a quiet life in the small town where both her husband and my husband had been born. The doctor she went to was a small-town doctor, and he assured her that nothing was wrong.

Months passed but the lump didn't go away. In fact, it got bigger and began to hurt. And then, so much later, just as for my mother, it was already by then too late. The "nothing" that was cancer had spread far into her nodes.

When she was treated at the local hospital, stunned, she accepted the mastectomy and radiation, whatever the doctors did. But they didn't do the hormone receptor tests or give her chemotherapy. It was only when people like Keith's older sister, nurse Diana, raised the alarm that things began to change. Pat was referred to a London teaching hospital and the treatment suddenly improved. She carried on, became more outgoing, and looked pretty good for a while.

But then quickly, so very quickly, metastasis took hold. There was more radiation, lots of chemotherapy, and visits in and out of the hospital for months. The girls couldn't take in what was going on, and after a while Pat couldn't cope with the children she had borne. It went to her bones, to her brain. She was dead at thirty-four.

Her brother Tim, a veterinarian, had been desperate to do anything he could. He changed careers and enveloped himself in cancer research. Keith held it all together, but could so easily have fallen apart. Then his new wife, Christina, came along, and a new daughter, and Eleanor and Celia had mothering once again. But Pat, the woman whose face shines out so clearly from the faces of those two young girls, would never see her children grow up.

Jane Berlinka, the other woman whom memories of England evoked—her luck was different, she lived to see her son become a man. She was a friend who taught me more than she could ever know about how to live life after breast cancer.

I met Jane in 1978 through work, in those London days when I edited textbooks for colleges and schools. She was half Swiss, half English, a high school teacher at home in three languages. Her German course had been contracted by the firm several years before I'd been taken on, but mysteriously, nothing had happened to move it along. Mrs. Berlinka could be rather "difficult," or so I was told. Now that "difficulty" had fallen to me.

The problem, inevitably, centered on money. Jane's course was good and imaginative, but its three volumes called for a thousand drawings, costing thousands of pounds. There was no way, with such an outlay, that the publishing house would make the usual level of return.

It was at that time the firm's practice to ask the author to help defray such costs. The formidable Mrs. Berlinka would have to be persuaded to take a much lower royalty on the first printing, whatever the contract she had signed had said. I was now the one who would have to do the persuading, and I didn't like that prospect one bit.

I invited her out to lunch, thinking that a bottle of wine and a good meal between us might help. The woman sitting opposite me was fortyish, blond, her hair in a page-boy cut. Barely a trace of makeup was visible on very soft skin; nothing adorned the cool eyes that seemed to take everything in. I hated the task before me, and had to steel myself to speak, but I told Mrs. Berlinka exactly what the firm had proposed without any vague excuse. When I finished, I waited for the explosion to come.

But the messenger remained intact.

"Look, I'm relieved that finally somebody wants to get on with it and publish my course," she told me in perfectly modulated English with just a hint of a Continental accent. "I've heard nothing for months. Of course I don't like the new arrangement, but I'll agree to it. I don't want to start all over again, to waste more time going somewhere else. You've been straight with me. I think I can work with you."

She smiled, we sat back, drank the wine, and began to talk. I found myself liking the rather difficult lady rather a lot.

I don't recall how it came out, at which meeting or when— perhaps it was during that very first lunch. Certainly I don't know whose secret was shared first. But Jane and I discovered we both knew something of breast cancer, she from her own experience, and I from my mother's.

We became close friends, despite the decade and a half age difference, and David and I were charmed by her Swiss–Russian–Jewish husband, Jose. He was another amazing linguist, incredibly lively, highly strung, an actor who had transmogrified into a journalist. Both of them seemed more at home in the cafes of the Left Bank than in the pubs of North London, but no matter. They had had their years on the Continent and would return to Paris one day. It was important for their son, Daniel, that they be in England.

Jane had had the mastectomy a few years before, and when we met, everything seemed to be fine. She and Jose did everything, went everywhere, saw all the new plays and films. She jogged every day and cultivated her garden, read voraciously in three languages and published books using two. She headed a large languages department and found time to write poetry, doted on the precocious Daniel, and ran her house like a Swiss clock.

I can't remember when it happened, when she noticed the telltale pain, when something showed up in her bones. She fought the metastasis fiercely and, once out of the hospital, walked until she could jog again. She traveled even more, seemed even more committed to teaching and to writing. She had to go into the hospital from time to time but resumed full life again as soon as she could.

As the years passed, days started turning into weeks spent at the Royal Marsden, the major cancer hospital in London. But although she grew noticeably shorter and a little stooped, her spirit kept her going. We were living in New York by then, and she and Jose visited us and fell in love with the city.

I remember one day we ate lunch in the boathouse in Central Park and then walked for a long time amidst the trees and talked. What we talked about was the future, we didn't dwell on the past. Jane would not give up, nor could I give up the idea that she would be the one who would survive. She would beat breast cancer, grow old, live to see Daniel's children come into the world.

But after they returned to London, Jose started phoning us at odd hours of the day or night. He was a man who lived on talk, and now he needed to talk out his fears. Unlike my mother and Pat, the cancer was not spreading to Jane's brain, but her bones were crumbling, she was in constant pain. Walking became difficult, and finally a wheelchair appeared. Still she and Jose made it to the National Theatre; still she sat in the garden and wrote. But then she could no longer hoist herself in and out of the chair, could no longer get to the bathroom on her own.

It was late summer the last time we spoke across the Atlantic. Her voice sounded different, dry and slurred. It wasn't just the painkillers, it was more than that; her spirit had been shattered beneath the bones. When he came to stay with us in New York that Christmas, Jose told us she welcomed the release at the end.

I wonder what Jane, Pat, my mother would tell me now if they could. My memory of their words and deeds is only partial and imperfect at best. As a grown woman, it was Jane whom I came to know better than the other two. She had demanded for herself, and lived, an active, fully rounded life. She and Jose were one of the most loving couples David and I have ever met.

Some of her poems speak of sadness and terror. One, entitled "Fear," goes like this:

> A little rodent
> Gnaws at my spine,
> Patiently,
> Secretly.
> Were it not for the odd jab of pain
> I wouldn't know it was there.
>
> A little serpent
> Coils round my brain,
> Silently,
> Artfully,
> And if there's a moment when I forget
> It pierces my brain with its teeth.

Those emotions were not, though, until the very end, what we saw in her life. I have been lucky thus far, far luckier than the others, luckier than most whom cancer has touched. Luck brings with it certain responsibilities. I know for Benj, for David, for others, for myself, for the memory of those who went before, what must be visible in my return to life.

Chapter Sixteen

PERHAPS IT WAS THE JUMP-START COLD OF THE NEW YEAR getting into everything, or more likely it was simply the healing passage of time, but whatever it was, toward the end of January, some of the nerve endings on the left side of my body that had lain numb and dormant since the operation suddenly tingled into feeling again. About the same time, other impulses began to make themselves known with an intensity they had not shown these past four months, as I became aware of a curious kind of restlessness within me.

Benj, cancer, and the house had been occupying every minute of my time, but the habits imprinted by twenty years of working life are not easily erased. Despite all the busyness at home and the overwhelming delight I took in my son, I'd been growing a little impatient and irritable during the past few weeks. David and I both realized that the part of me used to the exercise of work was calling to be pushed back into action once again.

And so one morning, while Benj was sleeping, I walked into the study, sat down at the computer, and turned it on. True, I was due to go back to the office in a couple of weeks—at the beginning of February—and was still feeling very tired, so in one sense I told myself this was a crazy thing to do. I could have left all that still needed doing in the house, left David and Ben behind, and gone off for a week or two's break to rest and prepare for reentry into the working world. But at that point, I could not detach myself from either the boy or his father for very long, and David could not take any more time off from his job until later in the year.

So I sat there facing the computer, hands on the keyboard, the screen a perfect blank. I looked out the window at the bare branches of the mimosa tree and wondered if all that had happened had rendered me dumb, for along with the restlessness, with the recognition that I needed the mental and social stimulation of work, had come the deep dread that I would not be capable of writing anymore, of filling that screen with words enough to express anything again.

During the past few weeks there had been moments when I had felt almost paralytic with fear about working life. Would the turmoil of the preceding months interfere at every juncture, scramble my thoughts like static on an old radio set? How would I be able to get up the speed that a journalist requires, get back into the swim of the publishing business, meet the iron deadlines of a weekly magazine? Had I forgotten how to talk or listen to people, make sense of what they said, turn it into pages covered with words?

And yet, as I sat in the drafty, beautiful room that I still could not believe had become my study—a room in which Margaret Reid might have felt at home—and slowly took in the smoothly carved mantelpiece, the celadon walls with their Chinese scrolls, the shelves and shelves of books, I felt the need to grasp on to words not to make sense of what others had said, but to grapple with the changed world that latterly had come to be my own.

I remembered stumbling across an ad in a magazine three months before, an ad about mothers and daughters that had struck me enough for me to have ripped it out and stored it away in a file. The file had survived our move intact; I found it quite easily, in fact. When I pulled out the folded page, I felt the same shock of recognition, the wonder at the power of the advertiser's words to speak in such unimagined circumstances directly to me. I began to write, the sentences coming in spurts, some tumbling onto the screen like a running child, others edging out tentatively in the painful slowness of an invalid's pace. I sat there for several hours, feeling a kind of urgency, feeling not fully in control of myself. When I got up, the winter day was darkening already, and I had written the first few pages of what, unknown to me then, would later become this book, pages that even now remain remarkably unchanged.

I mentioned to David during the next few days that I was spending time scribbling at my desk, and he seemed glad. Later, when I showed him what I had done, he read the words and told me, "This is very different from what you've written before, my darling. It's strong stuff."

He smiled encouragement, but I seemed to sense a slight hesitation in tone, a kind of puzzlement, an almost imperceptible movement of the head. He didn't say anything further, but months later told me that he had worried if looking inward, churning everything up, might not prove too much at that point, might keep me from emerging back into the world. His worries, though, did not last long, for the outside world quickly enough began to reassert itself. The office beckoned.

The scribblings were put aside, although in my head some random jotting continued. I did not go back to them properly again for another six months, when the urge to do so finally proved too great, after much else had happened and it was time to turn inward again. But pouring out that first chapter helped release something in me, even then helped to differentiate my mother's experience from my own, and also served to break through my fear of the blank page and help me feel I could take up writing again.

Certainly, as far as the magazine was concerned, it was time. I had had more than the usual maternity leave—much more. Six weeks was the norm; occasionally an extra six weeks was granted without pay. That's what I had arranged in my life before cancer. After everything blew up and my recovery proceeded so slowly, I had asked my boss, Daisy, to see if the company would agree to an extra four weeks of disability leave without pay. It was hard on her and on my associate editor, Maria, who between them were covering for me, shouldering the burden without complaint. They agreed to give me more time, and so the company did, too.

A few days before my return to the office, Daisy phoned to make sure all was well. "How're you doing, Gayle? Everything okay?"

She said it with the kind of enforced casualness people now universally adopted, the underlying seriousness of the taken-for-granted question never anymore being in doubt. During the months I'd been away, I'd seen Daisy, Michael, and Maria from time to time, and I'd spoken off and on with John, the editor in chief, and Isabell, his secretary. They, the publisher, and several members of the personnel department were the only staff members who knew exactly what had happened. I could not have asked for better colleagues. Like those who populated David's small office, they were always there when needed, but never invasive in their concern.

However, going back to the office meant seeing more than just a handful of people, and as my return approached, I grew more and more anxious about meeting them all again. When asked about my sudden leave-taking, Daisy had provided answers at the time, speaking vaguely of "complications." But I knew that some of my colleagues and cronies in the gossipy publishing business had persisted in wondering why I had disappeared weeks before my maternity leave was to have begun and why I had remained silent ever since. People had remarked on my longer-than-usual leave and the fact that I hadn't brought the baby into the office to show him off. What would I say to them, how would I seem to them, could I bear to go through another round of explanations?

My mother, of course, silenced by the custom of the day and her own inclinations, had talked about the cancer with very, very few. Her daughters had not been among them. I asked David what he thought—should I talk or hold my tongue?

In his lawyerly way, he reviewed the pros and cons of each option, and seemed to favor talking. But then he finished by saying, as
I suppose I knew he would, "It has to be your call, my darling, and
if you decide to speak about it, only you can determine when you
should."

Some of my close friends thought I should sail into the office
brandishing photos of Benj and shrug off any questions, not tell
anyone else about the cancer, about this thing that had so pro-
foundly changed my life. "Look, people won't treat you normally,
there'll always be that barrier, we all have such a fear of cancer. It's
like a kind of taboo. If you talk, some of that fear will attach itself to
you. Anyway, it might not be good for your career," several counseled.

I remembered that group discussion we had had in Sloan-Kettering and those two women—the one adamant about keeping herself
to herself and the other, arguing equally passionately about opening
the eyes of the world to the urgency of dealing with breast cancer
by opening up our stories to anyone who would listen. I had come
down on the side of the latter, but when it was time to put that
conviction into action, self-consciousness seemed to overtake me,
self-confidence seemed to slip away.

I dressed very carefully that Monday morning. Although I had
gotten used to the prosthesis during the past weeks, and once or
twice had almost forgotten that it was there, I was very conscious of
its foreignness that morning. I looked in the mirror and noticed the
slight asymmetry that others would probably never see, and
reached inside the pocket of the bra to make sure both snaps were
closed. Then I rooted about in my toilet bag for cosmetics and put
on more makeup than I normally would have worn.

I felt the uncertainty of leaving the baby and the house clutching
at my heart. What was I doing, going back to the office with this
little child to look after, when so much of my maternity leave
hadn't in fact been taken up with mothering him at all? And yet I

knew that this was something I had to do, for myself, for my husband, and yes, for my son. I wanted him, fiercely wanted him, to have a mother who felt a full person in herself.

And so I set out, with the uneasy sense of retracing steps taken long before. I arrived at the building and felt like a dreamer as I passed through the big entrance doors, for although so much had changed within me, everything seemed untouched, unaltered there. Why should I have expected anything to have been different, after all?

And yet, when I got out of the elevator and walked to my cubicle and saw my name on the partition wall, when I glanced at the posters and postcards that I had stuck on the walls months and months before, I could not shake off the feeling of disjunction, of being a traveler from another world come back to look at a place I once had known years and years before. And so almost immediately I went to see Daisy, to see Michael, to hug them, to feel the reality of them, to have their chat fill up the panicky silences in my head.

I returned to my desk after that and began to go through the piles of mail, but within an hour I was to discover that the changes I had been undergoing in my own life were not the only changes that had been afoot. John, whom I had looked for but who was not around when I arrived, suddenly called all of us senior editors into his office.

"I've just been told that I am being replaced as editor in chief," he said to us, as we stood there, mute. A new group publisher had been appointed a few months before I went on leave, and as so often happens in the magazine world, he had decided to bring over the editor from his previous journal to head our establishment.

I realized with a start how very lucky I had been. If this had happened three or four months before, how much less certain it would have been that I would be sitting here now. It was John, after all, who had given me my first break, who had taught me how to be a journalist, who with Daisy had brought me onto the staff. If

the timing had been different, the worries that so many cancer patients face—would there be a job to come back to after the treatment and recuperation—would inevitably, amidst the unknowns
of a new regime, have been mine as well.

At the editorial meeting later that afternoon, everything was in
turmoil. There was so much for everybody to take in, so much that
was unsaid, uncharted. Already it was clear by the glances, the silences, the tenor of their questions that some saw the glimmer of
opportunity in the new order, whereas others could not compre-
hend the passing of the old. But in the midst of it all, John somehow
managed to look in my direction, to smile, and to open his heart
and extend with quiet grace the official welcome back.

The general nervousness in the stuffy, enclosed room jumped
like electric current from one person to the next. With John's
words, I felt supercharged by the extra burden of knowing that the
moment had come when either I should speak and get it over with
or should keep silent about what had happened in my life.

I had at least to say something, to respond to the generosity of his
gesture at such a moment as that. I could hear my voice quavering,
"Well, my return to the office has been a little more momentous
than I had expected." There was soft, uneven laughter. "It certainly is something of a strange return, but let me tell you, it's been
a very strange four months. I know many of you wondered why I
seemed to have fallen off the face of the earth in September, why
I've not been back during the past four months to have lunch or at
least show off the baby, why I've been gone so long. Well, that's
because I didn't just have a baby, I had cancer as well."

The words were out and I felt a tremendous relief, even as I saw
the momentary incredulity, heard the surprised silence of the men
and women seated all around me.

I said a few more words to fill the void and tried not to wonder
whether anyone was glancing furtively at my chest, attempting to
gauge its symmetry or lack thereof. I tried not to dwell irrationally

on the prosthesis, on whether it might slip out of the pocket in my bra. Although I knew it would be painful to have to repeat the story over and over again to colleagues and business acquaintances as I had done to doctors and nurses and hospital bureaucrats, to family and friends, I was glad I had chosen to speak about the cancer, to be a kind of witness, a simple advocate, to tell the truth.

I sat back and the meeting continued on its curious way. Not all in the usual day's work, I thought to myself. Clearly we were living in interesting times, as the Chinese so often say.

It was late afternoon by the time I returned to the cubicle—only an hour to go before packing up. I sat facing the paper towers that had risen all over my desk, but couldn't settle to anything. My eyes kept straying to the big office clock counting out minutes along the far wall. I wanted to rush back, see the boy, talk with his father. Too much had happened for one day.

On the subway home, I slumped with tiredness. With all that had occurred during the past months, how could I let myself be unnerved by office events? And yet I felt a profound malaise. My mind would not switch over to anything else.

I waded through the human tide on Lexington Avenue, nego-tiating the three blocks from the station to the house with a kind of desperation. And then I was through the door and washing the subway off my hands and reclaiming the baby from Amira's arms. I brought Ben upstairs to the rocking chair and together we sat.

I began to sing "Froggy went a'courtin'," one of the childhood songs that had mysteriously found its way back into a front com-partment of my mind. Eyes that had turned deep brown, like my own, smiled up at me. I transferred the baby to my shoulder and now saw him from the side, saw wide eyes peering out from be-neath incredibly delicate arches of eyebrows, opening to the myriad curiosities of his little world. I loved that look, that angle, the quiz-zicality of his expression.

He was such a good baby, no rumbling colic, no screaming. So easy. And suddenly his face, his smell, his little sounds were all that was there. This child I was meant to comfort instead brought unimagined comfort to me. David would be home soon. Other things could wait.

Chapter Seventeen

WINTER PASSED, SPRING ARRIVED, AND THE HEAT OF SUM-
mer could already be felt on that day early in May when the invita-
tion arrived. I had been feeling my way, groping, stumbling, but
managing to hold my own: so many shock waves to be dissipated,
channeled into the recomposed ordinariness of a quotidian life. I
understood, now, more of the fine print appended to terms like
"working mother," "office politics," "running a household,"
"taking good care of yourself," even if greater understanding did
not always bring with it the requisite ability to cope.

The envelope was postmarked Philadelphia but it wasn't written
in my father's hand or that of one of my sisters. It came from my
second cousins, Eileen and Marcy, and invited us to a surprise party
in honor of their mother's seventy-fifth birthday. Ann had always
been more of an aunt than a first cousin to Sandy, Vickie, and me,
having been something of a younger sister to our father; they had
seen so much of each other as children, after all. Ann's mother had
died when she was just a baby, and relations with the stepmother
who followed were never very good, so long periods were spent in
her aunt's—my grandmother's—house as a girl. She was skinny and
shy and full of dreams, a pale, red-haired, blue-eyed kid, quite unlike her rough-and-tumble Feldman cousins with their jet-black
hair and dark good looks.

The quiet, nervous kid surprised everybody, though, with a
tough core of stubborn grit. She fell wildly in love, left Philadelphia

behind, traveled with her husband in an old jalopy making for the golden land. Unheard of, unimaginable, in a family such as that. Her two daughters were born there, in California; the war ended for her there; the letters crossed back and forth. But somehow the new life in Los Angeles was not as straightforward as she would have wished. Perhaps she was a Philadelphia girl after all. Perhaps it was time to go home.

And so she did. That is how so many Saturday nights of my early childhood came to be spent with my parents and sister Sandy visiting Cousins Ann and Mort, Eileen and Marcy, in Logan, that older part of Philadelphia where they had settled down. Our father's elder brother, Uncle Ben, and his wife, Aunt Betty, and their youngest son, Michael, regularly joined in.

There was a porch there, at Ann's house, where we children would play during the long summer evenings of grown-up talk. The porch had fat white columns brushed by a sidewalk canopy of dense, damp leaves, leaves that glistened coolly in the light and shadow of the streetlamps after the sudden strong rains had passed. The trees were old there, unlike the fast-growing evergreens dug into the cleared land of our new home. They were city trees, smelling of age and wisdom, of people living in houses planted closely together many years before. They gave off a wonderful fresh scent as well, and sometimes the essence of their smell seemed to take over our young souls, open us up, make us yearn for something larger than ourselves, connect us to the unseen rootedness of all life.

Ann left the trees behind, left Logan, and moved to a new development like ours a year or so before Vickie was born. Our mother entrusted us to her care while in the hospital with our new sister. Later, seven years later, she turned to Cousin Ann again. "Keep an eye on the girls," were the few words she managed to say that one time, before all was gone.

As the years passed, Ann came to be known in our immediate family as "the godmother," she who had to be obeyed, the female

230 presence who intervened in our affairs, like it or not. The tentative slip of a girl had become an extremely forceful woman, opinionated, involved in her community, one who believed herself mandated to do good. Now three quarters of a century old, she was still extremely active, absolutely undulled by age, and a summons from her—or on her behalf—was a thing to be reckoned with, something you could never ignore.

During the past months, I had been in close touch with my father and sisters. They had visited me a number of times and we had spoken on the phone every week—more frequently than before. I had talked with the extended family and had received their cards and letters and all the comfort they had brought. Now, courtesy of Ann's birthday, a meeting of the whole Philadelphia clan had been set for early June, when David and Benj and I would have to face them all in the flesh.

Crowds have never been easy for me, even when populated by loving ranks of family members. Indeed, I've always found the prospect of weaving through either massed contingent—American or English—slightly daunting. Now it seemed even more so.

I played out the scene in my head. We would arrive and immediately be swept into the whirlwind of hugs and kisses, the din of contrapuntal voices, only this time the bodies and voices would press closer still than usual. Benj would be admired and touched and held and he'd be nonplussed by it all.

"Oh, isn't he wonderful. Finally, a boy after all these girls in the family. What a *schöne punim*, what beautiful eyes!" That's what my relatives would say to me. I would feel proud and protective, glad that at last they were all able to meet him. And then they would turn their gaze from him to me and I would feel my spine stiffen, the smile set like cement about my lips.

With the best of intentions they would be so worried and concerned. They would all, I knew, be remembering my mother.

Some would take me aside into a corner, ask questions, want to probe into the gory details of what had happened. Others would smile, shake their heads in wordless sympathy, and be shy and awkward, not knowing what to say. The emotion would flow from every one of us. I would have to reassure them all, distance the ghost of my mother from hovering at our sides, prove that really, really, I was not at death's door *quite* yet. It would be a piece of work, no doubt about that, and David would be in on the job just as much as I.

The Saturday dawned hot and clear. We would drive down and spend the night with Sandy and Steve, Melissa and Jessica, in their brownstone near the Philadelphia Museum of Art. Vickie lived nearby and she would join us there for supper. The following afternoon we would all set out in convoy for the far northeastern suburbs, for the party that would take place at Eileen's house. Then David and I would peel off with the baby and make our way back to New York early in the evening, happy to have seen everybody, completely talked out.

We made good time on the New Jersey Turnpike that morning, and as we drove along it felt as though we were negotiating a series of locks on a long canal leading backward in time to childhood. The road between New York and Philadelphia was as it always had been, with only the starting point and destination reversed. We passed through industrial sprawl, eerily ugly, aglow with sulfurous, infernal fires, then marshland that gave way to suburban towns and malls, on to farmland for a while, followed by suburb once again.

We knew our journey was coming to an end when we entered the strip zone, its topless joints and peep show signs and hourly motels clinging to the highway, pathetic outcrops of a larger landscape of rusted cars, ragged weeds, windblown balls of trash. Then we skirted Camden, the city across the river where Joe Feldman had been born, desolate and largely abandoned, the heyday of the

Campbell kids long gone. And then the Ben Franklin Bridge rose up before us, and there it was, stretched out below, Philadelphia, the City of Brotherly Love, my hometown.

"How far away, Philadelphia, Pa.," went the Rodgers and Hammerstein song from *South Pacific,* sung by a young man who had also left his home oceans and continents behind. Although I have lived away from it now almost as many years as I called it home, although from those early years, after my mother died, I so consciously set about distancing myself from it, going abroad, changing the way I spoke, changing so much about myself, I nevertheless recognize that I am bound to Philadelphia. It is a source of strength, connecting me to my past, to the bedrock of genes and experiences and people and places from which I was formed.

As we crossed over the bridge, I turned to look at the fine, straight profile of my husband seated up front. David glanced back in the rearview mirror at the baby and me. He focused on the car seat and smiled.

"Well my Benj, this is a very important place we are entering, you for the very first time, my little chap. This is the place your mama comes from, where your mama and I met a long time ago. You'll know more about that some day."

I peered down at our boy as my fingers skimmed the soft, dark down that had replaced his original crop of hair. His gaze locked in on mine precisely, absolutely, as only a baby's can. Then a sudden chortle erupted, as plastic keys clutched in a small curled hand began to wave.

I looked up again, through the window. The emotion rose within me as it always has, every time I've returned and seen the skyline, the two rivers threading through William Penn's "green country town," the cobbled streets and pleasing symmetries of the small colonial houses, the river drives crisscrossed by lacework bridges, the art museum like a Greek temple atop its little hill. There is so much that is lovely in a city too often maligned, places that gave me a sense of beauty and greatness and wonder, of history and a world to strive for beyond the confines of our suburban enclave. Philadelphia is the vessel holding all the precious and painful memories, the mysteries of childhood. It's where I went to college and discovered yet more worlds, where I met a young Englishman, fell in love, and found a partner for life.

It is also the place where my mother is buried, where I come to stand by her grave once a year to say Kaddish, the ancient Jewish prayer we recite when remembering the dead. My last visit to the cemetery had taken place the previous May, when Benj was growing inside me and there seemed to be no clouds on the horizon even as we passed through the cemetery gates.

That day, I went not with David but with my mother's first cousin Fritzie. I had phoned her and made the date—she lived near the cemetery and would pick me up from a small suburban station and accompany me there. Afterward we'd have lunch and she'd drop me late in the afternoon at Sandy's house in town.

I had contacted Fritzie, with whom I had gotten reacquainted during the past few years, because with the bloom of new life upon me I had felt the need to learn more about the woman who had given me life. Fritzie was just about the only person I could think of who would be able to conjure up my mother from early on. We went to the cemetery, left our tears and flowers, and then went to a restaurant and talked.

"Your mother was such a lovely person," Fritzie said to me. "Your grandmother, she was tough, very stern, and what she said ruled the house. I was always a little afraid of her. Bossie was a very good daughter to her, but she was warm, much warmer than Golde. And when she and your father got married, they seemed very happy together. But you know, I was quite a bit younger, and so there's a lot I don't know. I wish I could tell you more."

We stopped off at Fritzie's apartment, looked at old photographs, talked a little longer, went our separate ways. After that visit, I put

234   the memories aside. There was so much to get on with, a new life on which to concentrate. How little did I realize that, come autumn, the memories would fan through me like fever, unbidden, out of control.

And now I was visiting the cemetery again, this time with my husband and son, on this, our first trip to Philadelphia in nine months. Normally during such a period, we would have been in and out of the city on several occasions, but I had last set foot in my hometown two weeks before I was diagnosed with cancer. For long months thereafter it wouldn't have been very easy to return, but although I had felt the need to come back, to visit my mother's grave, perhaps too I had been putting it off the past few months. But now the time had come.

Shalom Memorial Park, it is called. We drove slowly through the entrance, Ben asleep beside me in the car seat. It was no special holiday, no particular occasion for calling on ancestors, remembering the dead, and so, as we wound our way along the cemetery drive, we passed only one other car. But we were glad to see that other family visiting that other grave.

We found the bronze plaque embedded in the earth quite easily. "Beloved wife and mother, Bernice Feldman, 1920–1967." Sculpted roses curled around one corner of the slab, and Hebrew letters were embossed diagonally opposite. The remains of real flowers poked out of the vase at its top, left there by my sisters a few weeks before, on Mother's Day.

Time seemed to come to a halt. There was always the same quietness, the sound of wind soughing through the trees, the dappled sunlight, the smell of freshly mown grass, damp earth. David stood beside me and we held each other, weeping silently.

Images flooded back, disjointed, random. My mother's frightened eyes that summer she came home from the hospital, the year before she died. The gray suit and rayon paisley blouse my mother's friend Sophie lent me, much too big for a thin fifteen-year-old frame, but dark and formal, something proper to wear at a funeral. An onyx pendant, an emerald ring, the few bits and pieces I had of hers, things I put away in jewelry boxes, things I could not bear to wear. The Friday night visits to the synagogue to say Kaddish for months after her death. Our trips as a family, when my mother was still alive, to her mother Golde's grave in a different part of the city. It was a much older cemetery, much less well cared for, where we knew to be quiet as we watched our mother sit on a stone bench, her head in her hands.

Although I'm not very religious, I go to services on the high holy days of the Jewish calendar, feeling ethnic, cultural, spiritual solidarity on Rosh Hashanah and Yom Kippur. In the afternoon, toward the end of Yom Kippur, comes Yizkor, a time given over to remembering the dead. I always make sure to be at a synagogue for that.

As I stood above my mother's grave with my husband at my side, some lines that form part of the memorial service came back to me. They ask the question like this: "If some messenger were to come to us with the offer that death should be overthrown, but with the one inseparable condition that birth should also cease . . . that never again would there be a child, or a youth, or first love, never again new persons with new hopes . . . ourselves for always and never any others—could the answer be in doubt?"

I understood so much more now, and at the same time so much seemed even more obscure. But at least one answer was clear as I looked across to my baby, my mother's grandson, sleeping quietly in the car. I bent down, plucked a few blades of grass, and scattered them over the grave, as, when I was still a small child, my mother had taught me to do. I stood up and David and I locked hands, walked back to the car, walked back to our boy. We would travel on from there.

Chapter Eighteen

"WE NEED A HOLIDAY, MY DARLING," DAVID SAID, STILL using the British term for a vacation almost seven years after we had decamped to the United States. Indeed we did, whatever the terminology. It had been a hard, hard slog and we could both, finally, leave our offices, take off with the Benj, move to a slower rhythm for a few weeks.

It wasn't the usual sort of destination for us: not Rome, not Beijing, not even London. Guess what? Life changes after having a baby. But we were looking forward to Cape Cod with as much eagerness as we would any of those more "exciting" places: two weeks by the sea, by the beautiful sea, together. The foreign parts would still be there when we were ready for them, a few years down the road.

It was the very end of June, three days before we were due to set off, when I noticed the thin, dark line directly beneath the nipple of my right breast. I stood peering at my image in the mirror, hardly taking it in, hardly taking my eyes away from what looked like crusted blood lodged in the fold at the center of my breast.

We had both been hurrying through the morning ritual when I walked out of the bathroom and into the bedroom to show David.

"D. Reid, I've just noticed something funny on my breast. It's dried blood, I think. Why don't you take a look," is what I said to him. I could feel the skin tighten around my cheeks, could see my husband suddenly slow down and listen to each word. His face turned gray. We stared at each other, realizing how far we had come. We hadn't felt this intensity of fear rising up through our bodies since the previous October.

"Yes, I see what you mean, my darling one. Can you remember, did anybody bump into you? Could it have been the baby, accidentally scratching or pinching you?"

"Well, Benj does sometimes pinch." I tried to grab on to one of the explanations. Yes, of course, maybe it was the baby. But the words rang hollow through our ears. I hadn't even reached my one-year anniversary yet.

I finished dressing. The clock, finally, inched past eight. Barbara, Jeanne Petrek's secretary, would have just started her office day. I picked up the phone and dialed the number that I knew by heart.

Barbara recognized the English accent at once. "Oh, hi, how are you? I'm sorry but Dr. Petrek is away on vacation. What's up?"

I felt even more afraid. Jeanne was away, she was away. What was I to do? I told Barbara, the ever-unflappable Barbara, what I was worried about.

"Well, you have two choices," she began. "Either you can go on vacation and I'll set up an appointment for just after you're back, or you can see the surgeon who's covering for Dr. Petrek, Dr. Patrick Borgen."

Barbara probably already knew what I would request. An appointment was fixed at Sloan-Kettering for late that afternoon. I held and kissed the baby and tried to let the clockwork of routine take over. I set out for the office and got through the hours without telling anyone of my fears. Work was indeed a blessing that day.

I felt the adrenalin rise as soon as I passed through the double doors into Sloan-Kettering. I went up to three, produced the blue card, was met by a nurse and showed into a familiar examining room. Soon a youngish, fair-haired man walked in carrying my file.

238   I heard myself laugh nervously. "Part of me feels a bit ridiculous coming here, creating a fuss over what's probably just a little normal secretion."

The doctor smiled off my panicky embarrassment and began to examine me closely. He didn't say anything, but walked quickly to a cupboard, extracted a bottle of liquid, some cotton wool, some swabs. Before I knew quite what was happening, he gently, repeatedly, wiped under my nipple. He looked closely again and then said, "Well, you can sit up now and get dressed. I'll be back in a moment."

It was a long moment, that minute or two, but when he returned, he smiled. "You certainly did the right thing in coming here; you shouldn't feel at all embarrassed. I think everything's okay, but there is something known as Paget's disease—in fact, there are a number of diseases with that name, because Paget was obviously somebody who liked to put his stamp on newly discovered conditions—anyway, it's a cancer that usually shows itself by blood coming from the nipple. But I was able to wipe the stuff off without any trouble; it came away cleanly and I don't see anything underneath."

"But what do you think caused it?" I asked him.

"Well, women do occasionally get discharges if the nipple is squeezed or pressed, even inadvertently. You told me when you first came in that your baby sometimes pinches you—that could have done it. And besides, your hormones have been all over the place these past months, which would make a discharge more likely.

"Go away and have a good vacation and forget about it. I really think it's nothing to worry about." Dr. Borgen paused, and then came the inevitable. "But if by any chance some bleeding recurs, it would probably happen in a couple of weeks. Call us right away; we might have to look further. I'll make a file note for Dr. Petrek so she knows about it when she returns."

I walked out to the lobby. My fingers shook as I put the coin in the pay phone. While the phone rang and the secretary answered and I waited to hear my husband's voice come over the line, I could see chemotherapy patients, their heads wrapped in scarves to hide the absence of hair, arriving for treatment. I could see people with IVs being wheeled down the corridor by nursing assistants. But I could also see the majority of women and men who were sitting in the large waiting area reading magazines, chatting, looking perfectly normal—healthy, even.

"Hello, my darling," came the tense voice on the other end of the line.

"We are going to have a really good holiday, D. Reid," is what I told my husband.

✿ ✿ ✿

And so we did, we had a lovely time with our boy in a cottage by the sea. And while we were there, and when we came back, nothing reappeared beneath my nipple, no telltale signs or marks of doom showed themselves in my body or in our lives.

But somehow, I could not shake off that moment of pure terror when I had first looked in the mirror and saw the blood; the fragile equilibrium we had struggled to reestablish had been disturbed, and small tremors of fear continued to rumble through me at odd moments of the day or night. I began to feel the need to talk to other people about the fear, about the inside of my heart and head. Although I was so fortunate in being able to talk things through with David, I felt, nevertheless, the need for a different kind of outlet. I wanted to find women who had had experiences similar to my own.

In New York it was not too difficult to find several organizations offering help. And so one hot August day, about a month after we had returned from vacation, I picked up the phone and dialed one of them. The woman who answered explained that her establishment ran different kinds of sessions to accommodate different kinds of needs. There were groups for the newly diagnosed, groups for older women, groups for women with metastatic disease. There was also a group for women with young children. That, of course, was the one for me.

Subsequently I was to learn of studies that have concluded that women who attend breast cancer support groups seem to have a greater likelihood of survival. Who knows, after all, how mind and body interact for good and ill? That Thursday evening, when I walked into the small room where several women were already seated, I was unaware of such statistics. I simply needed to talk.

The women were all in their thirties or early forties. Two of them had hair somewhere between fuzz and crewcut; they were each just finishing up months and months of chemo. The other two were obviously long past that. Anyone hurrying by them on the street would never have guessed how close those women had come to losing their lives.

The leader of the group, Karen, was one of those two, pretty, seemingly healthy in every way. She explained that one other woman, Linda—another newcomer—was supposed to turn up, but that we'd better begin since we were already running a little late. Although the others had all met at least once before, Karen started off the session by asking each of us to talk about when we were diagnosed, what stage cancer we had, what treatment we were undergoing or had gone through. Rather like habitués of Alcoholics Anonymous, we each had to begin by publicly acknowledging our unwanted membership in this club.

"I discovered my cancer four years ago, just before I gave birth to my second child," Karen told us. Clinically, I knew, she would be grouped the same as I, as having been diagnosed during pregnancy or lactation. Unlike mine, though, her malignancy was invasive. She had had a mastectomy and a very strong course of chemotherapy, and had opted, as well, for immediate reconstruction of one of the most complicated types, using her own abdominal tissue.

Mary, the woman with the crewcut, had been diagnosed seven months before with invasive cancer. She had been feeling awful from the chemo but was beginning, now, to feel a little better, the course having finally reached its end. "I just had to come to a place where people understand, where I don't have to explain anything," she said by way of introduction.

Terry was the woman with the fuzz. She herself was a doctor. The others all knew that piece of information; I was the newcomer and did not. When she saw my eyebrows involuntarily rise, she responded, "Yeah, you don't expect it to happen to people like me. But I woke up one morning and got into the shower and got out and looked at myself. I saw dimpling. And I thought, I *knew,* then and there, I had breast cancer and that it was probably pretty bad." Under the microscope, seven lymph nodes had showed invasion. Terry had chosen to have a double mastectomy—one prophylactically—and since her tumor was receptive to estrogen, she had also had her ovaries removed.

"I've had everything out that could be taken out, I've had heavy, heavy doses of chemo, and yet I feel so depressed. I'm a doctor and I know too much. I've got two kids and I'm worried I'm going to die and leave them without a mother. I need another dozen years to see them through school. That's all I want, twelve years."

We shook our heads. We each had done our personal arithmetic, calculated our secret calendars, worked out the minimum number of years we prayed and struggled to have. Those numbers were like magic incantations chanted deeply within us, ceaselessly, each day and night. We all of us would do anything to see those years go by, to see our children grow up. We had learned, unlike so many women our age, to welcome each birthday, to embrace each passing year. For us, getting older was something to be desired, a triumph, not something to be feared.

I told my tale next. I felt curiously guilty, having a prognosis seemingly so much better than the others', the only woman sitting in that room whose cancer had been noninvasive. But I was also the only woman there who had seen her mother die young of the disease. I talked about my recent scare, about my terror that somehow the doctors had missed a microinvasion, that somewhere a cell had escaped and was quietly doing its worst.

As I was finishing, the door opened and a dark-haired woman who looked a little older than the rest of us walked in and slowly made her way across the room. We all stared and tried not to. She was using a cane. That must be Linda, I thought to myself.

Ellen, attractive and in her early thirties, broke the momentary silence. "I was diagnosed almost two years ago, with invasion but clear lymph nodes. I've got a boy who's three and a half, and I'd like another child. My oncologist spelled out all the risks of another pregnancy, and said to wait at least till I had passed the two-year mark. Well, that'll be in two more months, and I'm torn, now that the moment has come. I just don't know what to do."

Karen turned to the newcomer. "Hi, you're Linda?" she asked. The woman nodded and Karen very quickly introduced us all and asked Linda to tell her story.

"Well, they told me I could try this group because, like you, I've got a young child, a boy who's three." Her voice was very quiet and seemed to quiver with the effort of pushing out each word.

"You see," she continued, "I started by going to another group last week, but that was all older women. There was one thing we had in common, though. We all had metastatic disease." She reached for a handkerchief and dabbed her eyes. "I'm sorry, although I guess I don't have to apologize here. The cancer's in my bones, in my spine. I'm not responding to chemo, and it's growing so fast. My husband isn't coping very well, and I don't know what to do for my boy." Her voice caught and she looked at us yearningly through red-rimmed eyes.

For a split second, an atom of time that would not have been perceptible to any outsider, each woman in the room froze as the

same terrified, ungenerous, utterly human instinct telegraphed
through her—thank all that I can thank that I am not Linda, and
please, please, please, don't let me be like her, let me be one who
will grow old, survive.

Then the gates of generosity, of warmth and caring, opened
wide. Each of us, immediately, tried to find some way to comfort
her. Karen mentioned possible sources of financial and childcare
help. The rest of us used the low points we had climbed out of in
our own struggles to try to bolster her shreds of hope. We offered
information and opinions about alternative therapies. We listened
when she wanted to talk some more.

That night I went home and thought of Linda and my mother
and Pat and Jane, all of the cancer-crushed bones and spirits I had
known. For the next three weeks I could not put Linda out of my
mind. Her face and words crept up on me over and over again, like
a wind that catches you unawares when just rounding a corner, the
shock of its power stinging through your cheeks long afterward.

I could not forget her either, that morning early in October,
when I walked slowly toward Sloan-Kettering's just-opened outpatient facility. I was coming for my "anniversary" mammogram at
the new breast center. It had been one year, give or take a few days,
since breast cancer had reactivated itself in my family tree.

I would have the mammogram and receive the radiologist's verdict. I would return and see Jeanne Petrek later in the week. My
friend Jean had told me about anniversaries when she had had hers
the previous December. "You begin to relive all the events of the
diagnosis, it's spooky and kind of horrible, then you get it over with
and you're okay." I would be okay, David had said to me. I had to
be okay.

There was no one else in the gleaming new waiting room. I had
opted for the first appointment. The woman led me into the cubicle and took the picture quickly. I knew how to stand, and there
was only one side to do. "The doctor will be in to see you in a few

minutes," she said. She went away, and I clenched my teeth, breathed very slowly, took in every angle of the room. Then the footsteps came, the door opened, and the doctor, another woman, appeared.

"It's fine, you're alright," she said to me. "Nothing suspicious." She smiled and left the cubicle. I could feel a few tears burst through in relief. I glanced at the bra on the chair, one side full with the prosthesis. Quickly I put it on. Quickly the other clothes tumbled over my head. I wanted to get out of there, to talk to David, and then to become, once again, just another person in another rush-hour crowd.

But three days later, as I waited to be called in to see Jeanne Petrek, I could not dissolve into anonymity. Nor could I banish all those memories: the fearsome sound of the radiologist's footsteps before she walked in with her good news; the sight of Linda struggling with her cane, her eyes so like my mother's; the crusty feel of the thin line of blood that had curled like a snake along the surface of my skin.

This would not be an ordinary check-up. It was my anniversary, after all. And it was more than that. One year before, the first time I had met the woman who would be my surgeon, she had shocked me at a time I thought I was beyond shock. Then, stepping back, she had told me to go away and not think for a year. When that period ended, I would come back and we would talk. The oncologists, Dr. Gilewski and Dr. Moore, had each in her own way said pretty much the same thing. Now the time had come.

While she was examining me, poking here, palpating there, Jeanne's unadorned comments came in the usual rush: "The mammo is fine, but I guess you know that. The scar's healed well, and I don't feel anything to worry about. Now, Barbara said you wanted to talk."

"Yes, that's right. A year ago you suggested that I have a prophylactic mastectomy of the other side, and then you said to wait a year and we'd talk about it. Well, the time has passed. I want to know what the risk factors are, I want to know how you think I stand. I'd like to hear some numbers."

"Weell," the midwestern twang made its appearance. "The chance of a recurrence from the original cancer, as I've told you, is pretty small. It's a new primary we're talking about. You've had ductal carcinoma in situ and lobular carcinoma in situ in one breast, you've got a strong family history, you've taken hormones, you got pregnant late. Let me think. I'd say there's a fifty to sixty percent chance, over the course of time, that you'd develop cancer in the other breast."

For a moment, I could not take it in. Fifty to sixty percent. I somehow had never reckoned on odds quite that high.

Jeanne continued. "Look, if it were to happen, it might not occur for eight years, fifteen years. And if you're lucky, it won't happen at all. But if you were to develop a new primary, the prognosis probably wouldn't be as good. However closely we monitor you and you check yourself, there's no guarantee that a second cancer would be found when it was still noninvasive. You were really lucky the first time."

"And if I were to have the prophylactic, what would the odds be then?" I asked.

"Oh, I'd say, only one in a hundred that you'd develop something from the original cancer. That's the best odds we can give."

"If you do a prophylactic, am I right in thinking that you won't have to take any lymph nodes, that there wouldn't be any danger of developing lymphedema in the other arm, that it's all a lot simpler?"

"Yes, that's right. It's all very neat. We're taking away normal tissue, not cancer. That's why it's something you can't exactly wait around to do. You have to do it when the breast is healthy."

I had heard the plain facts, stark and straightforward. She gave no opinion, no recommendation as such. The information was emotionally unclouded, and unclouded, my mind would have to make the decision.

David and I had already talked about it, especially since the preholiday scare. The thought of taking away healthy flesh, chopping off clean tissue, was even more barbaric and horrific than removing a breast in which cancer lodged. Two breasts were better than one breast, but one breast was better than none.

What would it be like to have no breasts at all, just two thick scars running across the skin of my chest? I knew my husband loved me and would stand by me whatever I looked like, but I also realized that somewhere within him he wondered, was nervous, about what he would have to face. And I had to admit that my sense of womanhood was comforted by still having one breast. How would I feel about myself if the other one were gone?

And yet, I already knew what I would do; I had known it, in fact, even before coming. David did, too.

I thought of Linda, I thought of my mother. I thought of Benj, whose first birthday we had just celebrated. Eight years, fifteen years was not enough. I would do anything to be around to see the boy I brought into the world grow up. I had a sacred responsibility to do so. And I also had a responsibility to myself. I didn't want to die of breast cancer. I wanted to live.

"Jeanne, I'd like to schedule the operation."

She glanced at me as she stood up, already on her way out the door to the next patient. "Yes, well, unless you or your husband is absolutely in love with your breast, I think that's pretty sensible under the circumstances. Go see Barbara and she'll write you in the book."

"In love with my breast"—I could hardly keep from laughing in spite of having just decided to put myself through the wringer once

again. That lady shoots straight from the hip, I thought. "In love
with my breast"—not bloody likely. In love with my continued
existence was more like it. Classic Petrek. Classic. I must go and see
Barbara.

Coda

THE DEED WAS DONE EARLY IN DECEMBER 1992 AND I'VE lived to tell the tale. Oh yes, it was strange to be a patient on Sloan-Kettering's breast floor once again. I passed through the same rituals, knew each step of the way. The fear of the anesthetic curtain coming down was there, so too the nervousness before the pathologist's report. And yet, in many ways, it wasn't the same experience at all.

In the panic-filled hours after I was first diagnosed with cancer, there was really no other option: a mastectomy was it. Later on, I could have chosen to gamble. There was no suspicion of cancer in the right breast. The decision to act preemptively was mine and mine alone.

The physical and psychological effects were quite different the second time around. A woman with only one breast can stand in front of a mirror and at certain careful angles, the image reflected back will have soft curves and roundness, an illusion of wholeness. Such a woman can still pretend. After my second stay in Sloan-Kettering, the mirror no longer held such illusions. That inexpressible, innate sense of femininity that comes from having breasts was gone. And yet the emotion that surged above the sadness, gave sense to it all, was the overwhelming feeling of relief. I had sacrificed healthy tissue to keep me healthy, had done all I could to help myself and my boy. I would not, now, develop a new primary breast cancer. It was the right decision. I had no regrets.

The physical recovery went a lot faster, everything from getting out of bed to being released from the hospital to regaining full use of the arm. The attitude of many of the doctors and nurses was different, too: they treated me with a kind of camaraderie. I was almost an insider, I pretty much knew the score.

I felt the responsibility of that knowledge when I looked around at my companions, who were all going through the trauma for the first time. During the therapy sessions, and in the evenings after our families had gone home, we had time to talk. I wanted them to see that somebody could get through, that there was life after breast cancer, after the disfigurement of the operation. I don't know if our talking helped them much—I hope so. Certainly, it helped me.

Many months have passed since then, and life has continued on its way. I don't wear a prosthesis anymore; somehow, the idea of using two seemed two too many for a small-framed body like mine. I've had to adjust my wardrobe a bit; only certain bathing suits will do. And there are times, now, when I turn to David before going out into the world and ask him if I look alright, posing the question with a little more seriousness than I was wont to do in the old days of easy fishing for compliments.

When I visit them for check-ups, my doctors still occasionally predict that one day I'll choose to reconstruct the breasts. I beg to differ: still no lover of the operating room am I. But who knows? Stranger turnarounds have occurred.

The level of tension in my day-to-day life has been raised a notch or two. I'm more likely to get tired and emotional than before. It takes longer for me really to relax, but I suppose that's inevitable in a way. And yet, I do feel deeply the full measure of my luck. The doctors all count me among that happy band—those who've had cancer and can consider themselves cured. They tell me I should go about my daily life . . . well, *almost* as before.

Of course, I have to watch my diet, taking little fat but lots of certain fruits and vegetables, anticarcinogens harvested from nature's bounty. Some weeks, though, I've been known to sneak in the odd bean or pea, to live dangerously for a day or two without the all-pervasive smell of broccoli or cabbage steaming through the house. I have even, on occasion, managed some "forbidden fruit"—a bit of cake, some pudding, a piece of pie. But for the most part, I am pretty careful. There is, after all, the wild card of that one wild cell to consider. Even if it doesn't hide in some dark corner of my body, the knowledge of its possible existence hides always at the back of my mind.

On the bad days, when I'm tired or under pressure or feeling physically low, the ordinary aches and pains of life translate themselves into fears of metastasis. Is that back pain really from the disc that slipped twenty years ago, or does it herald something far more sinister within my bones? Do the intermittent spasms of what I'm told is a nervous stomach indicate instead that ovarian cancer is taking hold? On days like that, I worry about everything I eat: too much fat? chemicals? pesticides chock full of carcinogens?

An awkward remark, a graceless joke, a stupid comment about boobs or tits: all of those, on such days, can set me brooding or fuming—equally bad. An advertisement for a dress I can no longer wear or a photograph of a woman with more than a modicum of décolletage can also make me feel acutely the sense of loss. When other mothers talk about ordinary life, unclouded expectations of seeing their children grow up, I can feel the sadness and fear creeping over me. On the bad days.

On the good days, I feel the joy of being alive, of strolling with my son through the park, of having a meal with my husband in our home, of chatting with my sisters or my father on the phone. Being able to put in a good day's work, to plan a trip, to see an old friend after an absence of several years, these are gifts I do not take for granted.

I like to sit in my study looking out the window, watching the world of the city go by. And I like to sit in our garden playing with our boy. Sometimes, when he's concentrating raptly on sorting through his basket of shells, or is happy making his little bus and car go round and round and round, I turn my attention for a moment to the sunlight filtered through the birch leaves, the gradations of color in the old brick wall, the patterns in the clouds passing overhead. Perhaps I notice more of the details than I used to, a little bit like a small child. And perhaps those moments of yearning and completion are some of the best that life can have.

The experience of cancer doesn't change everything, doesn't make every moment feel precious, doesn't sweep the pettiness, anger, frustration, the tedium in our less-than-perfect lives clean away. There are times when I feel consumed with anger about breast cancer itself, when I cannot understand why more isn't being done, why so many women still are silent, why hundreds of thousands will suffer and many will die before time and money and consciousness enough are devoted to finding a cure.

I look at my sisters and nieces and son—men very occasionally do get breast cancer—and pray that the future will be cancer-free for them. But despite the strong history, I don't know for a fact that my breast cancer was hereditary; only about five percent of cases can truly be attributed to an inherited gene. Still, research on that front at least is proceeding apace, and soon the gene will be identified and tests will exist that will bring with them new hope *and* new fear.

For until a cure—or, better yet, a way of preventing the disease—is found, a woman who is identified as carrying the gene will be faced with the choice I had to make after the first mastectomy: the uncertainties of careful monitoring or the prophylactic removal of her breasts.

Sometimes I sit and think back to what it felt like as a girl, when I watched breast cancer kill my mother. I think of what it feels like to have harbored it within myself. Sometimes I can hardly believe the life I am looking at is my own.

I think of the lessons I took away both times, of my mother and myself, of how our paths diverged, converged, diverged again. I know full well I don't have to be my mother, my life doesn't have to follow the course hers took, whether I spend the rest of it cancer-free or not. Yes, I am her daughter, but I don't have to be afraid

252 of a dark legacy anymore; I can think of her more as a person, less as a ghost. My mother gave me life, just as I've been blessed to give life to my boy. And I've learned from her life, as I hope he will learn from mine. For truly, I believe it's because I learned from the tragedy that befell her, that I am still alive today.

BACUP

Bath Place
Rivington Street
London EC2A 3JR
Tel: 0800 181199 / 071 613 2121

Cancer information service

BREAKTHROUGH

PO Box 2JP
London W1A 2JP

Raises funds for research into causes and prevention of breast cancer

BREAST CANCER CAMPAIGN

1 Oxford Street
London
W1R 1RF
Tel: 071 439 1013

BREAST CANCER CARE

5–19 Britten Street
London SW3 3TZ
Helpline: (071) 867 1103

Suite 2/8
65 Bath St
Glasgow G2 2BX
Tel: (041) 353 1050

13a Castle Terrace
Edinburgh EH1 2DP
Tel: (031) 221 0407

Offers emotional support and practical information to complement medical advice and nursing care. Also a resource for nurses and other health professionals

BREAST CARE CAMPAIGN

1 St Mary Abbot's Place
London
W8 6LS
Tel: 071 371 1510

Provides information on benign breast disorders to women and health professionals. Leaflets available on breast lumps, breast pain and nipple disorders

BREAST TEST WALES

18 Cathedral Road
Central Cardiff
CF1 9LJ
Tel: 0222 397222

THE CANCER HELPLINE

40–42 Eglantine Avenue
Belfast BT9 6DX
Tel: (0232) 663439

CANCER RELIEF MACMILLAN FUND

Anchor House
15/19 Britten Street
London SW3 3TZ Tel: (071) 351 7811

9 Castle Terrace
Edinburgh EH1 2DP
Tel: (031) 229 3276

Funds MacMillan nurses, including specialist breast care nurses, doctors and cancer centres, all within the NHS. It gives grants and offers information direct to patients through four associated self-help charities. It has also produced a leaflet on the minimum standards of care that breast cancer patients should expect.

EUROPADONNA

Via Ripamonti
66–20141 Milan
Italy

A European breast cancer coalition

THE PREMENSTRUAL SOCIETY

PO Box 429
Addlestone
Surrey, KT15 1DZ

A service for women with PMS who have distressing breast symptoms for which PREMSOC provides advice and help

TENOVOUS CANCER INFORMATION CENTRE

142 Whitchurch Road
Cardiff CF4 3NA
Tel: 0222 6198. Freephone 0800 526527

Provides information on all aspects of cancer, including care and support services available. Also offers emotional support and counselling

THE WOMEN'S HEALTH CONCERN

PO Box 1629
London W8 6AU
Tel: (071) 938 3932

Helps women seek treatment and care for gynaecological conditions.

THE WOMEN'S NATIONWIDE CANCER CONTROL CAMPAIGN

Suna House
128-130 Curtain Road
London EC2A 3AR
Helpline: (071) 729 2229
Taped message: (071) 729 4915